The Cross
and
the Cinema

THE CROSS
AND
THE CINEMA

*The Legion of Decency
and the National
Catholic Office for Motion
Pictures, 1933–1970*

JAMES M. SKINNER

PRAEGER

Westport, Connecticut
London

Library of Congress Cataloging-in-Publication Data

Skinner, James M.
    The cross and the cinema : the Legion of Decency and the National
Catholic Office for Motion Pictures, 1933–1970 / James M. Skinner.
        p.   cm.
    Includes bibliographical references and index.
    ISBN 0–275–94193–0 (alk. paper)
    1. National Catholic Office for Motion Pictures (U.S.)—History.
2. Catholic Church—United States—History—20th century.   3. Motion
picture industry—United States—History—20th century.   4. Motion
pictures—Censorship—United States—History.   I. Title.
BX1407.M68S55   1993
303.3'76—dc20   92–43431

British Library Cataloguing in Publication Data is available.

Library of Congress Catalog Card Number: 92–43431
ISBN: 0–275–94193–0

First published in 1993

Praeger Publishers, 88 Post Road West, Westport, CT 06881
An imprint of Greenwood Publishing Group, Inc.

Printed in the United States of America

The paper used in this book complies with the
Permanent Paper Standard issued by the National
Information Standards Organization (Z39.48–1984).

10 9 8 7 6 5 4 3 2

O, the immense amount of good that the motion picture can effect! That is why the evil spirit, always so active in this world, wishes to pervert this instrument for some impious purpose; it is for public opinion to support wholeheartedly and effectively every legitimate effort to purify the films and keep them clean; to improve them and increase their usefulness.

—Pope Pius XI, Encyclical *Vigilanti Cura* (With Vigilant Care), July 29, 1936

"You're not Catholic are you?"

I shook my head.

"You know what the Legion of Decency is?"

I nodded.

"These bastards can give you the fits, especially in towns with big Catholic populations. The Knights of Columbus come out in their uniforms and picket the theater. They'll have kids in parochial schools write letters to the theater manager begging him not to play the picture. The priests stand up on Sunday morning and tell the audience, the parishioners, to take the Legion of Decency pledge, and boycott any theater that plays the show for a year."

—Kroger Babb, in David F. Friedman, *A Youth in Babylon*

Contents

Photographs follow page 104.

Acknowledgments

My thanks are due first to Mr. Henry Herx and his staff at the Department of Communications of the U.S. Catholic Conference for Film and Broadcasting. There I had the kind of freedom to immerse myself in the archival material of the Legion of Decency that researchers covet but seldom achieve. My thanks are also due to the staffs of several specialist libraries: Dr. Nicholas B. Scheetz of Special Collections, Georgetown University; the staff of the Margaret Herrick Library of the Academy of Motion Picture Arts and Sciences, Los Angeles; and Mr. Fred Lombardi of *Variety*. Msgr. John J. McClafferty and Father Patrick J. Sullivan gave freely of their time to answer a multitude of questions on their periods of tenure with the Legion. I particularly wish to thank Mr. Martin J. Quigley, Jr. for reminiscences of his father's role and Charles A. Nugge of the U.S. Catholic Church Conference Office for Publishing and Promotion for permission to quote from Legion and NCOMP sources. Thanks also to the Museum of Modern Art Film Stills Archive.

My access to the Legion of Decency's records was contingent upon my respecting the anonymity of the reviewers and consultors. I have adhered to this condition with one exception, that of Moira Walsh, for many years the distinguished film critic of *America*. She made no secret of her association with the Legion and, in the circumstances, I felt it was pointless to conceal it.

As with all research in a foreign country, finances might have been a major problem. Research in New York and Washington was made possible by a Strategic Studies Grant from the U.S. Information Service. Further work there and in Los Angeles was made possible by grants from the Brandon University Faculty Research Committee. The manuscript was meticulously prepared by Janice M. Mahoney, Annelie Thiessen and Joan Thiessen of Brandon University's Arts Secretarial Pool.

Introduction

How the Roman Catholic Church, through its agency, the National Legion of Decency, dominated the American film censorship scene in tandem with the Production Code Administration, is the subject of this book. The period covered includes the early 1930s through the late 1960s. It is a book that I felt needed writing because of the paucity of material on the Legion. Amazingly, and despite its pivotal role in dictating the content of motion pictures for the best part of three decades, there exists only one full-length work on the subject. That is an unemendated doctoral thesis of barely forty-three thousand words by Paul W. Facey, S.J., dating from 1945 and therefore covering only the first eleven years of the Legion's existence, which is based almost entirely on published sources. Father Facey seems to have been allowed very limited access to Legion files, and its having received the imprimatur of the local archbishop, while not necessarily a point in its disfavor, is indicative of its "political correctness" in the eyes of the Church.

Most people over the age of fifty retain memories of attending the movies in what has been termed the Golden Age of the cinema, from the Depression era to the advent of television. My own experience is probably not atypical. Moviegoing then was a family affair. My parents first took me as a toddler to picture palaces that really deserved the name. These were a far cry from today's glorified shoeboxes clustered in multiplexes and increasingly located in sterile shopping malls. Then, most cities of any consequence boasted at least one and often more of these grand edifices, designed with a motif in mind—Egyptian, Chinese, Arabian or whatever took the owner's fancy—to provide a suitable setting wherein the collective imagination of the toiling masses could be whisked away to a fantasy world. Within their exotic walls hundreds or even thousands of seats accommodated the throngs for whom a night at the picture show was as natural and regular as church attendance. Programs were often changed biweekly and most comprised three or four hours of entertainment. Like stations in the

Paris Metro, each theater had its particular ambience. The odor of popcorn and stale tobacco mingled with detergent permeated the nostrils to the exclusion of all else. Formidable-looking women in uniform ceaselessly patrolled the aisles, beaming their flashlights at and temporarily blinding malefactors as they issued stern warnings about talking or draping one's feet over the seat in front. They were also puritan killjoys to the courting couples whose embraces invariably lost whatever attraction and momentum they might originally have had on account of the intrusive shaft of light.

An hour or so into the program the resident organist would emerge, phoenix-like, from the bowels of the stage, to play a medley of recent hits and old favorites with audience participation in a sing-along spurred on by a bouncing ball accompanying the words on-screen. The performance over, the performer would retreat into the stygian darkness from whence he or she came, with a well-practiced wave of one hand while continuing to perform with the other. As the evening progressed, irate mothers would come in search of offspring who had decided to sit through the main feature for a second time, which was a possibility then, since programming was continuous and unaccompanied children were seldom excluded. It all seemed (and probably was) a marvelous bargain for a fraction of what one pays today for a scant two hours of entertainment within the confines of what amounts to an expanded living room. These impressions bring others to mind: the gaudily decorated marquees outside with their parallel rows of electric lamps illuminating the program and its stars; the manager, dapper and neat in his tuxedo; the girl with the refreshment tray, standing in a spotlight, proffering a variety of candies and ice cream, designed to remind us of her glamorous equivalent on the screen selling a pack of cigarettes to a suave George Raft; the magical moment when the house lights dimmed and the curtains parted to bring us a Disney cartoon or an "interest" short followed by Movietone News that transported us to some part of the world quite alien to our experience; and, finally, breathless anticipation as the big picture was announced and we relished the prospect of being entertained by impossibly handsome men and beautiful women. Hollywood was, indeed, the dream factory and we were in its thrall of our own volition.

But dreams are mostly unreal, divorced from the verities of daily existence. Just how far those movies convinced us and to what degree we consciously and willingly suspended disbelief is hard to say. Some English brides of G.I.s were certainly misled as to what life on the other side of the Atlantic held in store for them when World War II ended and the time came to cross the ocean. Raised on this steady diet of escapism, they fondly imagined that their future existence in the American countryside would be a rural idyll of spacious ranch houses set amid spectacular scenery, peopled with elegant Joan Crawford and Bette Davis types, or an opulent Manhattan penthouse amid a forest of sky-scrapers in which a silk-clad Veronica Lake lounged. Reality seldom lived up to imagination. That was often a clapboard house with outdoor plumbing on the bald prairie where a sweat-stained husband battled isolation and the elements, or a sweltering Bronx tenement with no one in sight even faintly approximating, in looks and style, Alice Faye or Lana Turner. Had we collectively pondered a little, we might have concluded that the manner in which life unfolded was a far cry from its depiction on the silver screen, where conflict was resolved with remarkable ease in the space of less than two hours.

Most obviously—and with the advantage of hindsight—we might have pondered the absence of certain social and emotional problems. Venereal disease, abortion, birth control, sexual molestation of children and euthanasia were but some of the themes one would have searched for in vain in popular screen literature of the time. To be fair, in reality a conspiracy of silence surrounded these subjects. A curious prudishness reigned supreme. Salty language proliferated in most neighborhoods, but the foulest profanity uttered by the most weatherbeaten of movie seamen was "Darn." Pregnancy was shyly announced by wife to husband in some circumlocuitous manner by referring to an imminent "little visitor" or by knitting baby bootees. Once delivered into this world, the screen newborn could never be shown in the altogether. Indeed, it was impossible to discover many anatomical differences between the sexes beyond the swelling female bosom and hips, and both were kept decently covered. One could not even see a female navel in an American picture until 1961, when Christine Kauffman nonchalantly exposed her belly-button to the gaze of Kirk Douglas in *Town Without Pity*. Divorce was a permissible springboard for plot development but only if its awful consequences were visited on the guilty party and made plain for all to see; it was never an answer to marital unhappiness. Unrepentant protagonists, such as those who committed adultery, were invariably doomed to permanent unhappiness or even death—a reminder, as if we needed one, of the wages of sin. But most marital difficulties evaporated before the fade-out by a variety of plot mechanisms whose essential creakiness seemed insignificant when juxtaposed with the lovers' final embrace. The glow of happiness that embrace induced in the audience was supposed to obliterate disconcerting thoughts about the difficulties of everyday male-female relationships and send it home smiling.

Intellectuals might scoff at the naivete of the movies. Their propagation of a simplistic, melodramatic, Victorian set of values was sufficient to exclude them from consideration as a legitimate art form. That was true even of Chaplin and Griffith, who were later hailed as masters of the American cinema. There was some justification for this viewpoint. Technologically, the medium advanced from the primitivism of the early silents to the talkies in the space of thirty years. The literary quotient of the average picture remained so low as to be beneath the attention of scholars. The movies' vision was one of political and cultural conservatism that reflected the prejudices and beliefs of the majority of its predominantly proletarian audience. Industrially and scientifically, the United States might have been in the forefront of change, but culturally and morally it remained a backwater. European visitors never ceased to be amused by the spectacle of American mothers hastening to cover the top half of their female two year-olds at the beach, or the euphemism "powdering one's nose" as a prim substitute for describing a normal, everyday bodily function. Near total nudity was to reach the fashion pages and the beaches before it appeared on the screen. This innate puritanism might seem to be at odds with the concept of the glamor girl, and objectors could summon the so-called Hollywood sex symbols in their defense of the movies' daring. And yet, on closer inspection, there was an innate childish innocence to their characters. Marilyn Monroe might not be the girl you brought home to mother for Sunday dinner, but her appeal was of a credulous, nonthreatening sort. The fortyish Mae West was a travesty of female sexuality, and Jane Russell soon jettisoned the half-breed image of *The Outlaw* to become an athletic outdoor girl and even screen mother-confessor to Monroe. The really popular female stars of the domestic cinema projected an image of girl-next-door wholesomeness (Betty Grable, Judy Garland) and always appeared to be in the virginal state. Doris Day, the most successful female actress of the fifties, was regularly cast as the all-American girl who surrendered her maidenhood only after wedding bells had pealed. It was axiomatic that the threat to these values came almost entirely from foreign women such as Brigitte Bardot, Sophia Loren and Gina Lollobrigida, who arrived on these shores carrying their looser European morals in their baggage.

The American public was complacent to the point of defensiveness in its acceptance of chastity and associated rigid social mores on the screen. Movie moguls boasted of the family values to be found in their pictures. The list of those who fell from grace when their public personae failed to measure up to the screen image is long, starting with Fatty Arbuckle and continuing through Mary Pickford, Ingrid Bergman and even Julie Andrews once she shed her clothes and her sweet *Sound of Music* character. The files of the Legion of Decency yield very few expressions of protest against its imperious impositions. On the contrary, they contain pleas urging unceasing vigilance in combatting perceived immorality both on-screen and in the private lives of actors.

And so, as we sat in our seats in the theaters, we knew next to nothing and thought even less about the Hays Office, the Production Code and the Legion's ratings. That would not have been unpleasing to them, for all three subscribed to the "ignorance is bliss" philosophy. We were unaware of a mind set that was obsessed with the ideology of natural law and its literal application but paid scant attention to actual human behavior. A passionate kiss that lasted and lasted was wrong be it betwixt husband and wife or a pair of illicit lovers. A plunging necklines was forbidden whether its wearer was a slut or a "nice girl." Dance-hall women, we somehow came to know, were invariably loose. It was the appearance of morality that counted, not the underlying message. Film-makers learned to play the game. The pounding of waves on rocks, and the candle shooting heaven-wards were synonymous with passion and orgasm, but one had to learn these conventions by constant attention to the screen to be able to appreciate their meaning. There were a dozen different ways to suggest the unutterable. It was a permanent duel of wits between the Hollywood producers and the guardians of morality. The most formidable of the latter was to be found in the heart of New York City, its hierarchy dressed in black, its membership huge, its powers of retribution against transgressors of decency merciless, its agenda—to mold the content of American motion picture enter-tainment to its will.

The Cross
and
the Cinema

_____ *Chapter 1* _____

American Film Censorship
to 1933

In April 1896, in a thirty-second motion picture that appeared within days of Edison's first public film show in the United States, a portly, elderly gentleman twirled his moustache and proceeded to kiss a lady of indeterminate but equally advanced years.[1] The actual osculation lasted barely ten seconds. Nevertheless, what John C. Rice and May Irwin had restaged for the screen from their stage success, *The Widow Jones*, was condemned as shocking. "No more than a lyric of the Stock Yards," wrote one disgusted observer.[2] Less than a year later another assault on the sensibilities of the decent-thinking was mounted by an anonymous young woman in *Fatima Dances*. In a solo act that again claimed no more than half a minute of audience attention, the title character's enthusiastic gyrations exposed her calves as her skirt twirled knee-high. She then proceeded to cause her fully clothed stomach and bosom to move up and down in rhythmic fashion. Bowing to expressions of public indignation, the distributors of the offensive item attempted to mitigate the severity of this insult to good taste by having two sets of thick parallel lines drawn across the image of her body at strategic intervals. Thus were screen censorship and industry self-regulation born. They have dominated the American commercial cinema ever since.

More than any other expressive art form or popular entertainment, the motion picture has had to bear the continuous scrutiny of moral watchdogs. It would occasion outrage and recourse to protection of first amendment rights if bookstores, art galleries and the live theater were daily forced to exclude customers on the basis of age or have their commodities classified, emasculated and confiscated on the basis of content by governments or groups whose collective or individual identities were unknown to the general public. The movies have always had to labor under such restrictions.

Why this medium was singled out for such stringent control for the best part of a century is not difficult to deduce. The power of the visual image to move hearts and minds has long been recognized. But the distinctly plebian origin of the motion picture is an equally important facet. From the outset, movies were created for mass consumption with no pretensions to literary merit. Appearing in the last decade of the nineteenth century, they were, for America especially, a case of the right invention in the right place at the right time. For millions of new and recent immigrants, the silent film was an exclusively visual medium requiring very little fluency in a strange language, beyond recognition of a few words on card titles inserted intermittently between the images, and in this regard it was unlike vaudeville or the stage. It was also inexpensive—an important consideration for an impecunious segment of the population. The arcade owners who screened movies in tents, rooms and halls in those early years were content with a modest admission charge that gave the nickelodeon its name. But—and this was among the most alarming aspects of the new invention—it permitted the unchaperoned to sit alone in the dark and witness who knew how many unsavory and subversive images. As the preamble to the Hays Code—which appeared a generation later—would state bluntly, "Most art appeals to the mature. This art appeals to every class, mature, immature, developed, undeveloped, law abiding, criminal."[3] Classical music, painting, sculpture, great literature and drama were assumed to be primarily for the higher classes; movies pandered to the lowest. From this assumption it was easy to extrapolate the theory that since there were, numerically, more of the latter, mass resistance to suggestion would be commensurately feebler among these uneducated souls. Even in communities remote from what was perceived, at the turn of the century, to be a hardening process in ethical and moral values in the burgeoning, impersonal cities, the pernicious influence of the motion picture could be fairly indicted because of its accessibility and popularity. In short, it was the great unwashed who patronized the picture shows, uncritically and with deplorably enthusiastic regularity. It was the moral duty of their betters, protests from libertarians to the contrary, to save them from their baser instincts.

Early in the present century the censorious impulse came from politicians no less than clergymen. There were always votes to be garnered from an impressionable public by those who ostentatiously posed as guardians of morality. On Christmas Eve, 1908, Mayor George B. McClellan of New York City, with an eye firmly fixed on the next election, summarily closed all of the city's six hundred-plus movie theaters, citing both the potential fire hazard from the use of inflammable celluloid and the content of too many movies that were threatening to "degrade or injure the morals of the community."[4] Though an injunction obtained by the exhibitors thwarted the mayor's intentions, city council struck back in January with a by-law that excluded those under sixteen from attending unless accompanied by an adult. Undaunted, theater managers suddenly found legions of surrogate guardians within close proximity of their places of business to accompany the young to the box office and children just as quickly discovered long-lost "parents" as if by magic on the doorstep of the picture houses.[5]

Behind Mayor McClellan were clergymen anxious to cleanse the Augean stable of movie theaterdom if the doors could not be permanently bolted. A public meeting held in New York two days before Christmas in 1908 attracted spokespersons from the Interdenominational Committee for the Suppression of Sunday Vaudeville, and, among others, Canon William S. Chase of Christ Church, Brooklyn. Chase stoutly affirmed that his future life's work was to remove the filth purveyed by those who had "no moral scruples whatever," and were simply in the trade for the money.[6] Individuals from various denominations testified that the new-fangled invention was demoralizing children by encouraging degeneracy and keeping them from attending Sunday school. A countervailing note to this chorus of disapproval was struck by Dr. Charles Sprague Smith, founder of the People's Institute of New York, an adult education and social research institute. In the aftermath of controversy following the showing of *The Great Thaw Trial*, which dealt with the sensational Harry Thaw–Evelyn Nesbit case, Smith had formed a board of review to study the movie scene. Though acknowledging the film's shortcomings, the subsequent report was not entirely negative, seeing theaters as "places not to be condemned *in toto*; they are needed to meet the demands of the majority and attention must be given them in a constructive way."[7] This was balm to the wounded sensibilities of the industry and provided it with ammunition when the time came to rebut the charges laid against it. William Fox, whose name was later to be synonymous with a major studio, pointed to statistics that, if true, gave an indication of the enormous growth of the business in barely more than a decade. To close down the city's picture houses would mean a loss of $50 million a year and the livelihood of 40 thousand persons, besides depriving honest citizens of legitimate places of amusement.

Meanwhile, other jurisdictions were not idle. In 1907 Chicago's city council passed an ordinance giving the police powers of inspection and licensing of all films. Movies would be denied a certificate if the police chief found them to be immoral or obscene.[8] Major cities and states followed suit. The Pennsylvania format was a model for the rest of the nation. It comprised a state board of censors appointed by the governor, whose members were paid an annual salary and granted powers to inspect, cut or ban outright all unsuitable films and associated advertising material. By 1925 over ninety cities and more than a dozen states had censorship boards in place. Their efficacy in keeping disreputable fare off the screen varied from one locality to another. The sheer number of movies produced and the wide variation in quality proved too much for some to handle. The framing of suitable legislation that would stand up to court challenges tested the minds of lawyers. Inconsistent standards and personal prejudices laid the censors open to charges that they were provincial, narrow and lacking in uniformity.

Nevertheless, the motion picture industry received a blow in those early years from which it would take a generation to recover. It fell particularly hard on D. W. Griffith's *Birth of a Nation* and was administered by the U.S. Supreme Court. Griffith's epic of the Civil War and Reconstruction had generated controversy throughout the land for its denigration of blacks and its unabashed glorification of the Ku Klux Klan. The author of the equally racist novel, *The Clansmen*, from which it was adapted, the Rev. Thomas Dixon, sought to obtain the imprimatur of the Supreme Court, and especially that of the chief justice, Edward Douglas White, to disarm the criticism. Far from affording it the protection Dixon had anticipated, the Court unanimously and pointedly excluded all motion pictures from First Amendment protection, finding their exhibition nothing more than a business, pure and simple, originated and conducted for profit like other spectacles, and unlike the press, which was an organ of public opinion. Films were mere representations of events, ideas and sentiments, undoubtedly vivid and entertaining but also capable of evil because of their attractiveness and manner of exhibition.[9]

Certainly a significant premise to be drawn from the decision was that motion pictures were relegated to the level of a carnival act or circus performance, with no compensatory aesthetic or literary merit. It doomed the film medium to inferior status. Whatever noble thoughts could be expressed on the stage or by the printed word lay beyond the ability of the cinema, which was purely an entertainment and therefore not to be judged by the criteria applied to legitimate art forms. There was, too, a fallacy in the judgment that implied that the motion picture business existed for the sake of the profit motive while the press somehow operated at a more exalted level as a purveyor of public opinion, as if newspapers were not bought, sold and operated for financial gain. But the most sinister assumption in the verdict for the future of the American cinema was its capacity for evil in the hands of unethical, unscrupulous showmen. Constant vigilance would be needed to ensure that the public was protected from the insidious effects of subversive pictures—control of the medium at its source would prevent the cancer from gaining a foothold.

Of the First World War it has been truly said that it was rich in unintended consequences. Not only did it result in the disappearance of four empires, the triumph of Leninism in Russia and the rise of the United States to world power status, it caused a profound change in social behavior in America and elsewhere. The chaperon became a declining commodity as young women pursued more independent lifestyles. The old morality was everywhere questioned and found wanting. Americans of the postwar era, known variously as The Jazz Age and The Lost Generation, scandalized those of another generation by indulging in the consumption of bootleg liquor, dancing frenetically and allowing females to smoke in public. The mood of the times was caught by film producers and directors in titles that told all. Before Cecil B. deMille gained a reputation as a producer and director of Biblical epics, he made a name for himself with *Don't Change Your Husband, For Better and Worse* and *Forbidden Fruit*, all dealing variously with stuffy, hidebound males, free-spirited females, marital infidelity and the nonconformist behavior of hedonistic youth.[10] DeMille's success spawned imitators whose works were even less subtle in their glorification of the younger generation and its audacious behavior.

On the other hand, the forces of traditional morality were just as determined to preserve the old lifestyle, even if it meant using constitutional means to achieve that end. The Volstead Act that ushered in the prohibition era was but one expression of a trend toward the contraction of personal freedom of action. Women's hairstyles, clothing and swimming attire were also assailed, though much less successfully. The mass of the population had to be protected against crass materialism and its baser self. It was logical, then, that movies should continue to be scrutinized and, inevitably, found wanting. In 1920, for example, a study commissioned by the General Federation of Women's Clubs stated that 80 percent of all motion pictures examined were either "bad" or "not worth while."[11] The upsurge in crime that had followed the Armistice was attributed, in part, to the baleful influence of the movies. The increasing domination of the motion picture business by Jews, who had largely replaced the mostly white Anglo-Saxon pioneers, caused an escalation in criticism that had nasty undertones of racial and religious intolerance. Canon Chase called his supporters "Patriotic Gentile Americans," while a kindred spirit, the Rev. William S. Crafts, spoke of the need "to rescue motion pictures from the hands of the Devil and 500 un-Christian Jews."[12]

Hollywood itself had gained a reputation as a latter-day Sodom in the postwar era, thanks, in part, to the fan magazines that dwelled at length on the extravagant lifestyles and occasional sexual peccadillos of its stars. The studios delighted in publicizing the romances and unconventional relationships of their leading players. Mysterious disappearances of actresses, with hints of suicide, or of passionate affairs being consummated in distant, romantic locales became the stock-in-trade of imaginative press agents. Entranced by exaggerated accounts of unknowns who had risen from anonymity to instant recognition and fabulous wealth within a short time of arriving in the film capital, thousands of hopeful young women streamed into Los Angeles from all parts of the country with the same impossible dream in mind. Local charitable agencies and concerned individuals strove to cope with the disillusioned by kindly suggesting that they swallow their pride and return home, sometimes providing them with the wherewithal for the return fare, or, perhaps, finding them a menial job in the expanding economy. Inevitably, a few escaped or fell through this well-meaning social rescue net and turned to prostitution as a means of survival. The scene was set for scandal, and scandal duly obliged.

The first of four sensational occurrences in the early twenties involved Mary Pickford, known as "America's Sweetheart" for her appearance in a succession of innocuous melodramas where she was invariably cast as the spunky but innocently childlike heroine. In 1920 she shocked her fans by divorcing Owen Moore in Nevada and almost immediately afterwards marrying her lover, Douglas Fairbanks, Sr., who had projected a similar on-screen image of wholesomeness and virtue. At one point in the divorce proceedings, the state's attorney general had threatened to rescind the decree because of perjured testimony and fraudulent witnesses. Though the charges were dropped, the affair added fuel to the perception that the marital bond in Hollywood was tenuous, to say the least.

The Fairbanks-Pickford affair was soon eclipsed by the most shocking of all scandals ever to affect the film capital. The Fatty Arbuckle "sex-and-murder case," as it was referred to at the time, provided a field day for moralists of all stripes and, more than any other event, led to public demands for censorship and industry awareness of the need for self-regulation.[13]

In the summer of 1921 Roscoe Arbuckle, a baby-faced, rotund comedian whose popularity almost equalled that of Chaplin, was accused of having contributed to the death of Virginia Rappe. Rappe was not the ingenue the Hearst press, in best yellow journalism fashion, tried to foist on the public. A one-time actress, she had had at least two abortions before she met Arbuckle and was suffering from venereal disease, which she had not contracted from him. The actor had driven a group of friends from Los Angeles to San Francisco's St. Francis Hotel for a weekend of fun and heavy drinking. During the course of an evening, Rappe complained of pain in her lower abdomen. By the time a physician was called, she was dead. An autopsy showed a ruptured bladder.

It was the kind of story the newspapers relished. In lurid prose they recreated the scene in their own fashion—of a helpless young girl crushed beneath the body of the obese comedian bent on committing a sex crime. Arbuckle was eventually indicted for manslaughter. Two juries could not reach a decision; the third acquitted him after six minutes. But if the law found him not guilty, the public had already convicted him. As protest letters and petitions flooded into Paramount Pictures, the decision was made to withdraw all of his movies in circulation and write off, as a loss, his recently signed $3 million contract. Though Arbuckle picked up a little work here and there under an assumed name, his career as a major star was at an end.[14]

Wallace Reid, a matinee idol, had suffered a back injury in a train accident in 1919 during the course of filming *Valley of Giants*. Unwilling to lose shooting time, a producer had ordered the company doctor to give him an injection of morphine to kill the pain. Reid was soon hopelessly addicted to the drug, and although he managed to conceal the fact from the public, his costars knew that something was amiss. His need for the narcotic became greater as the years passed until the inevitable happened. He was discovered dead of an overdose in a sanatorium where he had gone, in desperation, to find a cure.

The unsolved murder of the English director, William Dean Taylor, crowned the shoddy edifice, as it were. The Lasky studios for whom he worked attempted to cover up the details with some success. However, the career of Mabel Normand, a talented comedienne who had been a favorite costar of Chaplin's, was quickly in eclipse, the result of her having been the last person to see him alive, and other bits and pieces of incriminating evidence, including monogrammed underwear, linking her to the deceased.

These were the most prominent scandals of the era, and they were sufficient to convince many that there was something rotten in the state of California. Invidious comparisons were made with baseball and the Chicago White Sox game-fixing scandal in the 1919 World Series. It, too, had demonstrated that some of the public's idols were human after all. More to the point, it had forced that sporting establishment to look beyond its ranks for a "morality czar" who could restore decency and credibility to the game. Perhaps the time had come for the film industry to do likewise and find a savior to lead it out of the Slough of Despond.

Its choice was a cheerful-faced, midwesterner with protruding ears and a shrill voice. Will H. Hays had many attributes that made him suitable for the task. He was an elder of the Presbyterian church and exuded an air of respectability. A career in law and local politics in Indiana had propelled him through Republican party ranks to the status of National Committee Chairman during the presidential campaign of 1920, which saw the election of Warren G. Harding. In 1921 Hays was made Postmaster General, a position that required both business skills and political finesse. His interest in movies as something more than entertainment dated from 1916, when he had been impressed by the use Woodrow Wilson's campaign managers had made of a short film promoting the pacifist inclinations of their candidate. Thereafter he treated newsreel cameramen with courtesy and respect, especially during Harding's own campaign. Like Lenin in the Soviet Union, he saw film as an important propaganda tool.[15]

The industry's major concern was to avert federal censorship and regulation of its business practices. In 1916, producers and directors had formed the National Association of the Motion Picture Industry (NAMPI). Somewhat belatedly, it adopted the first code, known as the Thirteen Points or Standards, which proscribed subjects such as white slavery, illicit love, nakedness, crime, gambling and drunkenness. These impossibly wide parameters guaranteed that it would remain a dead letter, since not even the major companies were prepared to abide by a strict interpretation of the rules. A measure of its failure was a move in both the Senate and House of Representatives to entertain proposed legislation to ban movies depicting crime and criminal characters. During 1921, thirty-seven states considered legislation that would restrict motion picture exhibition in one way or another through the creation or extension of existing censorship boards.

Thus it was in an atmosphere of trepidation and in the face of a common danger that members of NAMPI sent two representatives to Washington, D.C. in December 1921 to seek out Will Hays. As contemporary Hollywood wags put it, he was asked to become "czar of all the rushes," at the enormous salary of $100,000 a year. As an indication that a new leaf was being turned, NAMPI was abolished and its successor, the Motion Picture Producers and Distributors of America (MPPDA), established in March 1922, with Hays as its president.

It says much for Hays's strength of character that he imposed his personality and opinions on the industry from the outset, to such a degree that his name became synonymous with the office he ran. This "mail order Moses," who had come to lead the movie people out of a desert of moral opprobrium, was at his best in the early years of his reign, presenting an affable face to the public and, by his personal charm, helping to soothe the susceptibilities of innumerable pressure groups who felt bound to continue the fight against degeneracy. After one of his early visits to Hollywood, he told a reporter from *Time* that he had found the film capital free from vice. "No drinking—very little smoking. And as for the evenings—they're just as quiet! Why they're practically inaudible. No sound at all but the popping of the California poppies."[16] To gild this particular lily, he suggested a series of vignettes on the home life of the stars. Thus Alma Rubens was seen cuddling a puppy and talking trivia with her mother in the family kitchen while Marion Davies earnestly vacuumed a rug in her tiny apartment, scarcely aware of the camera's presence. That Rubens was dead of a drug overdose shortly after this appearance and Davies was then living in the sartorial splendor of San Simeon with her lover, William Randolph Hearst, were facts to be carefully concealed from the public. Byron Haskin attests to the sort of lifestyle that continued behind the careful window dressing. A pot-pourri of drugs was available at many of the parties thrown by stars and producers. Even the testimonial dinner for Hays himself was marred by the expulsion of several guests who had become inebriated from drinking bootleg booze from teacups at the catered affair.[17]

One of the first victories in the war against state censorship proved to be decisive inasmuch as no major state law to regulate film content was passed after that date. The battle was won in heavily Catholic Massachusetts in 1922, where secular and religious groups had agitated for a referendum on the subject. Treating it like a political campaign, Hays used all the skills he had honed in Washington, supplemented by dollops of industry money, to defeat the proposition by a two-to-one margin. The pitch to voters had included a plea that the industry be allowed a little more time to set its affairs in order. It was afterwards revealed that the press had been liberally courted with some of the $150,000 from the coffers of the MPPDA itself. But, above all, the triumph was as much psychological as it was practical in reinforcing the fear of government censorship in the public mind.

In June 1922 Hays organized a conference at the Waldorf-Astoria Hotel in New York, to which he invited two thousand representatives from over two hundred civic, religious, educational and service institutions. Always the politician, he saw the one way to blunt the edge of agitation for change in the current state of the motion picture industry was to meet the critics half way and co-opt them under some kind of umbrella organization that would then give advice to filmmakers and support them in the amelioration of content. One of those involved from the outset was the International Federation of Catholic Alumnae (IFCA), a women's group that was to play an integral part in the operations of the Legion of Decency some twelve years later. For the moment, the IFCA became part of a committee of twenty that in due course became the official Committee on Public Relations, whose main tasks were to register objection with the MPPDA over specific pictures of which it disapproved and to encourage the public to patronize those that merited support. The Catholic Alumnae ladies found themselves in the company of women from other denominations and representatives from the Boy Scouts, Campfire Girls and the American Legion.[18]

It may be questioned whether anyone who took part in the deliberations of this Committee on Public Relations was really clear what purpose it was intended to serve beyond improving the status quo, and certainly not all were in agreement as to how this might be achieved. From the outset there were accusations that it was nothing but a creature of the Hays Office depending on it for much of its operating expenses. More, Hays was always prepared to pamper its constituent members in a variety of ways ranging from the loan of recent feature films for conventions to arranging trips to Hollywood for individual executive members where the awestruck were given studio tours, met the stars and were wined and dined sumptuously. Unwilling to bite the hand that literally fed it, the Committee on Public Relations tried to elevate the viewing tastes of the public rather than engage in the unsavory occupation of suggesting cuts in films. Some member organizations issued lists of recommended pictures to subscribers, which the Hays office thoughtfully agreed to mail or subsidize. Recalcitrant organizations such as local chapters of the General Federation of Women's Clubs who still thought state censorship desirable, were denied the choicest fruits of cooperation.[19]

Nevertheless there were limits as to how far Hays could go in his manipulation of the new creation. Fainthearted doubts as to what it was achieving other than acting as a bulwark against external interference and as a smoke screen for questionable fare, conscientious scruples regarding the moral or legal justification for accepting industry largesse, divisions among committee members as to what constituted a good film worthy of recommendation, all combined to produce a degree of uncertainty about the future, with deplorable results. The first strain on the system came in the wake of the Fatty Arbuckle trials, when Hays tried to rehabilitate the disgraced comedian by suggesting that the ban against the exhibition of his pictures be lifted. As he wrote afterwards, "It seemed a relatively commonplace decision. . . . I merely refused to stand in the man's way of earning a living in the only business he knew."[20] But the American public, then as now demanding a higher level of morality from its screen idols and politicians than from its own kith and kin, was in no mood to forgive or forget. The *New York Times* reminded the Hollywood czar that he had been brought west to "deodorize the movies" and this was no time for permitting the whiff of scandal to return. The Committee on Public Relations hastened to adopt a resolution that the industry not exhibit any picture in which Mr. Arbuckle appeared. Fatty himself ended the brief controversy by directing low-budget films and promising not to return as an actor.[21] The demise of the committee occurred during the winter of 1924–25 over some members' objections to a plan by the major production company, Famous Players–Lasky, to make a movie version of the novel *West of the Water Tower*, an action thriller whose unsavory elements included illegitimacy, a clergyman with a tarnished reputation and a collection of fundamentalist, intolerant, mean-minded local citizens. When the company disregarded the protest from the Committee on Public Relations, two of the largest member bodies, the National Congress of Parents and Teachers and the General Federation of Women's Clubs, immediately resigned from the committee.[22]

Hays had another string to his bow, in the National Board of Review. Organized in 1916 by a group of interested citizens, it pleased the industry no end by adopting as its watchword the slogan, "Selection Not Censorship," and allowing its name to be used as an imprimatur in movie credits. Also commendable from the filmmakers' viewpoint was its insistence on cooperation rather than confrontation between the incipient forces of censorship on the one hand and the producers and exhibitors on the other. With its emphasis on better films, family values and children's matinees, it espoused motherhood issues, making it a difficult target for those who regarded it as another piece of window dressing rather than the genuine conscience of movie morality. The fact that its funding came largely from the fees it charged companies to evaluate the pictures gave further substance to the charge that it was a tame fox in charge of the chicken coop. That its standards were far more lax than those of most state and local censorship boards could not be denied. Author Garth Jowett quotes statistics from 1920 showing that while the Pennsylvania State Board made 1,464 cuts in 228 titles, the National Board of Review made only 47, and similar ratios pertained to other jurisdictions throughout the country, despite the fact that it subscribed to much the same set of guidelines as those used by the censorship board.[23]

The furor occasioned by the making of *West of the Water Tower* caused the MPPDA to act on its own behalf rather than depend on the support of associate organizations. The result was "The Formula," which came into effect on June 19, 1924. Each member studio undertook to send to the Hays Office a copy of every play, story or book that it intended to adapt for the screen, together with suggested emendations, comments or queries on portions that might give offense. In turn, the Hays Office would warn its constituents of works it deemed unsuitable for film adaptation. Had the industry proceeded with reasonable caution and tact in the spirit of The Formula, it is at least possible that it might have achieved a measure of success. The hue and cry for control had never been stilled despite Hays's best efforts. But caution and tact were foreign to Hollywood in the mid-twenties. A few complied initially but soon realized that the document had no legal weight and that the MPPDA had not, in any case, a means to enforce its will by way of financial penalty for nonobservance. Moreover, some companies acidly pointed out that they had already paid a stiff price for rights and had no intention of seeing their investment evaporate for ill-defined moral reasons. By tortuous argument they insisted that an unwholesome book could be transformed into a perfectly acceptable film given the proper treatment, while a change of title would make it more difficult for the public to connect the one to the other in its own mind. As for original scripts, The Formula did not apply at all, and these not infrequently contained as much objectionable material as an unexpurgated adaptation. Nevertheless, there was some degree of compliance. Between 1924 and 1930, 125 scripts were rejected—a move, however slight, toward self-control by Hollywood.[24]

Having taken a first step to disarm criticism, Hays next proceeded with the establishment of a Studio Relations Department in 1926. Under the chairmanship of Colonel Jason Joy of the defunct Committee on Public Relations, it was intended as a liaison between the studios and the various state and local censors. Joy listened to the latter and communicated their joint philosophies and standards to the movie producers. They, in turn, began to show him films prior to release and consulted about problem scripts, although this was still an informal procedure. It bore fruit to the extent that those who followed Joy's suggestions ran into less trouble with the authorities once their films were released.

Though sound movies are as old as the cinema itself, it was not until 1926 that their popularity began to establish itself. The advent of the talkies raised new problems. In the early days, at least, actors who had been recruited hurriedly from Broadway and vaudeville for their voices had a tendency to ad-lib their lines (Al Jolson's dialogue in *The Jazz Singer* is a case in point). The sheer amount of verbiage was in striking contrast to the paucity of the written word in the subtitles of silent pictures. The removal of offensive words or sentences not only might destroy the sense of an entire sequence but also would require expensive reshooting. What had been impossible or innocuous in a silent picture—the creak of bedsprings or the mouthing of a curse—now assumed a far greater degree of salaciousness. In October 1927, the month that saw the premiere of *The Jazz Singer*, Rule 21 of the MPPDA's Code of the Motion Picture Industry was adopted. Known less formally as the "Don'ts and be Carefuls," it was a category of eleven topics that must not appear in motion pictures and a further twenty-five topics that required special care in their presentation.[25]

Since these were to become the basis of the Hays Code three years later, an examination of the two lists provides evidence of the Hays Office's concerns regarding motion picture content. The eleven subjects to be banished irrespective of the manner in which they might be treated were: pointed profanity by either title or lip, including "Hell," "Damn" and "Gawd"; any licentious or suggestive nudity—in fact or in silhouette; illegal traffic in drugs; any inference of sex perversion (which meant homosexuality or lesbianism); white slavery; miscegenation; sex hygiene and venereal diseases; scenes of actual childbirth; children's sex organs; ridicule of the clergy; and willful offense to any nation or creed. Subjects to be treated with special care included: the use of the flag; arson; brutality and possible gruesomeness; sympathy for criminals; sedition; rape or attempted rape; first night scenes; a man and woman in bed together; the institution of marriage; and excessive or lustful kissing particularly when one character or the other is the "heavy."[26]

Just as it was similar in format to the old Thirteen Points of the National Association of Motion Picture Producers, so was it ineffective in creating the moral climate Hays had hoped it would achieve. For one thing, the list of "Be

Carefuls" was so long and broad in character that observance to the letter was impossible unless one was satisfied with the blandest of the bland in screen entertainment, or so producers insisted. For another, the public at large, as distinct from fuddy-duddy pressure groups, seemed to have been mesmerized by those early talkies and in no state of mind to raise serious objections as to their content. Filmmakers insisted that cutting or modifying offensive elements in sound motion pictures created the kinds of practical and technical problems that were easily surmounted in the silent era but were now difficult if not impossible to rectify. This was particularly true of the clumsy sound-on-disc process that Warners had popularized as Vitaphone. The sixteen-inch, ten-minute, long-playing records that were synchronized with action on the screen could not be modified at all once the recording had been made. Ominously, several producers refused even to consider the new code and wrote "Return to Sender" across the MPPDA envelope containing it.[27]

Thus, facing the scarcely veiled hostility of obdurate film executives and their satraps, this drive to clean Hollywood's house rapidly lost momentum. Culturally as well as geographically distanced from the centers of ecclesiastical power in their remote Pacific enclave, the movie men saw little need for any compromise with religious pressure groups and were determined to plough ahead with ever racier projects rather than accept the killjoy ordinance of a Presbyterian church elder. Joan Crawford's hot Charleston in her underwear in *Our Dancing Daughters*, Renee Adoree's near transparent slip in *Mating Call* and Jean Harlow's decision to "change into something more comfortable" before entertaining her latest boyfriend in Howard Hughes's *Hell's Angels* were all steps that a genuinely contrite Hollywood with earnest intentions to reform itself would at least have hesitated to take.

As the twenties drew to their close, it seemed Hays was incapable of controlling the industry he had been hired to police and reform. While the origins of the code that was to bear his name have been a matter of dispute, there were a number of circumstances that led to initiatives being undertaken by two outsiders that were to have immediate and far-reaching consequences for the American motion picture business. Together, they reflect a strong and continuous pressure by a variety of interest groups, each animated by a desire to clean up the movies once and for all.

In the first instance, there was a feeling that Hays had had a long enough tenure to achieve results. By 1929 he had been in office for eight years, yet the moral condition of the industry seemed as deplorable as when he first assumed the reins of power. His strategy of co-opting the enemy and subsequently killing it with kindness was tried once too often and exposed for what it was in an incident that occurred in 1928. Among organizations calling for government regulation of the industry at a national level was the Federal Motion Picture Council. Its membership encompassed politicians, business leaders, churchmen and leaders of women's groups. When Hays learned that it intended to hold a conference in Washington, D.C. to address the issue of government regulation, he contacted those who had had a connection with the industry, no matter how peripheral, and urged that they attend. Some of those so persuaded were fully subsidized from the coffers of the MPPDA. During the proceedings they attempted to monopolize the discussion by refusing to cede to other speakers and dwelled at length on the amenability of Hollywood to listen to reason. Before the conference ended, this delegation ostentatiously walked out and retired to a hotel room where the leader held a press conference. Reporters were told that representatives of prominent national organizations had left in protest because they had been unconvinced that regulation of motion pictures was necessary. Hays would later assert that the Federal Motion Picture Council's name was a misnomer and that it was unrepresentative of public opinion.[28] As Ruth Inglis succinctly put it, his "open door" policy continued to be a kind of trap door to siphon off criticism. But now that kind of criticism would not be stilled.

Formidable voices were added to the chorus of complaints. Senator Smith W. Brookhart of Iowa introduced a bill in March 1928 to have the Federal Trade Commission add the movie industry to the bodies it directly supervised, and saw the business maneuverings of Hollywood as a fight between rival Jewish factions. William Randolph Hearst, no paragon of virtue, to be sure, nevertheless promised to throw the weight of his newspaper empire behind any move for federal control. As if to corroborate what many Americans already suspected, foreign censorship boards from Canada to New Zealand made a record number of cuts in prints in January and February of the same year.

Ever since Warners' premiere of *The Jazz Singer*, the rest of Hollywood had remained skeptical as to whether sound would revolutionize the medium or wane and die like other fads. But by mid-1929 it was clear that the talkies had caught the public's imagination and rendered the silents obsolete. Now the rush was on to transform the industry. Talking pictures cost far more to produce and exhibit, since new equipment had to be installed in theaters and stages had to be insulated against extraneous noise. Uncertain as to content and conscious of the larger budgets the new format demanded, producers tried to play safe by filming successful stage plays imported from Broadway and London's West End. Themes and dialogue were, depending on one's viewpoint, more mature or more salacious than what had appeared in the common run of silents. Hays was aware of the "objectionable things" that were creeping into some of the pictures. The "Don'ts and Be Carefuls" had become a fly-stained poster, obsolete and largely ignored. What was required was a codification of iron-clad rules, a philosophy that enunciated their moral justification and machinery that would enforce their observance. A Motion Picture Production Code seemed the answer. A lay Catholic newspaper man and a theology professor were to supply it.

Martin Quigley (1890–1964), a graduate of the Catholic University of America, first experienced the nascent movie industry as a reporter in Cleveland, Detroit and Chicago. Marriage to an heiress enabled him to branch out into publishing and acquire the *Moving Picture World* and the *Exhibitor's Herald*, which he merged into the *Motion Picture Herald*, the prime trade paper in the nation by 1928. Two years previously he had launched a complementary career as go-between when he hovered around the filming of the Eucharistic Congress in Chicago. From then until his death he was to have one foot in the film world and the other in the higher reaches of the Catholic Church, of which he was a devout member.

Quigley never deviated from the idea that the movies were exclusively a popular entertainment and should have no pretensions toward advancing the frontiers of artistic achievement nor contain antisocial messages. The filmmaker's duty was limited to providing decent, wholesome material that was fit for family viewing and would mirror the values of the Catholic Church. A moviegoer should exit from a show as moral a person as when he or she entered. Surveying the rising tide of outrage, he conceived of a means whereby the industry would not only be brought to heel but would genuinely reflect what was best in morality as defined by his religion. There was, to be sure, a degree of altruism inherent in his participation. But by successfully dictating a moral code to a recalcitrant industry, he would increase his standing and that of his growing newspaper empire[29] and become the moral *eminence grise* of moviedom.

Quigley was an inveterate opponent of government censorship although he recognized that, by 1929, the local variety of state and city censorship was too well established to be removed. His fight was with the concept of federal control, which he dismissed as impractical in terms of cutting prints, and unworkable because political appointees would be the creations of the party in power in Washington and installed in positions of authority on the basis of political loyalty, not superior morality. His plan for the elusive goal of movies fit for the American public called for a self-administered code whose rules would be binding on all filmmaking companies and whose philosophy would be spelled out in detail. Implicitly, it would contain nothing inimical to the Church.

The crusade began in Chicago with his priest, Father FitzGeorge Dineen, an advisor to the city's censorship board and a family friend. Dineen suggested the Rev. Daniel A. Lord as best qualified to compose such a code. Lord's credentials were impressive. As well as being a theologian, he was a playwright and professor of English and drama at St. Louis University and had served as one of three technical experts on deMille's 1927 *King of Kings*, where he said mass before each day's filming. Despite initial opposition from Chicago's George Cardinal Mundelein, who had doubts as to whether the Church should become so involved in attempting to control the movie business, Lord and Quigley pressed ahead with their creation in the fall and winter of 1929. After a series of consultations with Hays, studio heads and producers, the finished article appeared for adoption by the industry in March 1930.[30]

The document was in two parts. The first comprised the Code itself, as drafted by Lord and Quigley, and the second was an addendum entitled "Resolution for Uniform Interpretation." It is instructive to note that not until 1934 was this combined text published in the *Motion Picture Herald*. Though Quigley never gave a reason for the delay, it seems reasonable to assume that both he and the MPPDA were unwilling to reveal its distinctly Catholic slant. After Quigley's action, the Hays Office added a segment containing the philosophical musings of the two authors of the Code, also dating from 1930. The revised document contained the Code itself, "Reasons Supporting Preamble of Code," "Reasons Underlying the General Principles" and "Reasons Underlying Particular Applications." Over the following six years, further additions would be made regarding crime (1938), costuming (1939) and cruelty to animals (1940), the last mentioned in response to public outrage generated by stories concerning the maiming and death of horses during filming of Warner Brother's *Charge of the Light Brigade* (1938). A perusal of the Hays Code leaves no room to doubt that the agenda was primarily concerned with sins of the flesh. Of the twelve categories defined, eight dealt with sexuality. The "Sex" category itself occupied more space than any of the others and covered the sanctity of marriage, low forms of sex relationship, adultery, scenes of passion, seduction and rape, sex perversion, white slavery, miscegenation, sex hygiene (including any reference to contraception or venereal disease), childbirth and exposure of children's sex organs. Even the "Locations" section referred exclusively to bedrooms, where the treatment "must be governed by good taste and delicacy" which, in effect, established the custom of twin beds for married couples. Sin and evil were permitted as valid dramatic material but there had to be a sharp differentiation between "sin which repels by its very nature" and "sins which often attract." If a film contained moral transgressions, compensating moral values had to be inserted as a counterbalance. Quigley and his co-religionists had a clear idea of what would no longer be permitted. The list included marital separation and divorce as solutions to marriage breakdown, adultery as acceptable behavior when a partner could not obtain dissolution of the marriage, birth control, euthanasia or suicide as a viable outlet for ending unendurable pain and ministers of religion as comic characters or villains. Pregnancy and childbirth were to remain indecorous subjects and referred to in as circumlocutory a manner as possible. Nudity, whether complete, partial or in silhouette, was expected to disappear from the screen immediately. Over and above these specific exclusions, the Code was intended to place under careful scrutiny the stylistic approach to every subject.

Hays greeted the Code as "the very thing I had been looking for," and he may have genuinely viewed it as a way to disarm criticism, but the Hollywood chiefs had a different reaction. For them it was just another public relations gimmick, the latest smoke screen that would placate an ever-restive public but allow them to continue as before. Lip service might be paid to the Code by joining in the applause, but otherwise it would be strictly business as usual. Or not quite. The advent of the Great Depression following the Wall Street crash of October 29, 1929 had signalled tough times for the movie moguls as it had for the economy as a whole. The collapse of the economic system came at a particularly inopportune time for the film industry. The adoption of sound pictures had forced massive expenditures on new theaters—$160 million in 1928 alone. Production costs doubled or trebled as the new technique demanded insulated sound stages, more sophisticated processing laboratories and scores of miscellaneous, pricey innovations. It has been calculated that the average budget for a feature film rose fivefold between 1920 and 1930, or from $60,000 to $300,000. In the euphoric atmosphere that initially greeted the talkies, it was assumed that the film business was somehow immune to the disasters that were occurring in other segments of the economy. Attendance figures appeared to substantiate the optimism. Between 1927 and 1930 weekly viewing rose from 57 million to 90 million, despite an increase in admission prices. It seemed that not even the new-fangled radio, once dreaded for its perceived impact in keeping potential customers at home, could stop the onward and upward march of the movies.

Unfortunately the slump's impact had only been delayed. By 1931 the relentless grip of depression began to tighten around Hollywood. If confirmation were required of a gloomy diagnosis of the situation, it could be found in weekly ticket sales. Between 1931 and 1933 admissions fell almost as rapidly as they had risen in the previous four years, so that, by 1933, they were just slightly ahead of the 1927 figure, at 60 million. The steady rise in theater construction was reversed, and 4,800 cinemas closed their doors. Under the impact of these doleful statistics, the financial health of the studios rapidly deteriorated. Paramount, which had ended the twenties as the most powerful movie corporation in America with the continent's largest theater chain and a worldwide distribution system, found it harder and harder to meet its enormous mortgage payments for acquisitions. An $8 million profit in 1930 had become a staggering $20 million deficit by 1933 despite a 33.3 percent cut in budget for filming, an overall reduction in salaries and the sale of its share in CBS for $41.2 million. Paramount went into receivership and its debts were turned over to court-appointed trustees.[31] Fox entered the thirties in the worst shape of all the major studios with a hand-to-mouth policy of repaying debts through short-term notes. Its losses rose to $11.5 million by 1932 and the holding company for its theaters went into receivership. Warners, which might have been expected to weather the storm better than most because of its early espousal of sound, piled up losses similar to those of its competitors and survived only by paring budgets to the bone and divesting itself of 300 of its 700 theaters through closures and termination of leases. In short, the Depression years witnessed a torrent of red ink on most balance sheets in the film capital.

Faced with this financial sea of troubles, Hollywood determined that sensationalism and exciting action in greater quantities were required to lure the missing millions back into their picture palaces. Those bogeymen of the censors—sex and violence—were to dominate screen fare for the period 1930–34. Films were racier and more explicit than ever before during this four-year period, giving rise to the inaccurate but well-recognized phrase, "precode picture," as a synonym for outspoken entertainment.

A popular genre of the era was the gangster film as exemplified by *Little Caesar* and *Public Enemy*, which established the careers of Edward G. Robinson and James Cagney respectively. Though the law invariably exacted moral retribution in the final reel, the wealthy, hoodlum heroes of these and dozens of imitations led lives of excitement amid plush nightclubs and bulletproof cars in the company of beautiful and sexually available women. Morality groups might fulminate against them as primers for juvenile delinquency and draw dark comparisons between their inherent anarchic immorality and the increase in actual crime in the streets as practiced by Capone, Dillinger and their ilk. But the moviegoing public found a narcotic in thrillers that banished from the mind, for a few hours at least, the cruel world of soup kitchens and Hoovervilles that lay beyond the Bijou and the Ritz.

One aspect of the Depression years that provided a plot mechanism for precode movies was the "fallen woman" syndrome. As despair grew and poverty and hunger became realities, social workers observed that more and more working class females were having to resort to prostitution to support themselves and their children. So it was with the Marlene Dietrich character in *Blonde Venus*, a wife who became a kept woman for the sake of her husband and a hooker for the sake of her child. Not all of the screen ladies of the night were so basically virtuous. Some simply thirsted after fantasy and reaped the consequences or drifted into the profession through moral turpitude. Whatever the motive, the public's appetite was whetted by titles like *My Sin, Tarnished Lady* and *Hot Stuff*. But of all the females who roused the censors' ire, none drove them to greater heights of apoplexy than Mae West.

With her plain looks and buxom figure, West was a far cry from today's concept of a screen beauty, and by the time she began her movie career she was already middle-aged.[32] What alarmed her detractors most was her flippant attitude toward sex. The subject had never been absent from the American screen, to be sure, but it had always had an aura of high seriousness or mystical allure. West made it funny and sinless and led her audience to understand that it felt good. Her stage plays had given some indication of the double entendres and other assorted bits of ribaldry to be expected, and she did not disappoint with her screen debut in *She Done Him Wrong*. With a heroine described as the finest woman who ever walked the streets and a supporting character called Russian Rita who dabbled in white slavery, the tone was set. Scarcely had the outrage subsided than West was back on the screen as Tira, a part-time lion tamer, and hoochy koochy dancer, and full-time seducer of "chumps" in the accurately titled *I'm No Angel*. Paramount complied with some suggestions from the Hays Office regarding songs and dialogue. Mae's collection of records, each titled according to the home town of her latest victim, was changed from "No One Does It Like That—Man" to "No One Loves Me Like. . . . " but the method by which she lured hot-blooded businessmen to her bed was unmistakable. Above all else, she was always in command of the situation. She was her own woman.

That, perhaps more than her memorable one-liners, disconcerted the male-dominated censorship establishment and was an important factor in her persecution.

Nothing succeeds like excess. Studio heads looked enviously at Paramount's experience with Mae West and, if they had not already done so, decided to throw caution to the winds. Few films seemed complete without a studied contravention of the Code. Warners' musical, *Golddiggers of 1933*, had a flimsy plot based on the premise that showgirls need sugar daddies as a matter of course if they want to succeed. In one of the major musical numbers, "Petting in the Park," a sinister dwarf ogled dancers as they changed out of their wet clothes behind a thin screen that allowed them to be seen nude in silhouette. Later he supplied Dick Powell with a can opener, the better to get at Ruby Keeler who had donned a tin suit to try and keep roving hands at bay. MGM's *Tarzan, the Ape Man* showed a lightly-clad Jane indulging in some horseplay with Tarzan in a jungle pool and permitted the couple to live together at film's end without benefit of clergy. Al Jolson's *Wonder Bar* was submitted to Hays minus a scene that was added for its general release in which an effeminate man broke in on a dancing couple and waltzed off with the male partner. Greta Garbo administered a slap in the face to that section of the Code referring to low forms of sexual relationship in *Queen Christina*. The Swedish monarch, dressed as a man, agreed to share a room for the evening with John Gilbert. She subsequently revealed her gender and spent an ecstatic night in his bed.

Not surprisingly, the chorus of disapproval over movie licentiousness became a shrill scream. At the same time that Mae West was urging Salvation Army officer Cary Grant to "Come up sometime, and see me" in *She Done Him Wrong*, Henry James Forman's book, *Our Movie Made Children* (1933) was alerting the public to the terrible damage being visited on the nation's youth by motion pictures. Forman's tirade was a deliberately sensationalized condensation of a number of academic studies financed by the Payne Fund. The authors of these studies had found great difficulty in assessing the impact of motion pictures on children and adolescents because of the multitude of other influences on the emotional growth of the young. Forman chose to ignore their tentative conclusions. In breathless prose and by taking phrases out of context, he recounted the incidence of insomnia, rapid eye movements, excitability and other undesirable effects on teenagers from exposure to current Hollywood fare.[33] Within eighteen months the book had gone through four printings, was widely reviewed and discussed and held up as a salutary warning that something had to be done immediately. With Roosevelt newly installed in the White House, it became fashionable to look critically at the recent past and demand a new beginning. With increased federal government involvement in hitherto sacrosanct areas of private enterprise, there seemed to be no reason to exempt the movies. A series of articles by Fred Eastman in *Christian Century* complemented Forman's "discoveries." Eastman was also inclined to tamper with the findings of others in his zeal to prove that movies were to blame for loss of parental authority, delinquency and sexual promiscuity. The cure for the disease was ostracism of its source. The impetus for a moral crusade had to come from an institution with power and respect. The Catholic voice, which had not always been in the forefront of demands for screen censorship, was being heard more loudly. In her October 1933 address to the National Council of Catholic Women, its president, Mary G. Hawks, echoed the views of those present that the movies were "a menace to the physical, mental and moral welfare of the nation. . . . Constant exposure to screen stories of successful gangsters and 'slick' racketeers, of flaming passion and high-power emotionalism may easily nullify every standard of life and conduct set up at home." Her solution was "to use the facilities of organization" to educate public opinion and to boycott bad films.[34] Though she could not have known it, this plea was close to being answered.

Quigley was understandably mortified by developments of the previous three years, which had seen his and Lord's brainchild ignored and derided.[35] By mid-1933, however, he had located an ally in the black heart of the industry to assist him in bringing a contemptuous Hollywood to heel. This was Joseph Ignatius Breen, a fellow Catholic, whom Hays had hired as a public relations advisor, a position Breen had previously held with a coal company. By sheer force of personality Breen climbed the corporate ladder to become Hays's assistant in charge of West Coast operations, while retaining a healthy distaste for the mostly Jewish studio heads and their arrogant ways.[36] He longed for an opportunity to deal with the problem at hand that would enable him to repudiate his boss's kid glove approach and inaugurate a policy of his own. He had been unsuccessful in controlling the excesses of the recent past, partly because of his subordinate position and partly because Hays's remonstrations to end the cycle of salaciousness were met with a few token gestures that seemed to appease the chief. He was also exasperated by the conciliatory attitude of James Wingate, a New York censorship board director whom Hays had appointed as head of Studio Relations. Wingate's tough reputation in the East seemed to melt in the California sun. A few cosmetic changes here and there seemed sufficient to satisfy him—as Paramount discovered when it submitted a revised *She Done Him Wrong.* In substance Breen's policy was to utilize the monolithic structure and power of the Catholic Church in association with Quigley. The Protestant denominations in the country were fragmented and doctrinally at variance with one another; his church spoke with a single voice. But first it would be necessary to convince the hierarchy of the necessity of permanently involving itself in the unsavory chore of laundering the film business.

NOTES

1. There is a rival to Koster and Bial. Some historians are inclined to believe that Woodville Latham used his crude Eidoloscope to project moving images on a screen in his Frankfort Street office in New York on April 21, 1895. See Charles Musser, *The*

Emergence of Cinema: The American Screen to 1907 (New York: Charles Scribners' Sons, 1990), p. 94.

2. *The World*, April 2, 1896. Four stills of the sequence are reproduced in Kenneth MacGowan, *Behind the Screen* (New York: Delta, 1965), p. 95. It may be viewed in its entirety in Blackhawk's *An Edison Album* (16mm).

3. The Code and the written rationale accompanying it are reprinted in full in Leonard J. Leff and Jerold L. Simmons, *The Dame in the Kimono: Hollywood Censorship and the Production Code from the 1920s to the 1960s* (New York: Grove Weidenfeld, 1990), pp. 283–89.

4. Edward de Grazia and Roger K. Newman, *Banned Films: Movies, Censors and the First Amendment* (New York: R. R. Bowker, 1982), p. 10.

5. Garth Jowett, *Film: The Democratic Art* (Boston: Little, Brown, 1976), p. 112. The *New York Times* reported on December 25, "Picture Shows All Put Out of Business."

6. Jowett, p. 111. Chase would carry his campaign into the 1920s and lambaste the newly appointed Hays for inducing voters to act "contrary to the leadership of the Churches."

7. Ruth Inglis, *Freedom of the Movies: A Report on Self-Regulation from the Commission on Freedom of the Press* (Chicago: University of Chicago Press, 1947), p. 75.

8. For an account of the early work, including legal activity of the Chicago board, see Richard S. Randall, *Censorship of the Movies* (Madison: University of Wisconsin Press, 1968), p. 11.

9. The test case was *Mutual Film Corporation v. Industrial Commission of Ohio*, 236 US (1915). Mutual bought prints and distributed them throughout the state. For a full examination of the issue, see Ira H. Carmen, *Movies, Censorship and the Law* (Ann Arbor: University of Michigan Press, 1966), pp. 12–16.

10. For a reevaluation of Cecil B. deMille, especially for his postwar dramas, see Ian Christie, "Grand Illusions," *Sight and Sound*, vol. 1, no. 8 (December 1991), pp. 18–21.

11. Inglis, p. 63.

12. De Grazia and Newman, p. 23.

13. The case is dealt with extensively in *Single Beds and Double Standards*, one episode of a thirteen part film/video series *Hollywood: A Celebration of the American Silent Film*, produced by David Gill and Kevin Brownlow. Thames Television, 1980.

14. For Rappe's career see David A. Yallop, *The Day the Laughter Stopped* (New York: St. Martin's Press, 1976), pp. 108–110.

15. Jowett, p. 164. Hays would recount in his autobiography: "I had been raised in a Christian home, and while I am not a reformer, I hope that I have always been public spirited. It required no great insight to see that the young movie giant might grow up to be a Frankenstein. And precisely because I was not a reformer, I dreaded the blunders the reformers would make in dealing with this new and vital force." *The Memoirs of Will H. Hays* (Garden City, N.Y.: Doubleday, 1955) p. 44.

16. March 3, 1923.

17. *Single Beds and Double Standards*, reminiscence of Byron Haskin, a film director then at the start of his career.

18. Inglis, pp. 100–103.

19. In the winter of 1924–25, the National Congress of Parents and Teachers and the General Federation of Women's Clubs parted company with Hays over his refusal to prevent Arbuckle from attempting a comeback.

20. De Grazia and Newman, p. 27.

21. Will Hays alludes to these criticisms in his *Memoirs*, pp. 322–23.

22. Inglis, p. 113.

23. Jowett, p. 130.

24. Hays, p. 353; Inglis, pp. 113–16.

25. Reprinted extensively in Inglis, pp. 114–15.

26. *Colliers* (November 24, 1934) opined that they echoed the oft-repeated advice of mother to daughter, "Don't forget to stop before you've gone too far!"

27. Leff and Simmons, p. 7.

28. Department of Research and Education, Federal Council of Churches of Christ in America, *The Public Relations of the Motion Picture Industry*, pp. 92–93, 113–14.

29. De Grazia and Newman, p. 332.

30. According to Leff and Simmons, Hays leaked details of the Code to *Variety*, allowing it to "scoop" Quigley's *Motion Picture Herald*. This would help explain a certain mutual coolness.

31. Douglas Gomery, *The Hollywood Studio System* (New York: St. Martin's Press, 1986), pp. 31–32.

32. The huge success of her stage play, *Diamond Lil*, in 1928 commended her to Carl Laemmle, Jr. of Universal, but Hays poured cold water on the idea of a film version.

33. "The Payne Fund Reports," *Journal of Popular Culture*, vol. 19, no. 3, (Fall 1991), pp. 127–40.

34. National Legion of Decency file, "Morals and the Movies." In addition to Legion and NCOMP files grouped alphabetically according to film title, the Legion of Decency archives also contain miscellaneous folders, some dated and under general category headings, mostly from the late 1940s. Much documentation was apparently discarded during office reorganization in the mid-sixties. This material is located in the Department of Communications, Office of Film and Television, U.S. Catholic Conference Center, 1011 First Avenue, New York, N.Y.

35. Leff and Simmons, p. 35.

36. Quigley Papers, Box 3. Breen to Quigley, March 28, 1933. He expresses disgust at the ostentatious displays of wealth in the film capital while the rest of the nation is wracked by economic depression. The Martin Quigley, Sr., Papers are located in the Special Collections section of Georgetown University Library, Washington, D.C. They have been available to researchers since 1990.

_____ Chapter 2 _____

The Social Setting for Control

Seed that falls on stony ground, as the biblical parable relates, has little chance of germinating. The Legion of Decency might likewise have fared poorly as a religious pressure group in an industrially-advanced, secularized, Western society had the soil not been well-prepared. It may be instructive, therefore, to examine the origins and nature of such preparation.

In the opening decade of the twentieth century, the Roman Catholic Church in the United States was an Irish immigrant institution above all else.[1] Although other nationalities were represented of course, those of Irish descent dominated. This dominance was partly the result of the Irish establishing themselves in significantly greater numbers than other ethnic groups in previous centuries as a consequence of transportation from England for real and imagined crimes and, more recently, through the historical circumstance of massive immigration subsequent to the potato famine, partly because their proficiency in the English language removed a barrier that other, foreign-speaking elements of the population had to surmount; and it was partly a matter of tradition. To follow in the footsteps of a compatriot was the model for many an aspiring priest and his proud parents. The Irish-American cleric, like the Irish-American policeman, was to become a familiar character in popular literature and on the screen. The jovial Barry Fitzgerald of _Going My Way_ and the granite-jawed, two-fisted, fighting father portrayed by Pat O'Brien in _Angels with Dirty Faces_ were etched in the American mind as archetypes.

Historically, Ireland failed to have a thorough-going Renaissance. As a small island under English conquest since the end of the twelfth century, it remained mired in a medieval past. The flowering of an indigenous culture had occurred there in the early and high Middle Ages, but withered thereafter. What followed during the Enlightenment was alien and imposed from above by an English-born aristocracy that held the local population in contempt. Nor did it percolate far down the social scale. The repression of Catholicism during and after the

English Reformation by means of a subservient parliament and a savage penal code accompanied by the imposition of Anglicanism as the official religion meant that, among other things, the rococo and baroque splendors of the continental church passed Ireland by. On a psychological level, it deprived the native-born population of much of an aesthetic experience. That had to wait until the dawning of the present century, when independence from England became a distinct possibility. But for the hundreds of thousands who had already crossed the Atlantic for a life in the New World, never to return, the possibility of an aesthetic experience was not shared. The Jansenist influence of the priesthood, trained in a quasi-puritanical tradition, imposed its will. With no indigenous architectural tradition of decorating its churches grandly, and with the acceptance of a narrow asceticism that had no parallel in industrialized western Europe, Irish-American Catholicism possessed a bleakness of outlook masked by a superficial geniality. Beneath the veneer of the jocular, loquacious Paddy lurked a darker, tormented soul.

The traumatic results of the famine of 1845–46 left their mark in other ways. Whether or not it has complete validity, a popular contemporary interpretation held that disaster had been visited on the Irish peasantry because a rapidly expanding population caused farmers to subdivide their land among their too-numerous offspring at death. This was the root cause of subsistence agriculture. The postfamine solution—primogeniture—also created problems. Landless younger male offspring had limited options as they approached adulthood: the priestly life, the military, farm or domestic service or migration as unskilled manual laborers. None of these held out the promise of wealth, so Irishmen postponed marriage until they had the wherewithal to support a wife and family. Sexual continence before marriage became institutionalized, and illegitimate children were the visible betrayal of that imposed lifestyle. Such modes of behavior, dictated by conditions in the Old Country, were carried to the New World and, while sharply modified by succeeding generations, their vestiges impacted on Irish-American society well into recent times.

In the first three decades of the twentieth century, the Catholic Church in the United States was in a paradoxical situation. On the one hand it was a truly monolithic structure, the largest single, undivided denomination on the North American continent, with around 20 million adherents, heavily concentrated on the East Coast and the Midwest, with a growing constituency in the Southwest (See Table 1). It was regarded with pride and envy by the Roman hierarchy for its discipline, its wealth and its ability to flourish in a country where separation of church and state was a cornerstone of the constitution. How it had managed to survive and expand without any state subsidy was remarked upon by doomsayers during the turn-of-the-century crisis in France, where the Gallic church's inability to stave off separation was regarded as tantamount to financial suicide. The energy and vitality of the American clergy were attributed to the very fact that the Holy Mother Church had to fend for

Table 1

Membership in the Roman Catholic Church in Twelve Leading States and Dioceses in 1936

State		Diocese	
New York	3,075,428	Chicago	1,086,209
Pennsylvania	2,275,062	Newark	1,056,518
Massachusetts	1,696,708	Boston	1,027,969
Illinois	1,448,650	New York	956,686
New Jersey	1,390,428	Brooklyn	915,192
Ohio	1,052,101	Philadelphia	835,332
California	987,902	Pittsburgh	656,007
Michigan	800,917	Hartford	627,848
Wisconsin	741,563	Detroit	565,221
Connecticut	635,750	Cleveland	522,854
Louisiana	632,583	San Francisco	454,927
Texas	604,308	Buffalo	408,349

U.S.A. total: 19,914,937

Source: U.S. Dept. of Commerce, Bureau of Census: Religious Bodies, 1936, vol. 2

itself and could not depend on handouts from the government. Self-reliance was its salvation.[2]

On the converse side, American Catholicism regarded itself as being in a permanent state of siege, beleaguered by a host of enemies who lost few opportunities to condemn it. Some were ideological—humanists, intellectuals, sociologists and the like; others were institutional, like certain fundamentalist sects. Anti-Catholicism predated the American Revolution by more than a century, with anti-Catholic penal codes in operation in many of the original thirteen colonies. Only one of the fifty-six signatories of the Declaration of Independence belonged to the Church of Rome. Religious bigotry simmered beneath the surface, breaking out into occasional violence, as in 1842 when a mob ran riot in Boston following an attempt by a local bishop to exempt Catholic believers from reading a Protestant version of the Bible in schools. A block of stone, donated by Pope Pius IX for the Washington Monument in 1852, was seized by an irate Protestant mob who dragged it to the banks of the Potomac River and tossed it in. Irish and southern European immigrants, who crossed the Atlantic in record numbers between 1840 and the outbreak of the First World War, provided an impressive addition to the existing Catholic population. Nevertheless, the newcomers, overwhelmingly lower class, were excluded from positions of power in government, business and academe by a society where mainstream Protestant elements unarguably dominated.

In 1852, amid suspicion of nonsectarian education and as an indication of this siege mentality, the First Plenary Council of the Baltimore diocese (dubbed by its detractors, the "Yankee Rome") resolved to create a parochial school system both as a reaction to its perceived domination by Protestant elements and as a riposte to Horace Mann, who had begun the process of secularization of education a decade earlier. By 1884, the Third Plenary Session was sufficiently gratified by results to demand that Catholic parents send their offspring to church-run schools where feasible and to decree that no parish could rest content until it had adequate space to satisfy those needs. These decisions were of incalculable significance for American Catholicism. Physical energy and financial resources were channeled into a pedagogical structure that made the Church a significant temporal as well as spiritual power in the land. As one observer has noted:

It meant a poor body of immigrants would have to make great sacrifices to build their own schools. It meant that nuns would have to be recruited and trained in large numbers to staff the schools. It meant that these nuns would have at least as much formative influence on Catholics as priests did. . . . It meant that nuns would not be contemplatives in America, not merely the teachers of young ladies from the upper class, but teachers of all Catholics, young and old, girl and boy. It meant that Catholicism would be in large part child-centered, its piety a feminine sort.[3]

The Church did not rest content with education. It created a separate society that supervised and cosseted its membership from cradle to grave. Orphanages, hospitals, newspapers, magazines, book clubs, fraternities—all paralleled those in the mainstream of non-Catholic life in the United States. It was possible for the children of devout parents, at least those living in the larger urban areas, to exist completely within what has been termed "a cocoon of Catholicism," growing up, studying, working, playing, socializing, marrying, breathing his or her last and being carried to a resting place within sight of fellow believers.

For the Catholic child, first exposed to the Church by having water sprinkled on its head shortly after birth, conscious awareness of the role of religion in life began around the age of five. In 1905, Pope Pius X, in his encyclical *Tridentia Synodus*, had stressed that, to be able to receive daily communion, the individual must be in a state of grace and have a proper intention of receiving. The daily communicant ought to be free of deliberate venial sin and should start to make fitting preparations for the ceremony. At this time, First Confession preceded First Communion and children experienced the sacrament of Penance around the age of fourteen. When the Pope decreed in *Quam Singularum* (issued in 1910) that children might receive First Communion at the age of discretion— between six and eight—there was a corresponding fall in the average age at which First Confession was to be made. With some preparation from nuns in the first two grades of elementary school, followed by tests on procedure and understanding by the local priest, youngsters took their initial steps toward the confessional booth, fearful or confident, ignorant or knowing, as the case might be. For most, there was something mysterious and magical about the experience.

The odors of the candles, incense, floor polish and perhaps even the tobacco from the stained cassock of the priest dimly framed behind the grating were often indelibly etched in young minds, and the whole resembled a first rite of passage into the adult world. Above all, it tended to make notions of sin and purity, damnation and salvation realities. Heaven, hell, limbo and purgatory acquired distinctive meanings reinforced by graphic, pictorial descriptions of those various milieus, all aimed specifically at that age group. An illustrated nineteenth-century pamphlet by a Father Furness provided an image of hell that was surely seared into the consciousness of the hundreds of thousands of grade schoolers forced to commit his cautionary stories to memory. Hades was described as a flaming oven where children of the damned screamed to be let out, beating their heads in vain against the red-hot door for eternity, or as a steaming kettle containing the scalded souls of those sinners within whose whistling sound were really the cries of doomed sinners. The truly blessed, like St. Theresa of Avila, could see grey snowflakes, falling from heaven to hell—signs of confessions badly made.[4]

Sin came in several well-defined forms, which the faithful were to recognize and shun. There were sins of omission no less than of commission, in descending order of seriousness from cardinal to mortal and venial. At a tender age, confession of a sin might amount to no more than owning up to the theft of cookies from a jar or money pilfered from a mother's purse or a slap of jealousy delivered to an envied younger sibling when no one was around to observe. But with the onset of puberty and vague stirrings in the body, it became a major preoccupation with both sexes. Not only was it a mortal sin to do something of a sexual nature to oneself or to others, it was a mortal sin just to contemplate execution of the proposed action. St. Augustine had decreed, in the fifth century, that impure thoughts were no less reprehensible than impure deeds if there was a lack of determination in conquering and banishing them from the mind. Sin, for him, reached its peak in sexual desire in which the indecent parts of the body were excited. For the majority of Catholic males, sex as sin contained its own vocabulary for matters such as homosexuality ("sexual degeneration") and masturbation ("to have touched oneself in an impure manner"). This last-mentioned, odious act whose divine punishment, it was rumored, might condemn the perpetrator to a lifetime of hairy palms and insanity, triggered off a nightmarish sequence in the weak-willed of temptation, commission, guilt, confession, desire and repeated action. The habit was just the first in the slippery slope of sexual perversion, many of whose variations were rendered all the more mysterious by the attachment of Latin names. Premarital chastity by both sexes was necessary to avoid the risk of perdition, since one often progressed from touching oneself in an impure manner to touching someone of the opposite sex in the same way. The Catholic Church placed a high value on virginity before marriage and the purity of both sexes at the altar was, in theory, a nonnegotiable *sine qua non*. On the other hand, the almost uncontrollable urge in a normal, hot-blooded male to sow his wild oats before embracing marital fidelity was viewed as a regrettable necessity. No such leeway was allowed the female of the species and the white of the wedding gown was a statement of the untarnished state. In any case, it was assumed that the "decent" woman, less sexually charged than the male, had a duty to keep him at bay at all costs and as best she could.

Marriage might relieve some of the tensions and anxieties felt by the engaged couple, but for true believers it brought others in its stead. The marital bond was indissoluble, as priests scarcely needed to emphasize to about-to-be-weds. Divorce was unthinkable if one wished to remain within the Church and an annulment was a rare, complicated and invariably expensive procedure for ending a relationship, which only the extremely wealthy could contemplate as a possibility. Mixed marriage was discouraged by the Church and generally frowned upon by parents who could see no good coming of it. However, when it did occur, both parties were asked for an undertaking that offspring of the union would be brought up in the true faith. Sex within marriage was primarily for the purpose of procreation, and contraception, except for the grudgingly allowed rhythm method, was another mortal sin that thwarted God's injunction to be fruitful, multiply and hold dominion over the earth. Not uncommon was the priest who made quiet but determined inquiries of the young, childless couple as to when they might expect offspring and issued an explicit warning before departing that they must not resort to measures of mechanical birth control. His dogged persistence might be resented, especially by the non-Catholic in a mixed marriage, but that was seldom a deterrent to the zealous clergyman. Abortion was no solution for unwanted children: it was a crime of murder so heinous that the Church felt it best not to draw the attention of the young to its existence. The desperate female who, like the old lady who lived in the shoe, knew not how to stave off further pregnancies might be advised to make herself less attractive to her spouse so that his urge to consummate the sexual act would be felt less frequently. Abstinence initiated by either party in this circumstance was morally acceptably behavior; but "accidents" happened, and among the working class in the cramped quarters of the teeming slums of Chicago or New York there were often pressing financial reasons for limiting families. Suicide and euthanasia were likewise proscribed by the Church even for the terminally ill and those in atrocious pain. God gave life and only He would take it away. Those who advocated either were branded as racial suicidists.

Still, unlike most of western Europe and Great Britain, where the Catholic Church saw a steady erosion in the numbers of the faithful especially after the First World War, American Catholicism experienced growth in the same period. Not all of it could be attributed to immigration from Central and South America and Europe. The explanation lay, primarily, in a hard-working, vigilant clergy and in control of education from infancy to postgraduate university level study. In a very real sense, too, the Church and its social agencies were a focal point for the rank and file. Newcomers to a locality—and Americans moved around their country proportionately more often than those of any other nationality—found a ready acceptance there. This was not always true of Protestant denominations where middle-class mores and manners seemed to predominate. The Anglican church, with its Waspish connotations and aura of bourgeois respectability, might deter participation by the less affluent in the life of the institution except in the more formal sense of Sunday attendance, and that for appearance's sake. Catholics, on the other hand, found an informal camaraderie in the church basement bingo game or, if male, in fraternal orders like the Knights of Columbus, named after the one credited with bringing Catholicism to the New World.

For Catholic parents, schooling was another tie that bound. It was not only education for this world but preparation for the next. Unlike their state equivalents whose clock-watching staff, it was perceived, had little interest in their charges before and after the school bell rang for the day, Catholic schools concerned themselves with the moral well-being of the child at all times. Nor had the teaching brothers and sisters friends of the opposite sex, spouses, offspring or domestic budget-balancing to compete for their attention. To critics of clerically dominated education this meant that a significant proportion of future generations was condemned to irrational biblical concepts, the remarkable doctrine of transubstantiation that asserts the bread and wine of the Eucharist become the flesh and blood of Christ during holy communion, and the primacy of the Pope over other Christian, spiritual leaders, all hammered into their submissive heads by sadistic nuns on a daily basis. But this was a minority opinion. Anticlericalism in the United States has never reached the heights of vilification that it did in Europe. Children who emerged after seven or eight years of "Romanist indoctrination" from St. Joseph's or Our Lady of the Sorrows were regarded by their contemporaries not so much as bigoted reactionaries and threats to the liberal-humanist tradition of Western thought than as brainwashed kids and staunch defenders of their faith and the moral order. In adulthood, products of the system would take a perverse pleasure in recounting how they had survived the experience. They would exchange tales of the thumps and slaps of grade school or the excruciating pain felt when a particularly vindictive sister sprinkled the hardwood floor with uncooked rice and forced them to kneel on it with bare knees for an hour. On the other hand, many remembered with real affection the personal interest of a kindly teacher in their emotional and intellectual progress. Few would deny that the entire pedagogical experience left an indelible mark.

The intellectual foundations of Catholicism were not under attack in the United States to anything like the extent they were in modern Europe where, in the same period, a direct line of anticlericalism ran from France of the 1880s to Spain on the eve of its civil war. Nonetheless, there was a populist campaign to keep the Catholic influence out of politics. Rural America had mounted a rear-guard action in the twenties that was, in part, anti-Catholic. The Eighteenth Amendment, which brought Prohibition, was its response to the hard-drinking, Eastern cities and a priesthood that, for the most part, found little wrong with the demon alcohol. Though the Ku Klux Klan was a post–Civil

War invention, the zenith of its power as a born-again organization occurred during the twenties. With a membership of around four million, it fought to maintain racial (i.e., Anglo-Saxon Protestant) purity against Jews, Catholics and city immigrants from "inferior" races. In 1928 these disparate elements found a target in Alfred E. Smith, the Democratic candidate for the presidency. Smith took pride in his immigrant, Irish-Catholic ancestry and of a childhood growing up on the sidewalks of New York. A statue of the Virgin was prominently displayed in his office. He refused to take seriously charges that he and the millions of fellow adherents to the faith were held in subservience to a foreign despot by a phalanx of bishops and priests working in cahoots with Irish-Catholic political bosses in city machine politics. Their doctrines and dogmas were a danger to the real America, or so ran the propaganda. If Smith were successful, the pope would have a direct phone link to the White House and the president would be on his knees kissing some cardinal's ring. Protestant marriages would be annulled and all offspring of these unions would be declared illegitimate. Washington would be renamed Piusville or St. Patricksburg. Everywhere free institutions would be in jeopardy from a papist plot that would have conquered America, insidiously, at the ballot box.

Smith had attempted to pour oil on these troubled waters in an exchange of correspondence in the *Atlantic Monthly*, sensing that, besides the hysteria, Protestant doubts were based on reason and raised in good faith. He tried to reassure critics that Catholics, in common with members of other denominations, experienced no conflict in loyalties between their religious beliefs and their political programs. In any controversy, freedom of conscience would be the watchword. A Catholic president would no more obey the papacy than an Anglican would obey the archbishop of Canterbury. This candor availed Smith nothing. Farmers, miners, textile workers, small-town businessmen and others who had not been beneficiaries of the boom of the roaring twenties looked to the future with apprehension and ignored this citified Easterner with his distinctive New York accent. The Anglican Bishop Cannon of Houston, peering through steel-rimmed glasses, opined that the translation into the social order of the teaching of Jesus Christ concerning human brotherhood was no longer the greatest moral problem facing the nation, but rather the prospect of all Americans becoming subjects of the pope. On election night the returns told Smith that the slanderous tide of religious bigotry had helped sweep Herbert Hoover into the White House. Of course, other factors had contributed to the Republican victory. A majority of Americans wanted to believe that the next decade would see a chicken in every pot and a car in every garage. The new president had confidently predicted a day when, with the help of God, poverty would be banished from the nation. Catholics were left to ponder ruefully that a majority of the electorate preferred to believe that Hoover's invocation had been made to a Protestant deity.

The faithful might be told that Smith was beaten by a cleverer politician riding on the crest of prosperity's wave. They refused to believe it and retreated ever deeper into their fortress of belief. The pervasiveness of spiritual and social shelter lent some credence to the charge that Catholicism in the United States was a thing apart from the mainstream of American life. Its literary tradition since the Great War certainly reflected a world of separateness and certainty. There the individual was above the perplexities of daily existence, confident that faith would guide him to a satisfactory goal. The pessimism of a Eugene O'Neill seemed almost un-American and certainly alien to Catholic ideals. The triumph of evil over good on stage or in the printed word was unacceptable. But if Catholicism was unable to do more than protest the literary world, it found itself in a more advantageous position over an area of popular culture, the cinema. Here, through a combination of fortuitous circumstance and determination, the Church was able to flex a formidably developed muscle and exercise leverage that it was denied elsewhere. Still, as the euphoria of the Roaring Twenties and The Jazz Age gave way to the Depression, few could have imagined that the clerical reach would become so formidable and all-encompassing.

NOTES

1. This chapter is mostly based on secondary sources, principally the following words: William M. Halsey, *The Survival of American Innocence* (Notre Dame: University of Notre Dame, 1980); Peter Occhiogrosso, ed., *Once a Catholic* (New York: Ballantine, 1987); and Quentin Donoghue and Linda Shapiro, *Bless Me, Father, for I Have Sinned* (Toronto: McClelland and Stewart, 1984).

2. In France there was a minor clerical fashion for "l'Americanisme." In 1897, the Abbé Felix Klein produced a French version of Walter Elliott's *Life of Father Hecker*, founder of the American Paulists, a book urging modernism in Catholic life. At the same time, the Primate of the United States, Cardinal Gibbons, warned the French hierarchy that nearly all of its ambitious projects in the United States had been undertaken with money contributed by the Irish, English and Polish. "The Italians and French never give to the Church because they know that in their countries the priest is paid by the government; they think of him as a civil servant; and it takes at least a generation to teach these immigrants the duties they owe to the American clergy." Quoted in Maurice Larkin, *Church and State after the Dreyfus Case* (Macmillan: London, 1974), pp. 159–160.

3. Gary Wills, *Bare Ruined Choirs: Doubt, Prophecy and Radical Religion* (New York: Dell, 1972), quoted in Donoghue and Shapiro, p. 61.

4. This and other cautionary tales appeared in a widely used high school textbook, *The Story of the Church* by the Rev. B. N. Forner, first published in 1935.

_____ *Chapter 3* _____

The Formation of the Legion of Decency

The chain of circumstances that led to the creation of the National Legion of Decency was lengthy and fraught with more dissension than Paul W. Facey's quasi-official historical account would indicate.[1] The gestation period between the conception of the idea and the emergence of a fully operational organization was more than two years, an interval that witnessed no small degree of animosity among segments of the Catholic Church and ended in mutual recrimination. The political infighting was conducted behind ecclesiastical closed doors but could not escape the scrutiny of the press entirely. This may have given the film industry a false sense of security. The portentous change in the method of controlling and dictating the context of American motion pictures was not fully appreciated until it was too late to mount an effective challenge. When Hollywood did waken to the threat, it found itself in thrall to a curious newcomer in the realm of control. The Legion's guiding spirits then watched with approval as another, effective set of shackles was added to the four-year-old Code. This was the Production Code Administration's seal of approval. By 1935, the triumvirate of the Legion of Decency, the Motion Picture Producers and Distributors of America and the Production Code Administration had succeeded in bringing Hollywood to heel, as Will Hays had never done.

It cannot be seriously maintained that, in 1933, the hierarchy of the Church was committed to a policy of the continuous supervision of film content. As the Depression continued to rage with undiminished ferocity, there were more important matters confronting it: hunger, poverty, unemployment for many of its adherents and even incipient revolution. Priests were thankful that theaters were open for long hours, charged little, and provided heat and shelter from the elements as well as a refuge from the park bench where the authoritarian voice of the cop to "keep moving, buddy!" was depressingly familiar. By and large, the higher clergy knew next to nothing about the motion picture industry. For a variety of reasons—custom, taste, inclination and education—the majority of cardinals and archbishops were not inclined to be inveterate filmgoers. The avalanche of gossip that poured from Hollywood studios and found its way to the public via the pages of the fan magazines was of no immediate interest to them, and their knowledge of the business side was limited to a pained awareness that acolytes of an alien religion had long since taken charge.[2] Still, the ever-increasing volume of denunciation by clergy of all denominations was resounding throughout the land. Nor was it surprising that it should be heard most acutely in the Los Angeles diocese of Bishop John J. Cantwell, for within that diocese lay the latter-day Sodom, the root cause of the malaise.[3]

John Cantwell, like many of his priests, was from southern Ireland. He was a political activist who excoriated the New Deal and political progressives, and espoused the cause of the Mexican Cristero movement, a right-wing antigovernment revolt. He was to hail Mussolini and Franco as upholders of national pride and self-respect. He asked to meet with Joe Breen in the summer of 1933 to express his dismay at the apparent impotence of the Studio Relations Department to arrest a downward spiral in the moral content of pictures of the last few years and to discuss some permanent remedy. It was clear to him that pronouncements by the hierarchy were as ephemeral as the day's newspaper headlines and just as useless. Direct action that would hit the moguls where it mattered most—in the pocketbook—was the only effective course. As Breen noted at the time, "He has set himself to do whatever he can to cope with the wrong kind of screen fare—and he has fire in his eye."[4]

Concurrently, in Chicago, where the city's censorship board was excising and banning on an unprecedented scale, Cardinal Mundelein had asked Father Lord to explain to the bishops at their annual conference in Washington in November how it was that the high hopes that he and Quigley had entertained for their 1930 creation, the Code, had been dashed. Lord was eager to vent his spleen. He listed 133 pictures released in a six-month period that contained, all told, 26 episodes built on illicit love, 13 where seductions had been accomplished, 12 where they had been planned and attempted, 2 depictions of rape, 1 of incest, 18 characters living in adultery, 7 characters planning to commit the sin, 3 prostitutes as central characters and 25 films that presented "scenes and situations and dances and dialogues of indecent or obscene or anti-moral character."[5] To alert the faithful to their obligations and reap publicity for some as yet undetermined action, the new Apostolic Delegate to the United States, the Most Reverend Amleto Giovanni Cicognani, was prevailed upon to indict the motion picture business in his first public utterance at a Catholic Charities convention in New York in October 1933. The occasion was well-timed, as it happened to coincide with the national release of Mae West's *I'm No Angel*. Members of the Church, he intoned, were called by God, the pope, the bishops and the priests to a united and vigorous campaign for the purification of the cinema, which had become "a deadly menace to morals."[6]

At the Washington conference, Cantwell dominated the proceedings. His trio of targets was the Jews, "instruments of debauchery" who had cornered all aspects of film production, distribution and exhibition; those filmic "artists" on both sides of the camera, who were "seventy-five percent pagan" and cared nothing for decency; and New York City, with an increasingly "European climate" that had become a breeding ground for pornographic writers who, in due course, exported their "morals of the barnyard" westwards.[7] These harsh words seemed to preclude any negotiation with Hollywood to try to rectify matters. Cantwell's fellow clerics were won over to his idea that ethical leadership by the bishops based on concerted action by the rank and file was the only course. While his precise intentions were not formulated, it seems that at that date he did not envisage the creation of a new institution to police the movie industry in perpetuity. His concern was to show malefactors that the Catholic Church had lost patience and intended to manifest its strength in some dramatic manner to be determined by an Episcopal Committee on Motion Pictures.

From its formation in December 1933, the Episcopal Committee labored under a fairly debilitating handicap, namely the lack of mandatory or legislative power as an adjunct of the National Catholic Welfare Conference. The latter dated from 1917–18, when it had been set up to deal with refugees and other assorted social and economic problems resulting from the First World War. Its weakness, from Cantwell's point of view, lay in the fact that bishops were at liberty to join it or not, and equally to accept or reject recommendations made by it or by an agency under its control. The four members of the Episcopal Committee, Archbishop John T. McNicholas of Cincinnati and Bishops John F. Noll of Fort Wayne, Hugh C. Boyle of Pittsburgh and Cantwell sought to solicit ideas that could be translated into concrete actions binding on all dioceses. But individual clerics were already striking out on their own. On May 25, 1934, Dennis Cardinal Dougherty of Philadelphia declared unconditional war on the movies by issuing instructions to the faithful in the city to "stay away from all of them. . . . This is not merely a counsel but a positive command, binding all in conscience under pain of sin."[8] The ban was still in force a year later. A month before its issuance, Msgr. John Hunt of Detroit, who had regularly lambasted the film capital from his pulpit, caused a list of over sixty titles that he deemed unfit for consumption to be published in the parish journal, *St. Leo*. But by far the most belligerent campaign against Hollywood was being waged in Chicago, where the heavily Catholic censorship board had gone to new extremes in rejecting and emasculating dozens of titles. It was not only the Mae Wests and *Wonder Bars* that fell victim. Two prestigious productions, United Artists' *Catherine the Great* and the MGM Greta Garbo vehicle *Queen Christina* were being denied exposure in America's second-largest city because "they exemplified the lives of women of loose morals and unbridled passion who breathe the atmosphere of foreign courts and indulge in practices that could never be squared with the principles of Catholic morality."[9]

McNicholas may well have felt that events were outdistancing his committee as he contemplated these and other examples of grass-roots activity. There was the possibility that whatever recommendations emerged from his fellow bishops' deliberations would be redundant. The choice lay between disbanding altogether and allowing each diocese to act of its own volition or carefully steering the rank and file toward a uniform policy applicable from coast to coast. With the latter in mind, he approached Martin Quigley in the hope that the newspaperman, bestriding the industry and the Church, would be able to reconcile the two. Quigley was ready to admit that the headstrong attitude of the movie moguls of the past three or four years had distressed him and conditioned the Church to distrust anything that came out of their domain. All the same, in Joe Breen there was a new broom at the Hays Office on the West Coast and it should be given a little time to sweep clean. Turning to the Philadelphia boycott, he warned the Episcopal Committee against placing too much trust in its efficacy or giving encouragement to imitators. It had given the industry a shock and led to a dramatic fall in receipts at the box office. But, in his view, its lasting result would be the opposite of what Dougherty had intended. The cardinal's stern warning had discouraged attendance momentarily, but no campaign could be sustained at such a fever pitch indefinitely. When enthusiasm began to wane, the public's love affair with the movies would reassert itself and people would start to trickle back, especially to those titles that had garnered a reputation in the interim for being unsavory. The theater owners would reap a delayed harvest in ticket sales, but more significantly, they would regard themselves as the ultimate victors in a conflict about which the Church would have to think twice before resuming. On a positive note, Quigley suggested that a single list of recommended pictures be drawn up by a reviewing board composed of priests or their appointees. It should avoid mention of specific, unsuitable pictures since that would only serve to draw attention to them. Instead, Catholics should be urged to stay away from any and all films not on the recommended list. In the weeks that followed, he enlarged on his idea for a reviewing board. While Hollywood, with typical greed and disregard for audience sensibilities, thought that every picture should be open to all segments of the population, there was an excellent case to be made for a classification system based on age. This would still allow it to continue to make adult films but force it to recognize that not everything should be seen by children. On the question of location of this board, Quigley was adamant that it should be headquartered in New York, geographically as distant as possible from the subversive influence of the film capital yet still in a city where the vast majority of movies, both foreign and domestic, had their American premieres.[10]

This was most reassuring for McNicholas, and the new pessimism in Hollywood about the effects of the Church's assault in Philadelphia where receipts had fallen by 40 percent in three months likewise bolstered his confidence in a challenge to the status quo as he prepared for the Episcopal Committee's meeting in Cincinnati. There, Quigley's program of action would be submitted. Uncoordinated campaigns were also beginning to be effective. Parochial school children paraded outside designated theaters with placards reading "An Admission to an Indecent Movie Is a Ticket to Hell."[11] A despairing Hays had told Quigley that the Catholic Church "could have anything it wanted," since the movie colony had "built up an enormous amount of ill-will which, if continued, would be destructive for business."[12] All the industry asked for was to be allowed to retain the right of self-censorship rather than be subject to federal control. Meanwhile, the Episcopal Committee had come up with the idea of a Legion of Decency that would elicit a promise or pledge from every Catholic contacted to abide by the following code of conduct as it applied to the movies:

I wish to join the Legion of Decency, which condemns vile and unwholesome motion moving pictures. I unite with all who protest against them as a grave menace to youth, to home life, to country and religion.

I condemn absolutely those salacious motion pictures which, with other degrading agencies, are corrupting public morals and promoting a sex mania in our land.

I shall do all that I can to arouse public opinion against the portrayal of vice as a normal condition of affairs and against depicting criminals of any class as heroes and heroines, presenting their filthy philosophy of life as something acceptable to decent men and women.

I unite with all who condemn the display of suggestive advertisements on billboards, at theatre entrances and the favourable notices given to immoral motion pictures.

Considering these evils, I hereby promise to remain away from all motion pictures except those which do not offend decency and Christian morality. I promise further to secure as many members as possible for the Legion of Decency.

I make this protest in a spirit of self-respect, and with the conviction that the American public does not demand filthy pictures, but clean entertainment and educational features.[13]

Thus the Legion was born. In a ground swell of enthusiasm, pledge-taking was held throughout the nation by a variety of effective, if uncoordinated, methods. Some cities had door-to-door canvasses, others asked congregations to stand and recite the promise during the Sunday service where peer pressure to conform was undoubtedly significant. Nonattendees were reminded of their duty in diocesan magazine articles and editorials. Priests and nuns called upon entire classes to make the commitment with an authority that few children were prepared to disobey. By the end of 1934 the results were staggering. According to Facey, between seven and nine million had taken the pledge, including two hundred thousand in McNicholas's own diocese.[14] Protestants and Jewish groups showing interest were also invited to administer a slightly modified form of it. However, if its stirring words energized the faithful, the reality of a national body with offices, staff, membership lists and the other paraphernalia of an organization was still some distance away; nor was there a consensus as to whether it would be a permanent body keeping an ever-watchful eye on the movies or a short-lived affair to be dissolved once the moviemaking sinners had repented and demonstrated this repentance by walking in the paths of righteousness. These issues passed from the cool deliberations of late fall in Washington to the clammy heat of Cincinnati in June. To help mend fences and prevent the spread of a cold war between Church and cinema, McNicholas asked Quigley to attend the Episcopal Committee's conference, accompanied by Breen as the MPPDA representative. They were the only nonclerics in the room, but in composition the gathering was 100 percent Catholic.

One of Quigley's principal faults was his inclination to attribute misguided motives to those who held contrary opinions or had ideas that had not occurred to him. The virulence of clerical assaults on movies, without distinction, alarmed him. He railed against Daniel Lord and the Chicago clique for their treatment of *Queen Christina*, asking rhetorically whether the intention was to allow on screen only characters whose practices could be squared with principles of Catholic morality. That kind of attitude had made them a laughing stock. Worse, it had convinced some in Hollywood that no accommodation could ever be made with the Church and that the only alternative was to ignore it, press ahead and let the public be the judge. That was especially dangerous because there had been no outcry from the mass of moviegoers. He was convinced that "millions of our own people either do not know when things have gone over the borderline or else they have just become so accustomed . . . that they have come automatically to accept them as being all right."[15] Turning to the assumed primacy of Chicago, he confessed that he could conceive of no way in which the whole campaign might more effectively be wrecked "than to have the American public learn that a single priest (Father Dineen) was setting himself up as a censor to govern motion picture entertainment for the whole country."[16] What neither Quigley nor the rest of those assembled could ever countenance was that the majority of moviegoers' contentment with current screen fare might indicate a policy of inaction.

Breen's role at the conference was, of necessity, a conciliatory one. Even more than Quigley, he was regarded by some of the clerics present as a lackey of the industry, and to have joined the publisher in an all-out attack would have jeopardized his recent appointment. He pleaded for time. The Code was sufficiently comprehensive to ensure that no unsuitable picture ever left the studios. The problem, as it had struck him when he first arrived in the film capital, was inadequate enforcement of existing edicts. To this end he made four dramatic pronouncements. First, the Studio Relations Committee would be abolished and its place taken by a Production Code Administration (PCA) which he, himself, would head. Appeals against adverse decisions relating to treatments and scripts would now be heard by the MPPDA's board in New York and not by a Hollywood jury of peers. This would not only strengthen the Hays Office but would concurrently remove control from producers, whose actions had been dictated by a need for mutual backscratching where each felt obliged to look kindly on the films of his fellow jurors lest his own come to be judged someday. Second, a penalty of $25,000 would be imposed for producing, distributing or exhibiting any picture that did not carry the PCA certificate and seal of approval. For a million-dollar production this might seem a trifling amount, but to make doubly certain that nothing would escape the net, member-controlled theater circuits were forbidden to book titles lacking the seal. Since the major companies controlled most of the first-run cinemas in the larger cities, the enactment effectively prevented all except independently made low-budget films from obtaining profitable bookings on general release—and these did not play in such venues. Third, reprehensible titles currently in distribution would be withdrawn. Finally, to placate anti-block booking groups, exhibitors could cancel up to 10 percent of each block of pictures from a specific company. Hays was able to boast that he now had a police department or, at the very least, "a civilian defense force" to uphold the law.[17]

If McNicholas was personally amenable to the program that Breen and Quigley had presented, there were still obstacles in the way of reaching a rapprochement with his fellow clergy. Eternal vigilance was the price one paid for eternally decent screens, according to Father Lord. The atmosphere of the past three years had conditioned him to distrust anything new coming out of Hollywood. He had never forgiven it for the manner in which it had mocked and disregarded his creation, the Hays Code, and he persisted in the conviction that Breen's latest gambit was "a matter of trying to cure a diseased patient. It had been in no instance a matter of prophylaxis."[18] Father Dineen was equally skeptical as he assessed the motives that had brought the two laymen to Cincinnati. Both depended, in their different ways, on the movie industry for a living. In Quigley's case there was a clear instance of attempting what Christ himself had declared impossible—the serving of two masters. Even as he was carping about Mae West's latest disgrace, *Belle of the Nineties*, and the sympathetic treatment of a king's mistress in *Madame Dubarry*, his *Motion Picture Herald* carried glowing advertisements for both. The more profitable the motion picture business became, the more his publishing empire flourished. For Cardinal Mundelein, acceptance of the duo's reassuring words was a clear case of the Church having to capitulate or rather of having been maneuvered into selling out. By demanding that it soft-pedal its antimovie campaign pending a trial of the new system, both men might undermine Cardinal Dougherty's uncompromising action, which was the only way to bring movie people to their senses.[19]

If the Chicago diocese hoped to intimidate Quigley by these salvos, it was not only dismayed but incensed by his next gambit. Quigley was adamant that the compilation of film lists and the rating of individual titles must be done in New York and nowhere else. His objection to the status quo was well-founded. The growth in the number of pledges being made by the tens of thousands flocking into the Legion each month had been accompanied by a commensurate rise in dioceses issuing their own classifications. Boston had joined Detroit, Chicago, Omaha, Denver and other cities in publishing its list of acceptable and objectionable pictures. Because each locality acted independently of the others, there could be no uniformity. Paramount's *Limehouse Blues*, in which Jean Parker, a woman of indifferent morals, is attracted to gang boss George Raft and has to suffer the wrath of his Oriental mistress, Anna May Wong, was lambasted as an inferno of miscegenation by Detroit but rated acceptable in

New York. The Russian *Three Songs of Lenin*, which Quigley described as "the most vicious Soviet propaganda picture which has yet been displayed in this country," was passed without comment by Chicago after it had been condemned as subversive in Boston.[20] And, of course, if one were a Catholic in Philadelphia, both films were out of bounds.

In November 1934, the Bishops' Conference in Washington placed the desirability of a uniform rating system near the top of its agenda. As might be imagined, Mundelein and Dineen were active behind the scenes lobbying for the Chicago list as the most stringent and therefore the one that ought to be most in tune with the mood of the seventy-eight clerics assembled. Much time was spent discussing the merits of a "black list" with specific titles singled out for condemnation over a "white list" that would approve the best and ignore the rest. Dineen argued that any imprimatur given to individual titles would be exploited by exhibitors in their advertising campaigns. Surely it was not the intention of those present to promote the well-being of a collection of Jewish businessmen who had lately thumbed their collective nose at the Church. His persistence won the day, when a motion to send the Chicago list to all dioceses to the exclusion of all others passed by a small majority. An exuberant Detroit then began issuing a blacklist of recalcitrant theaters that had refused to change their ways in addition to a similar catalogue of forbidden films.[21] But even as the vote was being taken, Quigley was laying plans to demonstrate the pernicious effect of Dineen's tactics on the Legion's future—and to undermine them.

As he saw it, there had to be a more credible alternative to Chicago and he was sure it existed in the International Federation of Catholic Alumnae. The oldest film reviewing group of the Catholic Church, the IFCA dated from 1924 when, from its office at 131 East 29th Street in New York City, it had begun to rate movies in one of two categories, either "suitable for church halls, Catholic schools or family night programs" or "suitable for mature audiences but inappropriate for church halls and school showings." It was very much a "white list" that praised the good and pointedly ignored the bad and the ugly. Though there was a chapter in Hollywood that regularly communicated with Cantwell, the ace in the hole for Quigley's purpose was its headquarters, located in New York. Under the chairmanship of Mary Looram, who had succeeded its ailing founder, Rita McGolderick, the IFCA was building up a staff of knowledgeable, dedicated reviewers and was willing to marshal its resources to undertake a more comprehensive evaluation of motion picture fare than heretofore, even to the extent of singling out unsatisfactory titles if the hierarchy insisted. Events also played into Quigley's hand.

While Chicago gave the outward impression of a cohesive operation under the constant, expert supervision of a bishop and a prince of the Church, aided by St. Louis's Father Lord and other luminaries, the reality was startlingly different. Compilation of the lists was the work of a single individual, Sally Reilly, at one time a stenographer in Dineen's office and subsequently a member of the city's police department, who spent her nights watching the films awaiting release and her weekends summarizing the ratings she had unilaterally decided to impose. She was not a person who easily took "no" for an answer, and she tended to wear her prejudices on her sleeve. One of those prejudices was a bitter hatred of things British. She blamed the English—and she was certainly not alone among expatriate Catholics and their descendants in this sentiment—for all the ills that had befallen Ireland for the previous four hundred years. When John Ford's *The Informer*, a critically acclaimed drama, set during the dying days of England's occupation of Southern Ireland and centering on the betrayal of an Irish activist by a fellow countryman to the military, came up for inspection, she unhesitatingly declared that it should be banned on the grounds that it was a vile calumny on the Irish Free State and its people. This was by no means the first or the most controversial of her decisions. In a three-week period in August 1934, she had meted out similar treatment to at least half a dozen films, forcing the temporary closure of one of the city's largest theaters for lack of anything new to show, and this despite the fact that all carried Hays Office seals of approval. When the public insisted on ignoring her condemnation of Somerset Maugham's *Of Human Bondage*, where a sluttish Bette Davis ruined the life of sensitive Lesley Howard, she started canvassing theaters with a view to instituting a boycott if they persisted in flaunting her edicts.[22] The editor of the Jesuit weekly, *America*, Wilfrid Parsons, communicated his dismay at the Chicago situation to Bishop J. Francis McIntyre, hinting that although Dineen would defend Reilly to the hilt if an attack were made on the competence of his female protégé, the situation was patently ridiculous and might rebound to the detriment of the Church if the press got to hear of it. The reason all of this had not been made public was clear, said Parsons. If the news leaked that she was moonlighting from the police department, she would almost certainly lose her job. "Apart from the fact that this makes a not very well-educated young woman the arbiter of morals for the whole country, it is inevitable that mistakes were made, some of which had to be corrected."[23]

This was grist to Quigley's mill and he was quick to exploit it. Though it would be hard to deny a measure of self-aggrandizement in wrestling the Legion away from Chicago and into his own bailiwick, he had a point. The problem with Chicago as a center for film censorship and classification was its location, midway between Los Angeles and New York and distant from each. Beyond geography, there was its economic and artistic isolation from the industry. Chicago had been a center for production in the early years of the cinema, but since the 1920s Hollywood had garnered the lion's share, while the financial matters were handled in Manhattan. The Second City was now no more important than, say, San Francisco or New Orleans. It was small wonder, therefore, that the Reilly list was, by turns, obsolete and incomplete. In a given month, seven of twelve features playing in New York were lacking her classification for the simple reason they had not yet reached Chicago. Of thirty-six on the condemned list, only three were current; the rest had been in general release for anything from six months to three years or had been withdrawn from circulation. But infinitely more serious, if true, for the reputation of the infant Legion was Quigley's assertion that Dineen and Reilly, unable to cope with the sheer volume of weekly releases, had attached ratings to titles that they had not even seen, relying on friends' opinions or reviews in order to reach their conclusions.[24] In a stormy after-dinner session at Loyola University in February 1935, Quigley forced the issue of Chicago's domination by asserting that untold harm was being done to the cause through incompetence and pig-headedness. Dineen countered by accusing Quigley of fomenting discontent so that the Legion could be moved to his backyard and placed under his thumb, just as he had manipulated Hays for his personal satisfaction. It ill-behooved such a person to cast aspersions on Cardinal Mundelein and colleagues when "the record of his publications for the past fifteen years in advertising and promoting for public entertainment the very worst pictures ever made laid him open to reproach. One would imagine that those volumes of glaring and at times shocking advertisements would deter him from such conceited boastings." He was, in short, "a menace to the unity of the Church."[25]

Having thrown down the gauntlet, the wild-eyed Chicago Irish, as Quigley now referred to them, behaved as if the issue had been settled and threw caution to the winds. Despite winning four Academy Awards, *The Informer* remained off-limits to the Catholic citizenry and the list of unsuitable titles showed no sign of shrinking, despite a definite bowdlerization and sanitization of film content by producers consequent to the newly invigorated PCA under Breen's iron hand. In a sarcastic speech on the stage of the Mastbaum Theater in Philadelphia, the manager dedicated its closure that night to Cardinal Dougherty and the Catholic Church's Chicago list, which, in combination, seemed bent on destroying movies as a family entertainment for Americans.[26] Still, Dougherty remained as obdurate as ever to pleas that he relax his ban. In reply to Harry Warner that he be allowed to discuss the issue of Warners' films, the prelate replied icily that he had had "more than enough of that subject" but would be willing to talk about "anything except moving pictures."[27] For Will Hays, the response was equally negative. "Even if theatres were to reform and not show objectionable films, the boycott would not be raised until I was convinced of their sincerity. Anyway, there was a recent article in one of our Philadelphia dailies to the effect that producers do not intend to discontinue scenes of seduction as they are too beautiful to be eliminated."[28]

Had Dineen proceeded with reasonable caution and tact it is at least possible that Quigley and his supporters might have wearied of the situation and conceded defeat. But caution and tact were both foreign to Dineen's nature and he was becoming increasingly convinced that a constant show of strength was needed to prove to Hollywood where the power lay. In consequence, as the year 1935 progressed he began to act recklessly with measures he contemplated were likely to advance his interests. Hearing of a vacancy in Breen's office, he wrote a glowing but unsolicited testimonial on behalf of Sally Reilly, as someone who had "developed an acumen in picking out violations of Catholic morality in pictures. Her experience here, in Chicago, would be invaluable. She is smart and well-educated and capable of editing lists."[29] Meanwhile he had asked the MPPDA to use its good offices to obtain prints of recent releases free of charge and to ship them to Chicago where they would be screened in convents, church halls and other institutions under his jurisdiction. Accompanying the request was the thinly veiled suggestion that compliance would put the industry in a more favorable light. This was quickly nipped in the bud by Breen, who issued strict orders that no such cooperation was to be forthcoming. Dineen was to be made aware politely but firmly that the MPPDA was not "as weak and acrobatic as he would like to have us think and that we are not afraid of him." But the most outrageous suggestion was that the PCA should consider using some of its budget to finance the establishment of an expanded Catholic ratings office in the Windy City, since Cardinal Mundelein had only been able to promise "a paltry $12,000."[30] With singular lack of tact Dineen lauded the idea for its added merit in stealing a march on New York, since all prints would henceforth come directly to Chicago from Hollywood and only afterwards be forwarded for national distribution.

It was clear to Quigley that Dineen was digging his own grave. The prospect of newly released movies piling up in Chicago while the formidable Miss Reilly alone, or in cahoots with her mentor, decided when she could spare the time to register magisterial judgment upon them convinced him that the time had come to act. He had friends in high places and now was the time to call on their support. Bishop Cantwell, who little realized in 1933 what he had set in motion, was easy to convince. He had been the recipient of Dineen's scorn when he had suggested that the Los Angeles diocese might be the most suitable venue for the Legion's reviewing board. Now he agreed that if his West Coast diocese was ruled ineligible because of its lack of immunity to potential Hollywood pressure, it ought to be in New York.[31] To McNicholas, Quigley rehearsed all the well-worn arguments. The city was the distribution point for films from all over the world; as companies of any consequence had their financial headquarters there, direct representation to responsible officials when instances warranted would be immediate; in Mrs. Looram's IFCA women's brigade the Legion had a ready-made review board, whereas an alternative venue would require recruitment of a green group. In New York State, Quigley had the ear of Edward Mooney, Bishop of Rochester and chairman of the Administrative Board of the Catholic Welfare Conference, as well as that of the rapidly rising Bishop Francis Spellman, whose well-publicized support of the Legion in decades to come would be unflinching and vociferous. Playing on his already manifest hatred of Communism, Quigley described anew how Chicagoan incompetence had allowed a blatantly propagandistic piece of Bolshevik brainwashing, *Three Songs of Lenin*, to play untrammelled. Either the picture had not been seen at all, as had happened with distressing regularity in the past several months, or else "it had been seen by a particularly stupid person."[32] The logic was too clear and devastating to be missed. In November the Episcopal Committee was prevailed upon to reverse its earlier decision, to vote for the extinction of the Chicago list and place all responsibility for the Legion's operation with an executive secretary, to be located in New York. His Eminence, Patrick Cardinal Hayes assumed the financial burden, which was to be underwritten by Catholic Charities. Premises and office supplies were also donated at 35 East 51st Street, not too distant from the formidable shadow of St. Patrick's Cathedral, and an executive secretary was hired at $1,000 a year to coordinate the work of the reviewers.[33] Mundelein, Dineen and Lord accepted the decision with ill-concealed anger. Having no representation on it, there was little they could do to oppose the Episcopal Committee, whose motion had been proposed by McNicholas. As they faced a bleak future, they quietly dissociated themselves from the Legion and cast around for a scapegoat, finding one in Wilfrid Parsons, who was dismissed from his editorship of *America* within a year. Though several reasons were given for the ouster, Parsons was convinced that the "Chicago–St. Louis Axis" never forgave him for helping "steal the Legion away to New York," and waged an unrelenting campaign to drive him from office.[34]

The Flame Within—Metro Presents Ann Harding in the richest dramatic role she has played since she abandoned the stage for the screen. Hers is a vital, convincing, dynamic portrayal of a famous woman psychiatrist whose work of untangling the mental cobwebs of others is more than a profession. Story value, directorial accomplishment and photography all match in excellence the superb portrayal of the entire cast (Herbert Marshall, Maureen O'Sullivan, Louis Hayward. . . . Excellent.)[35]

This gushing, 1935 review by the lady reviewers of the International Federation of Catholic Alumnae was by no means untypical of the approach to those films that it singled out for praise—and in most monthly lists they were numerous. The morally mediocre and the bad were simply ignored. The upbeat, sunny disposition of these reviews reminded some of the circumstances surrounding the origin of this ratings system, which lay in Hays's open door policy of the mid-twenties. Various civic groups had been invited to avail themselves of the opportunity to view the latest Hollywood products. However, as with other window-dressing ploys conceived by the MPPDA chief, there was a tacit assumption that only Hollywood's flattering side would be highlighted. Mrs. Golderick had been one of the first to volunteer her group's participation, and even when Hollywood's image became tarnished, she continued the cordial association. Nevertheless, as the Legion was in its gestation period and with movie blacklists emanating from various locales, Mrs. Golderick's Pollyanna-ish approach was questioned within the Church and in the press for creating possible confusion in the minds of those seeking guidance.[36]

When, in November, 1935, the IFCA was asked to assume the awesome task of becoming the guide and arbiter for the entire country, the Episcopal Committee made its attitude perfectly clear from the start. There was to be an end to eulogizing. In future, even the best films were to be passed over in silence or, in the words of the official communique, "It has been thought best never to give more than negative commendation in a general list."[37] If certain pictures were deemed worthy of positive praise, the initiative for so doing was to emanate from the local Ordinary, with the understanding that no effort be made to involve other jurisdictions. The course thus charted shows a deliberate striving after a happy medium between the savage negativism of Chicago and Detroit and the undue permissiveness of the IFCA in pre-Legion times. Despite suggestions that it endorse the positive and show itself as a promoter of the better examples of film art, the Legion refused and, except for a very brief interval, as will be noted shortly, hewed to a noncommittal policy for the best part of three decades.

In the declining years of the Legion of Decency, the IFCA would be castigated by elements of the trade press as a group of middle-aged ladies in tennis shoes with nothing better to do with their ample spare time than pontificate on movies.[38] But, in comparison to the general run of film censorship boards throughout the United States in the thirties and forties, membership in the IFCA demanded a taxing apprenticeship. In many jurisdictions, political affiliation or cronyism played a more significant part in being allowed to sit in official judgment on movies than did knowledge of the medium. Virginia prided itself on the fact that its all-female censorship board was never drawn from the Republican party, reflecting the state's undying allegiance to the "Democratic Solid South" since the Civil War ended.[39] Those on the staff of Chicago's censorship board were overwhelmingly the wives of police officers who had the ear of their local ward boss, while the board in Memphis, Tennessee was chaired by the infamous Lloyd T. Binford, who boasted of his fifth grade schooling and whose reign spanned half a century, dating from 1928. Staffed with kindred spirits, its whimsical decisions reflected a Reconstruction-era mind set that banned a Hal Roach comedy for showing white and black school kids playing together because, as the decision read, "the South does not recognize social equality between the races, even in children." Similarly, the routine excision of song and dance numbers by blacks was justified on the grounds that "there are plenty of good white singers for musicals."[40] Mrs. Looram's Ladies, as they came to be called, were called upon to undergo an altogether sterner and more cerebral indoctrination.

The prerequisite for a potential member was graduation from a parochial high school, Catholic academy or liberal arts college. That was expected to have provided the basis in Church ethics and philosophy on which formal training in film evaluation would be built. By 1938 the procedural structure for producing trained staff had been finalized. The raw recruit, who was usually in her twenties, was required to spend six months under the wing of a veteran classifier, to accompany her to weekly previews and to participate, no doubt tentatively at the outset, in group discussions of specific titles just seen. An opinion to justify the chosen rating, formed in isolation from her compatriots, was solicited from the beginner, after which her mentor would report to Mrs. Looram on her suitability for permanent membership in the IFCA. The seductive, subliminal strength of the movies to infiltrate the heart, subvert the mind and undo all her careful years of moral upbringing and training was a constant danger. To guard against it and create an awareness of the snares that lay in the path of the unsuspecting, newcomers to the Catholic Alumnae were required to digest the contents of works by four authors. In the most important of these, *How to Judge the Morality of Motion Pictures*, the general principles enunciated were almost certainly the fruits of years of vigilance.[41] The preface stated the stark choice to be made between "entertainment which tends to elevate or to relax men and women physically tired with the duties and occupations of everyday life," and "entertainment which tends to lower their ideals and moral standards of life." Motion pictures were to be evaluated not primarily as entertainment but for their influence on morals; if false, they could only degrade. Turning to specifics, the anonymous writer defended the Legion's stance on salaciousness, which it defined as any appeal to the lower instincts such as might be made by protracted and lustful intimacies between the sexes and by disrobing scenes or by other suggestive sequences." While not narrow-minded, and cognizant of the beauty of the human body, "the Legion recognizes the serious moral danger to those seeing it exposed . . . under attractive circumstances."[42]

The main portion of the pamphlet addressed itself, by implication, to the greater proclivity for emotionalism and compassion evidenced by the "weaker sex." Though these traits were understandable and, on suitable occasions, praiseworthy, they were more often a manifestation of the frailty of feminine nature, which had to be recognized and strengthened at all costs before the business of film evaluation could begin. There followed instances of plots that made powerful arguments against accepted moral standards and might cause a vulnerable soul to change her convictions about right and wrong. Exaggerated sympathy for an adulterous man or woman might make for hatred of the faithful, if boorish, marriage partner. "Picture A," for example, was a deeply moving triangle story:

It is entirely devoid of salacious details but it proposes the doctrine that when a man's wife is selfish and unsympathetic, he is entirely justified in turning to another woman for love and happiness. In short, the film condones and justifies adultery. It does this not by ethical arguments but by emotional appeal. Deeply stirred by the picture, many of those witnessing it are apt to sympathize with the hero, approve his conduct and thus change their former convictions. They may be led to believe that under certain circumstances adultery is excusable. Here is a false moral standard, wholly at variance with traditional beliefs.

"Picture B" was the story of a young romance:

Because of some circumstance—parental objections, let us say, or lack of money—the hero and heroine are forced to postpone marriage indefinitely. They are young; they are persuaded that they cannot live without each other; they refuse to await marriage. Here is a film which by its sympathetic treatment presents most speciously the doctrine that sex experience is but the culmination of true love. It preaches that true lovers would be fools to defer it until marriage, and that pre-marital relations in such cases are pardonable. Because the hero is attractive and the heroine beautiful, the audience is inclined to sympathize with them and even approve what they do. It may be persuaded that deep and tender love excuses sin. Here, again, is a false moral standard, wholly at variance with traditional morality.

Other cautionary examples followed in similar vein. In the majority of these cases attention was drawn to the immoral behavior of "modern" women, be they mistresses defying convention, independent-minded career climbers sacrificing their virginity for advancement or "worldly-wise, impertinent wise-cracking types" playing off one suitor against another with no thought for the decorum becoming their sex. Such behavior on-screen should not be allowed to flaunt itself, since it would be contagiously destructive of true moral values of a Catholic audience. Though the pamphlet contained one instance of the superficial attractiveness of criminal behavior by a male gangster, the emphasis was squarely on the machinations of the latter-day Eve as temptress or innocent gone astray. For a picture to pass muster, the wages of sin visited on the woman for her transgressions not only had to be onerous but seen to be so.

Richard Dana Skinner's *Morals of the Screen*, written at the behest of the National Council of Catholic Women in 1935, was also required reading. While elaborating on a similar theme—the dangerous appeal of so many contemporary film scripts—it went further in stressing the obligation of evaluators to abide by strict doctrinal parameters. It cautioned that "any Catholic group attempting to judge the morality of a given (photo)play must be willing to base its judgment solely on the Catholic standard of morality and must not be surprised if this brings a storm of protest from those individuals and groups who have an entirely different standard."[43] Though most Protestant denominations still disapproved of divorce in the thirties, a number turned a blind eye to its depiction on the screen, where it was often the mainspring of the plot. For the Catholic viewer, on the other hand, the intrusion of alternative lifestyles, specifically "living in sin," promoted by secular interests, had to be recognized and guarded against. To illustrate the point, Skinner presented a script where "a woman who finds she has made a serious mistake in her marriage, has fallen in love with another man much better suited to her, and solves her problem by divorcing her first husband and marrying the other man." There could be no question of the immorality of her action, and it would demand a negative verdict from the Catholic reviewer. On the other hand, a photoplay that sought to justify a war of national defense would be a moral one for Catholics but highly immoral for Quakers. Spurious religiosity was another potential snare for the unwary. Without being specifically identified, Cecil B. deMille and his twenties versions of *The Ten Commandments* and *King of Kings* were almost certainly on the author's mind when he warned against the pernicious practice of employing indecent treatment in films purporting to have moral themes. The plight of Christian

martyrs at the time of Christ was frequently overshadowed by a "great splurge
of emphasis on the degenerate vices of ancient Rome, including even a display
of sexually perverted instincts." As Skinner warned, many were so completely
fooled by the alleged religious sincerity that they excused the indecencies as a
contrast to the heroism and sacrifice of the true believers. They should have
been aware that a moral theme was rendered unacceptable by the immorality
of its treatment and presentation. Nine reels of sin could not be excused by a
final reel of redemption.[44]

Martin Quigley's *Decency in Motion Pictures* rehearsed the arguments of the
two previous booklets and gave a superficial, condensed history of recent censorship developments, but his hand was also in evidence in the most honored
and respected of the four pieces of required reading material for Mrs. Looram's
Ladies. This was the 1936 papal encyclical, *Vigilanti Cura* ("With Vigilant Care")
of Pope Pius XI. There appears to be no conclusive evidence that the pontiff
took the initiative to issue it on Quigley's direct recommendation, but the
outcome may have been influenced in a circuitous way. Quigley had often
expressed dismay that the Church seldom paid much attention to the motion
picture as a means of communication, preferring to concentrate on the printed
word. There was no equivalent of the *Index Prohibitorum* for celluloid. In *Motion
Picture Herald* editorials and public speeches he impressed on audiences the
potency of the relatively new medium and the need to control it. Pius was not
slow to acknowledge the Legion's existence, having paid public tribute to it in
1934. In the fall of 1935 Bishop Spellman accompanied the Vatican Secretary
of State Eugenio Cardinal Pacelli (shortly to become Pius XII) on a cross-country
tour of the United States, and it is conceivable that the issue of Quigley's
disquietude over Rome's myopia was raised then. Martin Quigley, Jr. is in no
doubt that his father was a major influence in what bore the imprint of the
papacy: "The encyclical came out of my father's mouth."[45]

If anything was calculated to set the keystone on the Legion's legitimacy and
disarm criticism within the Church it was the *Vigilanti Cura*. In lauding the
improvement of movies from a moral standpoint, it emphasized the Church's
contribution rather than the industry's:

The bishops of the United States were determined at all costs to safeguard the recreation
of the people in whatever form that recreation may take. Because of that vigilance and
because of the pressure which has been brought to bear by public opinion, the motion
picture has shown improvement from the moral standpoint; crime and vice are portrayed
less frequently; sin no longer is so openly approved or acclaimed; false ideas of life no
longer are presented in so flagrant a manner to the impressionable minds of youth.

Pius went as far as to exhort other nations to follow America's lead and create
their own Legions for higher standards, although in approving of government
censorship elsewhere he went beyond Quigley's concept. That an IFCA classifier

with her intensive apprenticeship completed should regard herself as part of an exclusive team is not to be wondered at.[46]

While it was anticipated that, under Breen's reinvigorated regime in Hollywood, the majority of films would be sufficiently lacking in controversy or salaciousness to pose no problems to reviewers and therefore fall neatly into a Legion category, provision was made for the handful that offered difficulty. In problem cases the executive director felt able to cast a decisive vote that was usually acceptable to Mrs. Looram and her committee, but provision was made early in the Legion's history for recourse to an ancillary group if there was a possibility of deadlock or serious disagreement. These were the consultors. At the outset they numbered twenty and comprised a mixture of Catholic laymen and priests, with the latter in majority. Though the civilian segment was described as being a cross section of society, it was heavily weighted toward the great and the good, with a preponderance of "respected business and professional men" whose opinions did not deviate markedly from those of the Legion's regular staff.[47] Not until the late fifties was its composition to change markedly in favor of professional film writers and teachers and students of the cinema of both sexes. The cavalier attitude that the new breed was then to exhibit toward movie morality caused a permanent rupture and led to the severing of ties between the IFCA and the Legion. But that lay in the future.

The ratings system under which the Alumnae operated was arrived at after some discussion of fine moralistic points. Originally the intention was a three-category classification: A—Not Disapproved; B—Disapproved for Youths with a Word of Caution Even for Adults; and C—Disapproved for All. This was voted by the Episcopal Committee in November 1935 as being sufficiently comprehensive. Class C films were irredeemably bad and should be boycotted. The punishment to be meted out to the theater exhibiting one was at the discretionary power of the bishop. It could range from an admonition to the faithful not to attend the offending picture under pain of sin to a quarantine of all cinemas in the manner of Cardinal Dougherty. Later, the Legion would orchestrate campaigns against individual recalcitrant theaters of chains. At the outset, however, there were voices both within and without the Legion decrying the lack of a residual classification for those films that did not belong in the C category but presented major moral problems beyond those that made them unsuitable for children and youths. For some, the obligation to avoid certain movies was the same as the obligation to avoid occasions of sin. The gravity of the obligation depended on the gravity of the danger to which a person deliberately or carelessly exposed himself. The B rating signalled danger: B means Bad. But for others, a finer gradation was required, which would single out acceptable titles and place them in two categories: A-I—Morally Unobjectionable for General Patronage, and A-II—Morally Unobjectionable for Adults. While children would not be excluded by reason of an A-II classification, "charity and prudence would dictate that all individuals and especially parents and those having in their charge children and adolescents, inform themselves of the moral nature of a film before seeing, or allowing their charges to see, individual motion pictures."[48] The B classification would then cover titles Morally Objectionable in Part for All. In February 1936, this four-category system was adopted.

The gap between a high A and a low C was a grey area that made good grumbling material for fastidious theologians. When a Legion member asked whether it was right or wrong to attend a B movie, the official reply suggested that it was best to play it safe and not expose oneself to potential moral danger unless the film in question was exhibited with proper safeguards and controls. When pressed for a definition of these, the Legion found itself in deep theological water. It recommended that all Catholics stay away, though the obligation to do so was grave or light depending on whether the objectionable element constituted an approximate or remote occasion of sin. Fine intellects asked how an obligation could arise from a recommendation, especially since the definition of the former was too subjective and indefinite to be of any moral value, and certainly beyond the ability of the average lay person to fathom. Similarly, the terms under which a picture should be exhibited to permit viewing without danger were ill-defined. The act of attendance at a B film stemmed from a morally evil decision on the part of the prospective viewer in some respect. Aside from the circumstances and intentions of the person watching the picture, the very act of being present during its projection was a sin.[49] In the early years, at least, the Legion erred on the side of prudence in its prodigal recourse to the controversial B rating, using it mostly for pictures which, while keeping within the confines of the Production Code, dealt too light-heartedly with themes such as promiscuity, the martial bond, separation and the acceptability of divorce.[50] *The More the Merrier* (1942), an otherwise innocuous comedy, trivialized marriage by having the heroine, Jean Arthur, go to the altar with Joel McRea for propriety's sake as much as for love after she had sublet a bedroom to him in her tiny Washington apartment. It was rated B accordingly. Despite misgivings in some clerical quarters, the system remained unchanged until 1957, except for the addition of the Separate Classification, as will be noted in the next chapter.

A related problem was the appearance of controversial players in innocuous films. Mae West's notoriety was universally recognized, and her early starring vehicles with their bawdy content had been hastily withdrawn by Paramount in deference to Breen's new regime. Her later efforts, those dating from 1935, and the sanitized *Belle of the Nineties*, dating from late 1934, were bland by comparison. The question was whether her continued presence on the screen was an ever-present reminder of an unregenerate past and thus should not be tolerated. Rita Hayworth's well-publicized pregnancy as a result of her liaison with Aly Khan and the subsequent birth of Yasmin (who, wags insisted, should have been named Too Soon) before they made their marriage vows confirmed suspicions among the high-minded that screen sex symbols were poor role models. A third instance occurred in 1950 with Ingrid Bergman. She had deserted her husband for Italian director Roberto Rossellini and borne his child out of wedlock. The simultaneous appearance of their picture, *Stromboli*, raised the same question in acute form.[51] The Legion decision in all instances was to judge the play, not the player, as long as the immorality of private life was not mirrored in the movie. While the sexual peccadillos of actors and actresses were not a crucial factor in judging a movie, the accompanying advertising was carefully vetted. After interminable negotiations with Howard Hughes over *The Outlaw*, the issue of its release with a B classification was delayed until the more lurid stills and posters featuring Jane Russell were redesigned to the Legion's satisfaction. As author Richard Corliss explains in a similar context, an otherwise innocuous but serious study of Balinese voodoo customs, *Wajan, Son of the Witch*, had its rating lowered from A-II to B because of the refusal of the distributor to alter publicity material. Captions such as "Mystic Powers," "An Ecstatic Romance of Bali!" and "Frenzied Rituals" were the sole reason for the lower classification.[52]

The choice of an executive secretary to guide the Legion in its first tentative endeavor of supervising and imposing a film classification system on millions of the faithful was not taken lightly. The Episcopal Committee was cognizant of the fact that most priests knew next to nothing about the workings of the motion picture industry or the Production Code that purportedly controlled it. Like their superiors they had little patience with the tinseled world, so unreal and so alien to the plebian concerns of the local parish. It was acknowledged that a nodding acquaintance with the communications media would be a definite asset for the new position, allied, of course, with a grounding in moral theology.

The selection of the Rev. Joseph Daly seemed an admirable one from both vantage points. His doctorate in philosophy marked him as fit to interpret the finer points of the moral content of pictures, while his media experience as a regular speaker on the weekly radio broadcast, "Church of the Air," had brought him into contact with the production side of a business that, in terms of popular entertainment, was not entirely unrelated to the cinema. The remainder of his time he divided between teaching at Mount St. Vincent's College and priestly duties with St. Gregory's Church in Manhattan.[53] Unfortunately, Daly was to have a brief, uneasy and harassed period in office and would leave within less than a year of his appointment. The problem centered on the degree of authority the occupant assumed he had as distinct from that which the Episcopal Committee intended to grant him. At the outset, Archbishop McNicholas seems to have viewed the position as something on the order of a glorified clerk, dealing with office correspondence, arranging previews and overseeing the publication of the IFCA listings, but leaving the Committee to arrive at all the important decisions. As early as November 1934, he had cautioned against appointing a New Yorker because, in his opinion, the Church in the city had a distressing, if unconscious, tendency to incubate ambitious spirits that brooked no authority and abrogated to themselves the direction of whatever organization was placed under their supervision.[54] The unprincely stipend of $85 a month may have been intended to be both a disincentive for prospective candidates accustomed to Manhattan living costs and a declaration of what the job was worth. It was certainly indicative of the shoestring budget on which the operation would continue to be run for its entire existence.

It may be questioned whether McNicholas's concept of a supervisor only nominally at the head of a powerful pressure group would have stood the test of experience, but Daly effectively torpedoed the idea at the outset by demonstrating that he would be neither lackey nor discreet administrator. He had seemingly taken to heart Father Francis Donelly's statement in *America* that "Catholics do not expect dancers to be costumed like Admiral Byrd or all stories to be like the Rover Boys." His concept of the Legion was that of a trailblazer in the field of film appreciation. In overseeing the content and moral quality of motion pictures, it had a golden opportunity to elevate the taste of millions for whom going to the picture show had never been any more than a mindless pursuit. Too, the artistic attributes of a film were of equal importance to the moral content and it behooved the Legion to distinguish between the meretricious and the brilliant work of a Jean Renoir or Sergei Eisenstein. What better way to serve the cause of cinematic art than for the Legion to issue a Gold Medal Award for the most outstanding picture among those it reviewed each month?

Quigley was understandably upset by Daly's crusade, since he held an old-fashioned concept of the movies as cheap, noncerebral entertainment for the untutored working class that should profess simply moral virtues. To venture into the rarefied atmosphere of film aesthetics was asking for trouble, not least because so many of these doyens of the cinema held up for praise by intellectuals were political left-wingers and religious agnostics. The Spanish-born Luis Bunuel with his anarchist connections and sly digs at the Catholic Church to which he had turned traitor was a case in point. Renoir's Popular Front propensities and thinly disguised anticlericalism were equally distasteful.[55] Moreover, prizes to films or filmmakers would bring the Legion into closer contact with the industry when there ought always to be an arm's-length relationship. Faced with Quigley's displeasure, Daly's initial reaction was to ignore it. When the publisher insisted that he was set on a dangerous course, Daly retorted that he would not be bound by the orders of a layman who had almost split the Church in two by his highhanded behavior over the Legion's location. To make matters worse, he washed the Legion's dirty linen in public by telling anyone in the Hays Office who would listen that he was within his rights in conducting business as he saw fit without busybody Quigley poking his nose into the daily routine. Then he turned his attention to the consultors, the Legion's second chamber of opinion. He could see no point in their existence, since contentious issues could and should be settled by the IFCA's chairwoman and the executive secretary without recourse to the verdict of a heterogeneous collection of mostly cinematic illiterates, some of whom saw only the pictures they were called upon to adjudicate.[56]

Given these explosive ideas—consultors had been the brainchild of Cardinal

Hayes—it was not surprising that McNicholas felt alarmed. In trying to mollify Quigley he confessed that, although "Father Daly means wells, his judgment is not good. There is no hope of correcting a judgment that is natively bad or defective."[57] By summer's end there was a growing sense of mutual disenchantment. In November the break came over another of Daly's proposed innovations. He had never been happy with the bare application of a letter grade and the lack of an accompanying rationale for each film classified by the IFCA. To him it was yet another manifestation of Legion arrogance and self-imposed isolation from the creative side of the industry. He proposed that in future a "special estimate" be attached to every feature title, explaining why the specific category had been chosen. However, before submitting the idea to the Episcopal Committee, he had committed, as far as it was concerned, the unpardonable sin of canvassing Breen and some studio heads and producers for their reaction. To McNicholas's peremptory demand that he desist from conduct that threatened to rob the Legion of its independence, he reluctantly agreed, but not before observing acidly that "if we expect cooperation from filmmakers, it is only fair that we should give them some idea why the Legion approves or rejects their product."[58] Daly's fireworks might have passed unheeded in an obscure state censorship board, but in New York they were major news. One side had to prevail and it was to be the Committee. Within two weeks Daly performed his last service for the organization by tendering his resignation. McNicholas accepted it with alacrity.

In only one instance did the first Legion executive secretary acquit himself well in his superior's eyes. This occurred over the handling of the formidable George Bernard Shaw and a proposal to film his 1923 play, *Saint Joan*. In 1935 Paul Czinner had been chosen to direct his wife, Elizabeth Bergner, in the title role. For propriety's sake, Czinner had submitted the script to the *Azione Catholica* (Catholic Action) in Rome. The trial and execution of Joan of Arc had been a perpetual embarrassment to the Church for the five centuries since it occurred, and it sought to distance itself as far as possible from any visual reminder. Therefore, instead of the anticipated imprimatur, Czinner was issued a stern warning against having a bishop express regret at the Church's legal inability to burn the Maid of Orleans at the stake, together with a list of unacceptable words, including "archbishop, "deadly sin," "holy," "sacred office" and "infernal." Only a final version containing nothing capable of damaging the Church's prestige would satisfy Catholic Action. Unfortunately, when Shaw himself decided to enter the fray, he confused the issue hopelessly by equating Catholic Action with a similarly named but dissimilar organization in the United States and linking both to the Hays Office and the Legion:

Through a body of amateur regulationists and a list of words varying from State to State and even from city to city, the anarchists, the pugilists, the pornographers can easily drive a coach and six, as it is useless to check up on the letter if the spirit still eludes.

But the serious plays, like *Saint Joan* get stopped because they take censorships completely out of their depth.[59]

Daly rushed to the defense with a letter to the *New York Times* in which he stoutly repudiated allegations of amateurism in the ranks of the IFCA while taking aim at the playwright's well-known inclination toward socialism by accusing him of radicalism. Shaw found the whole experience richly entertaining and responded with malicious glee that the concept of a decency police force was a splendid idea and wished more power to its elbow.

In retrospect it would be hard to accuse Father Daly of anything worse than being ahead of his time. If the heresy of one generation has a habit of becoming the orthodoxy of the next, his concept of the Legion of Decency bears it out. A quarter of a century later, there would be a frank acceptance of its need to shrug off an image of negativism and instead encourage public appreciation for the art of the motion picture. The insular policy would be jettisoned in favor of a system of awards to individuals and films that would recognize their contribution to the growth of the medium with scant attention paid, in some cases, to the moral infelicities of award winners. All that lay in the future, of course. For the present, the Episcopal Committee turned to the task of finding someone it hoped would be a noncontroversial replacement. Its choice fell on Father John J. McClafferty, a priest in the Department of Social Action with Catholic Charities in New York. Though his first love was social work with the poor, a career to which he would return in middle age, he agreed to step into the breach on short notice.[60] The appointment proved to be a happy one for all concerned. McClafferty acquiesced in Quigley's concept of how the Legion should work, always deferred to his superiors and never raised any of the contentious ideas that had marred his predecessor's tenure. The organization kept a decent distance between itself and Hollywood. There were not even overtures to producers to excise unsuitable scenes but rather the initiative was left for them to approach the Legion if they desired a more lenient rating. Financial embarrassment resulting from a threatened boycott would be the whip that would drive them to seek reconsideration. And so, to the general relief of the Church hierarchy, the Legion put the contretemps of the previous two years behind it and embarked on a policy and a period of comparative quietude that was to last until the early fifties.

NOTES

1. Paul W. Facey's doctoral dissertation, *The Legion of Decency: A Sociological Analysis of the Emergence and Development of a Social Pressure Group* (New York: Arno, 1974), makes no reference to the feud that developed between the New York and Chicago factions over the Legion's location. Facey is also silent on the causes leading up to Father Daly's sudden resignation over matters of policy and principle.

2. The fight over implementation of the Production Code was regarded, at the time, as an appeal to "Patriotic Gentile Americans" to help endorse Judeo-Christian values.

See Leonard J. Leff and Jerold L. Simmons, *The Dame in the Kimono: Hollywood Censorship and the Production Code from the 1920s to the 1960s* (New York: Grove Weidenfeld, 1990), pp. 10–11.

3. For a thumbnail sketch of Cantwell and his milieu, see Mike Davis, *City of Quartz* (New York: Verso, 1990), pp. 330–35.

4. Facey, p. 45.

5. Ruth Inglis, *Freedom of the Movies: A Report on Self-Regulation from the Commission on Freedom of the Press* (Chicago: University of Chicago Press, 1947), p. 123.

6. The complete text can be found in *Le cinéma dans l'enseignement de l'eglise.* (Vatican City: Commission Pontificale pour le Cinéma, la Radio et la Télévision, 1955), pp. 234–35.

7. Ibid., p. 266.

8. *Catholic Standard*, May 25, 1934.

9. Martin Quigley Papers, Special Collections, Georgetown University, Washington, D.C. (hereafter QP), Box 1, Quigley to Lord, July 7, 1934.

10. Ibid., Quigley to Lord, July 8, 1934.

11. Inglis, p. 124.

12. Leff and Simmons, p. 43.

13. The wording of the pledge would remain unchanged until 1957. See Chapter 7.

14. Facey, pp. 57–59.

15. QP Box 1, Quigley to McNicholas, May 29, 1934.

16. Ibid., Quigley to McNicholas, August 20, 1934.

17. Edward de Grazia and Roger K. Newman, *Banned Films: Movies, Censors and the First Amendment* (New York: R. R. Bowker, 1982), p. 43. The Studio Relations Department became the Production Code Administration on June 22, 1934.

18. QP Box 1, Lord to Quigley, August 6, 1934.

19. Ibid., Dineen to Wilfred Parsons, August 24, 1934. The letter concluded: "It's the old story verified many times over that if Martin does not dominate a situation, he becomes disgruntled." Dineen and Lord flatly accused Quigley and Breen of substituting the PCA seal for a Legion imprimatur as an acid test of morality. See Wilfrid Parsons Papers, Georgetown University, Washington, D.C., Box C-50, Parsons to McNicholas, March 24, 1934 and Box D-204, Lord to Parsons, August 30, 1934.

20. Ibid., Box 2, Quigley to Bishop Francis Spellman, January 16, 1935.

21. *Variety*, January 29, 1935.

22. Ibid., July 17 and August 14, 1935.

23. QP Box 2, Parsons to McIntyre, December 12, 1934.

24. Ibid., Quigley to Samuel K. Wilson, August 20, 1934.

25. Ibid., Dineen to McNicholas, February 19, 1935.

26. *New York Times*, March 2, 1935. Also QP Box I, Quigley to Will H. Hays, March 15, 1935.

27. QP Box 2, Dougherty to H. M. Warner, undated.

28. Ibid., Dougherty to Hays, October 8, 1934.

29. Ibid., Dineen to Joseph Breen, June 5, 1935.

30. Ibid., PCA interoffice memorandum, Charles Pettijohn to Emma Applanalp, June 6, 1935. "The trouble is Father Dineen just wants to snap his fingers when he feels like it and expects us all to jump through hoops."

31. Cantwell had originally suggested a Los Angeles office with a staff of 250. QP Box 1, Dineen to Breen, November 1934.

32. QP Box 2, Quigley to Mooney, January 16, 1935.

33. Ibid., McNicholas to Quigley, November 24, 1934. A selection was to be made from within the Baltimore diocese.

34. Ibid., Parsons to Quigley, May 24, 1956.

35. National Legion of Decency files (hereafter NLOD). Miscellaneous file, 1934–46: Endorsed Motion Pictures, June 1935, vol. 4, no. 6.

36. Ibid., Memorandum from Father Patrick J. Masterson to Monsignor Gaffney, December 28, 1948.

37. Ibid., Miscellaneous file, 1934–46. November, 1935.

38. Criticism of the IFCA, heretofore muted, became more vociferous during the fifties. See, for example, *Motion Picture Exhibitor* editorial, "Mrs. Looram's Ladies and Other Reviewing Groups," vol. 54, no. 8, June 22, 1955, p. 35.

39. *Variety*, April 29, 1964.

40. *Colliers*, "Who Censors Our Movies?" May 6, 1950, pp. 38–40.

41. The eight-page pamphlet was subheaded: *A Popular Guide to Right Standards in Motion Picture Entertainment, Authorized by the Episcopal Committee on Motion Pictures for the Legion of Decency* (N.p.: n.p., n.d.).

42. Ibid., p. 8.

43. It was published by the Lay Organizations Department of the National Catholic Welfare Conference.

44. Richard Dana Skinner, *Morals of the Screen*, (N.p.: n.p., 1935), p. 5.

45. De Grazia and Newman, p. 44. Martin Quigley, Jr. confirmed this impression in a conversation with the author.

46. The text of the encyclical is published in extenso in *Le cinéma*, pp. 23–42.

47. NLOD, Miscellaneous file, Legion, 1934–46 (undated).

48. Ibid.

49. These opinions were submitted at the request of Masterson by John C. Ford, S.J., in "Moral Evaluations of Films by the Legion of Decency," NLOD, Miscellaneous file, Legion, 1934–46, (undated).

50. NLOD, *Annual Report*, 1940, p. 4.

51. NLOD file, *Stromboli*. The appearance of a Domincan, Father Morlion, in January 1950, as a friend-cum-apologist for Rossellini and Bergman aroused deep misgivings. He was candidly advised by Francis Cardinal McIntyre not to involve the Los Angeles diocese in any discussion of the picture. Patrick Masterson, then Legion chief, deplored his view of the love affair as "gossip of no consequence" and feared that his utterances could be "seriously detrimental to the Legion." Masterson to Spellman, February 3, 1950. The film was a financial flop.

52. Richard Corliss, "The Legion of Decency," *Film Comment*, vol. 4, no. 4 (Summer 1968), p. 31.

53. NLOD, Miscellaneous file, Legion, 1934–46.

54. QP Box 1, McNicholas to Quigley, November 24, 1934.

55. Bunuel's surrealist *L'Age d'Or* and the oblique criticism of peasant religious fanaticism in *Land Without Bread* were early examples of the Spaniard's ability to offend.

56. QP Box 1, Quigley to McNicholas, April 13, 1936.

57. Ibid., McNicholas to Quigley, September 30, 1936.

58. Ibid., Daly to McNicholas, November 2, 1936.

59. Corliss, p. 57.

60. Author's interview with Monsignor McClafferty, April 1991.

_____ *Chapter 4* _____

Early Days

It says much for the contrite, reformist attitude displayed by Hollywood from 1935 onward and the zealous application of the Production Code by Joseph Breen that the first few years of the Legion were remarkably free of controversy. Some pictures had been withdrawn and were destined not to see the light of day for a generation; others were aborted in the script-writing stage because of the impossibility of creating a finished product acceptable to the Production Code Administration; still others were scrubbed clean before being allowed to venture into first-run release.[1] The very existence of the duumvirate in Los Angeles and New York kept several projects from being considered. As the English trade magazine, *Film Weekly*, wryly put it, in a chastened film capital the old order had changed. Will Hays had been reduced to playing a figurehead Hindenburg to Breen's more activist Hitler.[2]

There was, of necessity, a blacklog of pictures to be classified by the IFCA as the Legion's official reviewing arm, but the dramatic change in the movies' moral content from just two years before made the task less onerous than might have been anticipated, as was shown in statistics for the period February 1936 to November 1937. Of 1,271 titles reviewed, 1,160, or 91 percent, were approved in the A-I and A-II categories. Only 13 were C-rated, and that figure would have been much lower but for two categories, independent productions and British and European pictures. Some of these had been in circulation since the early thirties. Those from the independents were either sex hygiene movies—of which more later—or "nudie cuties," ostensibly claiming to proselytize viewers to the healthy life through sunbathing, as it was decorously described. Like the nudist magazines displayed in the more disreputable outlets, they were eagerly sought after by brazen adolescents whose conversion to naturism was a remote possibility. And, like the magazines where the genitalia of the models were airbrushed into invisibility, the films failed to deliver the goods. Full frontal nudity and touching were absent. Instead, the characters played interminable games of volleyball and table tennis or simply lay around carefully posed. Even so, to have sought a seal for *Elysia* or *Unashamed* would have been an exercise in futility for their promoters, who were resigned to playing cat-and-mouse games with morality squads. The staying power of foreign language titles could be attributed to their art-house status in repertory theaters where they could be periodically revived, like a Shakespearean play or an Agatha Christie thriller on the stage, for the delectation of true movie aficionados. With few exceptions these C-rated pictures played in small cinemas to select audiences, either in the original language version for ethnic groups or subtitled for the rest. In either instance, their exposure was limited to around one hundred cinemas mostly in larger cities of the East and West Coasts.

In its inaugural sweep of reprehensible overseas pictures, the Legion fingered several classics. The 1930 German *The Blue Angel*, where Joseph von Sternberg played directorial Svengali to a young Marlene Dietrich for the first time, was condemned for its relentlessly sordid cabaret atmosphere and the ultimate degradation of Emil Jannings as the fastidious Professor Unrath, brought low by the sluttish Lola Lola. Similarly, Charles Laughton's critically admired portrayal of the Tudor monarch in the British-made *The Private Life of Henry VIII* (1933) failed to pass muster because of the king's leering demeanor, which reaches its apogee in his wink to the camera before entering the bedroom of his fourth wife, Anne of Cleves. With the need to sire a male heir on the distinctly plain-looking lady, he sighs to the camera, "Ah, the things I have to do for the throne of England!" Hedy Lamarr's notoriety in the Czechoslovakian *Ecstasy* (1933) preceded her move to the United States. Her nude swim and subsequent romp when a stranger gathers up her clothing, and her facial expression during sexual intercourse guaranteed that the Legion would be at one with Breen in his hostility:

It is a story of illicit love and frustrated sex, treated in detail and without sufficient compensating moral values, the portrayal of the mare in heat, and of a rearing stallion, the actual scene in the cabin where the woman's face registers the varying emotions of the sexual act—all are designed to stimulate the lower and baser elements and are suggestive, lustful and obscene.[3]

Though Lamarr's millionaire husband would attempt, in vain, to buy up and destroy all existing copies of the film, and though a severely truncated version was eventually licensed by the New York Board of Regents in 1940, the Legion, as was its custom with a title once it was in general release, refused to remove the Condemned label.

BIRTH OF A BABY

The appearance of *Birth of a Baby* late in 1937 presented the Legion with the first major classification problem in its brief existence. It also compelled the origination of a completely new category of classification.

Birth of a Baby would initially be lumped with other sex hygiene films, or "white coaters" as they were referred to in the trade because they invariably included an actor dressed as a doctor dispensing wisdom. The Legion's suspicions of the genre were well founded. Even in the silent era, sex hygiene shows had been a stock-in-trade of the more disreputable independent movie promoters. Cheaply made, indifferently acted and invariably accompanied by lurid, carny-style publicity, they played in sleazy theaters in the more disreputable parts of town or in remote areas where the forces of morality and the law took longer to track them down. Often they disappeared as quickly as they had arrived, only to resurface in a nearby locale. Their titles kept changing, both to confound the authorities and to lure suckers back to something they had already paid for. One of the more notorious was *The Story of Bob and Sally*, which was variously known as *Dust to Dust* and *Joys of Motherhood*. They violated at least two of the Production Code provisions, that sex hygiene and venereal disease were not to be subjects for motion pictures, and that scenes of actual childbirth, in fact or in silhouette, were never to be presented. These caveats meant that these pictures would never receive nationwide exposure on any of the major circuits. Few, beyond their promoters, were prepared to argue their fundamental seriousness and good intentions.[4]

Birth of a Baby was different. It came with impeccable credentials, having been conceived by Mead Johnson and Company, manufacturers of baby foods and other items for infants' diets. The company's intention was to make a feature-length picture that it would distribute to physicians at no charge, providing them with an educational aid for their female patients and at the same time help foster goodwill between the company and the medical profession. Christie Productions, a maker of short comedies, won the contract, and it was filmed in the late winter and spring of 1937 at their Long Island studio and at Cornell Medical School. It ran for seventy-two minutes and cost $50,000 to produce. Mead Johnson's name was not mentioned in the credits or elsewhere.[5] Because the original was in 35mm, it seemed logical to give it a commercial airing before donating 16mm copies to doctors and assorted health agencies. Copyright was taken out in the name of the American Medical Association, with all profits going to the U.S. Public Health Service and the U.S. Children's Bureau. It had the imprimatur of several eminent gynecologists and public health directors.

The film centers on Mary, played by professional actress Eleanor King (who was to become pregnant herself during the ensuing furor). Her ignorance of the basic facts of life cause her to listen closely to her mother-in-law, Mrs. Burgess, as she explains menstruation to her daughter. Mary suspects she might be pregnant and confides in Mrs. Burgess, who urges her to see a physician while assuring her that birth is a perfectly natural process. In the office Mary is given an examination, fully clothed, shown the sequence of conception and fetal development via a series of diagrams, and fitted for maternity garments by a nurse. The birth takes place at home with more diagrams of the baby's passage to the outside world. The most controversial part of the film is a twenty-second, live-action sequence where the baby's head is seen emerging from the mother. The new mother is given her infant to nurse, in a long shot that does not reveal her breast. Her husband is then allowed to enter and embrace his wife who, we are told, will remain in bed for ten days to recover. Everything has gone nature's way.

At issue in the struggle to bring the movie to the commercial screen were two mutually antagonistic concepts. "We are born between feces and urine," asserted St. Augustine, who had little to say in favor of women of any age. If there was not an actual stigma to being pregnant in the thirties, there was an aura of embarrassment akin to having bad breath or pimples. Mothers-to-be went to great lengths to conceal their expanding girth and the term *confinement* had real meaning then as a period when decent women should refrain from appearing in public to advertise their condition. "We'll guard your little secret!" boasted one manufacturer of maternity clothing. The processes of pregnancy and delivery were intensely private events to be cloaked in respectful secrecy. To be sure, they were among the facts of life but were best left to parents to explain to their offspring when they judged fit. Opponents of this attitude pointed an accusing finger at the results. Ignorance and fear were rife in the United States, which had one of the highest infant mortality rates in the industrialized world. Embarrassment was contagious, leading many mothers to shirk their responsibility when it came to informing daughters. Hypocrisy, outmoded puritanism and social taboos had for too long caused newly married women to contemplate motherhood with dread. Far too many entered the labor ward knowing little of what to expect. The film would provide desperately needed knowledge and reassure prospective parents.

Birth of a Baby was submitted by Sam Citron of Christie Productions to the Board of Regents of the State of New York on July 12, 1937. It was refused an exhibition permit on the grounds of indecency.[6] An appeal of this judgment was heard by the commissioner of education, Frank Graves, on November 5, at which time he not only upheld the recent decision but added that the picture was "immoral and would tend to corrupt morals." Graves later elaborated on his verdict before the Supreme Court of New York, insisting that "any picture which fixes the minds of spectators assembled in a mixed audience composed of both young and old upon the functions of female organs . . . is not only indecent but tends to stimulate morbid curiosity relating to sex that is demoralizing."[7] When the commissioner ironically prophesized that the result of such misguided liberality would culminate in the portrayal of the act of coition itself on New York screens, he could little have imagined that such would become the stock-in-trade of the city's pornographic movie theaters a generation later.

At this point in the proceedings, the Legion of Decency had not entered the controversy since it had not had an opportunity to view the controversial film, but it managed to hold two screenings in the last week of December, the first for IFCA reviewers and the other for consultants because of the explosive potential of the item. There was unanimous agreement by both groups that Graves had acted wisely. Movie audiences were an agglomeration of sexes, ages and temperaments, control of which would be difficult if not impossible in the confines of a commercial movie theatre. All that would result would be the arousal of morbid, prurient curiosity.[8] Support of the Legion's position came from the Jesuit weekly, *America*. Why is it, asked their film critic, that the purveyors of this type of product, who claimed to have a zealous regard for the public's health, never turned out pictures about indigestion or "How to Protect Your Daughter from Tuberculosis," but always foisted their sex-obsessed wares on people in some side street theater or ex-burlesque house with all its concommitant seediness? The people of New York City had protested against shadow obstetrics in a Broadway play the previous year and wanted no repetition.[9] Dr. Ignatius Bryne, a physician and Legion representative in Brooklyn, urged all decent women to band together and "tear apart any filmite" who dared belittle their sex by satisfying "a sex-crazed clientele for thirty pieces of silver." The evil effects of *Birth of a Baby* were hard to exaggerate, the doctor declared. They would plant the seeds of fear of marriage and childbirth among engaged couples just as surely as they played into the hands of birth controlists, those advocates of racial suicide. Then, lashing out at a development that had occurred in another medium, he demanded that the Legion extend its activities to the printed word and make that, too, a religious crusade.[10]

He was referring to a decision by *Life* magazine to run an illustrated feature on *Birth of a Baby* with thirty-five stills from the film, including three of the actual delivery. When the April 11, 1938, edition hit the newsstands, the police were on hand to confiscate the copies. Sales were banned in the Bronx, Brooklyn and Nassau county. Elsewhere in New York vendors were cautiously selling only to known customers from beneath the counter. Matters quickly reached such a peak that the managing editor of *Life*, Roy E. Larsen, took the place of one street dealer who had been charged with obscenity and sold copies until he, too, was arrested.[11] That, however, was not the end of his tribulations. In canvassing support for the issue, a number of public figures had been approached including Constance Armstrong, president of the Catholic Young Women's Club and a member of the Legion. Through a staff error, Armstrong's vehement condemnation of the film had been presented as an endorsement. The embarrassed publisher was forced to print an apology together with the text of a letter that the outraged Armstrong had written at the suggestion of her lawyer, blasting the film.[12] Some ten thousand copies of *Life* were confiscated in various parts of the nation and outright bans were imposed from Tennessee to North Dakota.

On the other side of the battlefield tempers were no less hot. The *New York Evening Post* reported that, instead of condescending pronouncements, the University of Minnesota Medical School in Minneapolis had adopted a logical approach by holding a screening for faculty, staff and students after which a vote had been taken as to the suitability of *Birth of a Baby* for public consumption. The decision had been 1,955 in favor to 40 opposed.[13] The *Daily Worker*, never slothful when an opportunity arose to embarrass the guardians of bourgeois morality, wondered whether New York had become the last refuge of the stork story.[14] Bosley Crowther of *The New York Times* and the doyen of film critics added his voice to those who demanded that the ban be lifted.[15] Eleanor Roosevelt, who had seen both the film and the article, was reputed to be in favor of both. Faced with this storm of yeas and nays, the Legion decided to have another look on March 18. It was one of the consultors, a priest, who suggested the application of a Separate Classification (S.C.) rating. He agreed with the majority of his colleagues that the picture might be a moral menace if shown theatrically. The young and the evil-minded would attend in the hope of sexual gratification from seeing a woman's sex organs exposed. On the other hand, were the Legion to impose its C rating, it should bear in mind that application was predicated on the intrinsic immorality of a film. To condemn a film that was intrinsically moral because of immorality extrinsic to it would be a departure from the spirit of the system of classification as laid down in 1935. To McClafferty's suggestion that some kind of rider be attached to the Condemned rating explaining the rationale, the priest replied that that would not change the nature of the verdict of intrinsic immorality. In any case, it was doubtful whether the public would read the fine print, as it were. If the Legion were to proceed with a C it would lay itself open to a bitter and perhaps not unjustified attack. That ignorance of even the most elementary facts of life was epidemic in American society could not be denied. The young and the ill-informed had a right to this knowledge and as every right postulated a corresponding duty, there was an obligation on the Legion's part to allow the imparting of that information. With adequate safeguards as to where and under what conditions *Birth of a Baby* might be screened, the S.C. label could be attached.[16]

McClafferty and his staff may have been influenced by another thinly veiled attack that came from the Federal Council of Churches, an umbrella organization for twenty-three Protestant denominations. The actions of those seeking to ban the picture, said an editorial in its *Newsletter*, were not only unwholesome but an altogether unrealistic contention undercutting the assumption that the educative process was carried out through a variety of outlets, both formal and informal. The dogma of the separation of entertainment from educational enlightenment had two obvious antisocial consequences. It would deny the most potent medium in existence to those who, from disinterested social motives, sought to use it. It would also allow the film industry to escape responsibility for the consequences of its product. To divorce education from entertainment in the development and enforcement of moral standards would seem comparable to the divorcement of business practices from social consequences, as the recent, unhappy Depression had exemplified. As for obscenity, the absence of elements that gave vulgar exhibitions like stripteases their salacious appeal was one of the more impressive attributes of *Birth of a Baby*.[17]

Special Pictures Corporation, the distributors, supplied the means that gave the Legion its rationale for applying the Separate Classifications for the first time. These were the stringent terms of the contract under which exhibitors would be bound to show the picture. It was a far cry from the "skindependents" tactics. All advertising would have to have prior approval in writing from the American Committee on Maternal Welfare; no feature-length film could be shown on the same bill, and even accompanying shorts would have to be approved; no commercial tie-ups were permitted; and managements were to use their discretion in admitting juveniles.[18] The Legion issued its S.C. label on March 31, 1938, though continuing to insist that the commercial cinema was not a suitable place for its showing. However, it was exhibited theatrically as this was the only way the distributor could recoup the money it had spent on a sizable advertising campaign. Despite the Legion rating, *Birth of a Baby* had a rough ride in parts of the nation, being banned by Pennsylvania and Nebraska, among other states.[19] The sober publicity and the aura of seriousness surrounding the screenings doomed it at the box office, a sad commentary on the reception given sex education movies that promised something other than titillation. By the end of the year it had disappeared from view.

Having tested the waters of the Separate Classification once, the Legion decided to apply the rating on two other occasions that same year, 1938. The Spanish Civil War was still raging and movies supportive of both sides in the conflict demanded attention. The most visible was *Blockade*, a fictional, romantic adventure yarn starring Henry Fonda as a freedom fighter and Madeleine Carroll as a world traveler who falls in love with him and his cause. The producer, Walter Wanger, had been forced by Breen to dilute the political content to such a degree that it was hard to tell whether Fonda was fighting for the Republicans or Franco. That the Republicans were Communist inspired and ostentatiously anticlerical was common knowledge in the United States, and *Blockade* was mired in controversy from the day of its release. The International Alliance of Theatrical Stage Employees, the movie projectionists' union, warned its members not to run this piece of subversive propaganda. In Boston, Baltimore and Chicago chapters of the Knights of Columbus staged rallies in front of theaters denouncing the false, atheistic and immoral doctrines in the picture. These actions reflected a more widespread persecution of survivors of the Lincoln Brigade, to an overwhelming degree composed of Americans who had volunteered for service on the Republican side and who returned from the war to have their passports lifted by the government. Privately, the Legion had no doubts that the picture was another manifestation of Hollywood ultraleft liberalism but it refrained from condemning it on the basis of political content. In applying the S.C. rating, it appended the explanation that "many people will regard this picture as containing foreign, political propaganda in favor of one side in the present unfortunate struggle in Spain."[20] A pro-Republican documentary, *Spain Fights On*, was similarly classified, but without a rider.

The Special Classification would be used with extreme parsimony in the years that followed. Indeed, it was not until 1953 and the appearance of *Martin Luther* that the Legion felt constrained to apply it again. The U.S.–West German semi-documentary, sponsored by five Lutheran organizations for its run in the

United States, proved to be a modest hit, to the pained surprise of the Legion. There were strong pressures for a Condemned rating from various parts of the country. William Mooring, whose film reviews in *Tidings* were characterized by a right-wing, McCarthyite stridency, sought to link the production to a perceived international Communist conspiracy: "If *Martin Luther* had been made by pro-Communists for the purpose of launching an attack upon the Catholic Church (the major Communist objective in the war against Christ), it could not very well have been contrived with greater subtlety nor with more characteristic style." Digging a little deeper, Mooring discovered that Alan Sloane, one of the writers, had "a long list of dubious political affiliations" and had been mentioned by name in "Red Channels." This referred to a notorious "Report of Communist Influence in Radio and Television" prepared by two ex-FBI agents that quickly became the bible of the media industry for ousting undesirables. Its underlying thesis held that Communists and fellow sympathizers were infiltrating the air waves to spread their subversive doctrines.[21]

Still, the link between Bolshevism and *Martin Luther* was tenuous at best and the Legion pondered the wisdom of using the Condemned rating to shield Catholics from brainwashing that was of a theological rather than a political stripe. Its Minneapolis representative disagreed. She could see no logic in a system that banned heretical reading material but might permit viewing of a picture "which, in its entirety, not only teaches heresy but bears false witness against the Catholic Church's teaching."[22] Roman theologians had long since attributed Luther's birth to the ability of the devil to use witches as an incubus. Should his spawn be allowed to masquerade on screen? Thomas Little, the Legion's executive secretary, was inclined to admit that *Martin Luther* could have a definitely harmful effect on "weak Catholics."[23] The censorship board in Quebec had shown one possible approach by limiting screenings to Protestant church groups, with admission restricted to parishioners holding tickets stamped with the words, "Catholics Not Admitted." That avenue was not open to the Legion. Behind-the-scenes pressure would later be applied to the booker of prints for the Army and Navy Motion Picture Service, requesting that he not rent the offensive title even though it had been granted a Code seal of approval. But, as with *Birth of a Baby* and the Spanish Civil War documentaries, there was no intrinsic immorality in the movie. In those circumstances, the S.C. label was the most that the Legion could do.

As the decade of the thirties came to its end, the National Legion of Decency could look back with unalloyed pride at what had been achieved. Membership was at a record level; the local chapters were in place and volunteers kept a vigilant eye on any releases that might slip by the New York office. Hollywood was, depending on one's viewpoint, cowed by the Production Code and the Legion, or living up to promises of better behavior like a chastened schoolboy. The advent of the Second World War meant that European pictures of the type that had caused most of the trouble would be an increasingly rare commodity, making the job of the Legion that much easier. In 1939 McClafferty was able to report to the Episcopal Committee that American pictures had shown a definite improvement in their moral quality in the past two or three years. The handful of titles emanating from the movie capital that had been threatened with a C rating had been hastily recalled and altered according to his dictates. Clean and decent movies were at last becoming a reality for American people.[24]

By the end of the decade, too, the fledgling organization was feeling confident enough to spread its wings and modify its policy of self-imposed isolation. Hitherto it had contented itself with classifying a film and then having nothing further to do with it. From this point it began to negotiate with studios, producers and distributors over terms for a revision of the rating if the initiative came from the industry. It held to its principle that it would not alter a classification once a picture had been put into national release. The rationale was that unscrupulous companies or individuals would milk a Condemned classification for all its worth and then accept the higher one once box office potential began to wane. They had to choose while their product was still playing in New York or Los Angeles. The initiative was not slow in coming from the other side, which was now only too cognizant of its adversary's formidable power. Between 1939 and 1943, all six domestically produced titles that were placed in the C category were appealed by their authors, and after withdrawal and cuts, raised in status.[25] What is equally instructive is that each had been granted a seal of approval by the Production Code Administration, which was evidence enough that the Legion was a tough revising chamber. The first of these chronologically, a Warner comedy, *Yes, My Darling Daughter* (1938), ran into trouble because of the unacceptability of the main theme—trial marriage. Ellen, the spirited young heroine, suggests to her fiancé that they go off for a weekend before he leaves for a two-year stint as an executive in Europe. His hesitation is countered by her insistence that, "We've got to have something beautiful and set apart so that in our hearts we'll know that we're really married." In the original version the young couple talked at length before retiring for the night, he to the outside porch behind a glass door, she to the cabin bedroom. The New York State censor and the Legion were at one in their objection to the concept. Additionally, for the Church there was the fine theological point that while the woman did not actually sin (they awoke in separate beds the following morning), she put herself in an occasion of sin. Further, said Father McClafferty, the convention that unmarried couples should never spend a lengthy period together unchaperoned and in a remote locale had been violated.[26] Six ultravigilant reviewers opined, via some circuitous reasoning, that a line of dialogue uttered by the feisty grandmother, "You know the only thing that puzzled me is why the good Lord invented such beautiful things as the trees and the flowers and the birds and then had to go and invent sex!" was potentially harmful to the Church's attitude that sex relations are good if performed within matrimonial bounds.

Faced with total exclusion from one of the nation's largest markets because of the New York State censor's disapproval, and with a Legion rating that would bar uncounted millions, Warners hastened to comply with suggestions from the latter to make it more acceptable. The cabin scene was severely truncated and a sequence added in which Ellen assures her mother that she did nothing wrong. Some 1,300 feet were excised, reducing the running time by a good ten minutes. Since not all of the complaints were addressed and the suspicion lingered that the heroine still hankered after a pretend marriage, the Legion would only allow a B rating.[27] Nevertheless, the New York State Board of Regents fell in behind, much to the relief of Jack Warner, who pronounced himself pleased with the compromise.[28]

The marriage sacrament came in for another dose of disrespect later the following year in an equally light-hearted comedy, This Thing Called Love, with a trio of seasoned players, Melvyn Douglas, Rosalind Russell and Binnie Barnes, who could be counted on to raise a smile from the slightest of material. The feminist ploy on this occasion was reversed—Russell insisted that she and newly wedded husband Douglas live a platonic relationship for three months following the wedding ceremony to ensure that they were really compatible in respects other than physical. After what the studio plot synopsis coyly describes as "a kissless honeymoon," Douglas begins to neglect his work and woos his secretary, the accommodating Barnes. The couples' impasse is ended through a creaky plot mechanism in which Douglas, for the sake of an impending business deal, is obliged to pretend that he is about to become a father. In the final scene, husband and wife are reconciled and retreat to the bedroom to make the pretense a reality.

With the reviewers split five-to-one for a B over a C rating, McClafferty decided to call in five consultors. Theirs was an even slimmer three-to-two margin for a B. What perturbed the Legion chief was that the rationales for both classifications were enough to merit condemnation.[29] Not only was there trial marriage without consummation, but equally reprehensible was the reason why the wife opened their bedroom door—for fear of losing her husband to another woman, not through recognition of her aberrant behavior in demanding a platonic relationship in the first place.

Puzzled as to why the PCA had granted This Thing Called Love a seal, Mrs. Looram tried, unsuccessfully, to get an explanation from Joe Breen. The chief was actually on vacation in New York visiting his old friend Martin Quigley.[30] Back in Hollywood, the vice-president in charge, Francis Harmon, confessed that his boss had been gravely worried about the picture and, after passing it, had warned other producers not to take his leniency as a precedent. The fact was that Breen was exhausted by the demands of the job. In one month alone he and his staff had had to examine 154 features and scripts. He was talking about retiring or assuming the position of production head at RKO. Said Harmon, scriptwriters were taking advantage of the old man's exhaustion to slip in bits of dialogue so filthy that Breen was unable to grasp the depths of their depravity.[31] When finally contacted at Quigley's home, he agreed that if he were on the Legion staff he would be torn between a B and a C.[32]

As if to add insult to injury, Columbia announced that the New York premiere would be held at Radio City Music Hall on February 13, 1941. Unlike the white elephant that it is today, Radio City was then a highly prestigious venue for showcasing new movies in the city. It also prided itself as a home of family entertainment. McClafferty felt that, with this latest effrontery, he had enough ammunition to act, and announced a Condemned rating on February 5. It was accompanied by a press release headed "This Thing Called Movies," in which he grimly reminded the public why the Legion had come into being in the first place. As for the movie companies, "If amnesia were setting it, it would be of a very inconvenient type, inconvenient for the coffers and accounts of producers. Decency still pays dividends; dirt pays deficits." Then, hinting at calling a boycott of the company's current films, he trusted that patrons would be discriminating in their choice of Columbia pictures when it came to patronizing new releases.[33]

The company was now thoroughly alarmed at what their harmless little comedy had occasioned. The manager of Radio City protested that he had never liked the picture and had tried to get out of showing it but was bound by a contract that Columbia insisted he honor. He could only hope it would die a quick death at the box office.[34] Nate Springold, the studio's chief in New York, complained that alterations to the print would cause difficulty. On the other hand, this was the first time his company had had a run-in with the Legion and he would not be the one to jeopardize future relations. He agreed to go over the script and make as many of the fifteen cuts in dialogue demanded as could be achieved without reshooting scenes. Among the lines that ended on the cutting room floor was, "No wonder she's tired, there's a convention in town." If the theme itself could not be changed, deletions apparently lessened emphasis on it.[35] Though the Condemned version did open on schedule at Radio City, a truncated one appeared a week later with a B, a reversal of Legion custom.

The legendary Greta Garbo was the third female in as many years to feel Legion wrath for what was to be her final screen appearance, in *Two Faced Woman* (1941). By chance, her costar was also Melvyn Douglas, playing the part of a philanderer who neglects his wife. To maintain his interest, Garbo pretends to be her single, slightly promiscuous twin sister, wears slinky dresses, performs a torrid dance and seduces him. The film was directed for MGM by George Cukor who had a reputation as a "woman's director" because he was supposedly more sensitive than most to the female psyche in that male-dominated profession. The PCA felt that a potentially indelicate subject had been managed with a delicate hand. But the Legion would have none of it. A total of sixty-nine objections were listed to scenes of unduly passionate lovemaking, objectionable dialogue, the low cut of a certain dress worn by Garbo and the casual treatment of marriage. Metro hastily withdrew the print and recalled Douglas to shoot an additional sequence that showed he had seen through the ruse of the twin sister business before bedding his wife and therefore was not guilty of conniving at adultery. This was sufficient for a B. A personal letter from Francis Cardinal Spellman to Louis Mayer recalling previous, amicable meetings of the two and presenting the Legion's case may have helped speed compliance.[36]

What may have been most responsible for raising the ire of Father McClafferty and his staff in all of these instances was the sex of the protagonists. All three were free-spirited women, consciously deciding to transgress the boundaries of traditional morality for their personal happiness and refusing to be shackled by the bonds of Christian matrimony when they were "given" by one man to another with all the passivity that entailed. Nor in any of the plots did they suffer for their willful action. On the contrary, each could count a small victory—the respect of a spouse for the independent behavior of his partner—a deviation from the Paulist concept of a married woman, to be sure. Too, their behavior seemed symptomatic of what the aftermath of Pearl Harbor had wrought.

The war years were not without their impact on morals and society. Just as the Great War had seen the demise of the chaperon, a rise in skirt lengths and the spectacle of women smoking in public, so World War II brought its own small revolutions. Sociologists remarked on the appearance of the two-piece swimsuit and its inability to cover as much female flesh as its predecessor, although it was justified on the patriotic grounds of saving fabric. To a far greater extent than in 1917–18, females were commonplace in the American workforce. Their relatively high wages gave them an independence of attitude and lifestyle that would have been unthinkable in the Depression era. What would also have been regarded as scandalous in the previous decade but was now accepted as a necessary measure was the publicity given to sexually communicable diseases and the need to report them. Moralists also pointed as much in sorrow as in anger to the soaring divorce and illegitimacy rates as the consequences of licentious behavior.

The new mood was especially evident in the entertainment industry. Parents were perplexed over the behavior of bobby soxers at the concerts of a frail-looking young crooner, Frank Sinatra, where screaming, crying and fainting by his fans were *de rigueur*. On the West Coast there was a revival of Edison's Kinetoscope and servicemen on leave lined up to peer through its tiny window to ogle bathing beauties in various stages of undress. Pin-ups were everywhere. Betty Grable's legs were insured for a million dollars, a wise investment since they had been reproduced by the million on posters that graced the lockers of fighting men in all four corners of the world. *Cheesecake* had entered the vocabulary with a vengeance and was instantly recognizable. Even Breen seemed unable to staunch the flow. One of his most extraordinarily liberal decisions since taking up the job was to give the green light to Preston Sturges's *Miracle of Morgan's Creek*, a comedy in which a frantic, slightly scatterbrained Trudy Klockenlocker (Betty Hutton) bewails the fact that she is pregnant by a now-vanished husband whom she had wed in a drunken stupor and whose name she can only vaguely recall as being "something like Ratsky-Watsky." It was in this atmosphere of liberality that independent producer Hunt Stromberg decided to film a whodunit, *The G-String Murders*, penned by the most talented and infamous of all striptease artists, Gypsy Rose Lee. Her knowledge of the business was encyclopedic; her ability to write a mystery story suitable for screen adaptation was limited.

If Breen and his office had had temporary amnesia in allowing passage of *Lady of Burlesque*, as seemed the case when it appeared with a seal, the Legion was in no such magnanimous mood. Moral standards would be maintained, war or no war. When first submitted, on April 27, 1943, reviewers were split five-to-three for a Condemned rating over a B for its double entendres, suggestive dances, indecent costuming and "sympathetic portrayal of sensuous entertainment."[37] Barbara Stanwyck's concealment behind a cardboard cutout of a heart gave the impression she might be nude underneath. Two lines of dialogue were considered particularly inappropriate: "It was just me taking natural advantage of the dark," and "That's not where you grabbed me." The Pickle Persuador routine might of itself be harmless, but showbiz types knew that *pickle* was synonymous with the male sexual organ. By the time Father Patrick J. Masterson, the Legion's new appointment as McClafferty's second in command, invited the consultors to deliver their second opinion, all of Mrs. Looram's Ladies had been converted to recommend a C rating and the consultors unanimously confirmed their decision. United Artists, which had agreed to distribute it, was sufficiently impressed by recent victories the Legion had scored over three major studios to wave the white flag in a gesture of surrender.[38] The company suspected, correctly, that the rating was as much a signal to the industry at large to desist from making plans for a cycle of burlesque movies, as it was a salutary example to imitators. It was indeed a tame entertainment that emerged after Stromberg made the necessary excisions. Gone was a shot of Barbara Stanwyck in a diaphanous gown; gone was a shot of the female chorus with their derrieres to the audience; gone was a bump and grind routine; and references to a male character having "left his motor running" and "taking natural advantage of the dark" were also left on the cutting room floor. The *New York Mirror*'s verdict on what remained was succinct: "There are scenes in which audiences of rational men are plunged into raucous excitement by the sight of girls clothed practically to the stifling point. There is not a single, solitary strip-tease from start to finish. In short, the film has nothing but a couple of killings to make your pulses pound. Hardly sufficient, really."[39]

The titillation may not have been sufficient for the millions of servicemen ogling real-life strippers from the Aleutians to Casablanca or peering through cigarette smoke at grainy, 16mm stag film loops. But among screen moralists, distrustful, and perhaps with good reason, of the Production Code Administration, the fate of *Lady of Burlesque*, and the warning to her potential imitators, was consoling. When Breen was questioned on his lenient attitude, he excused his conduct on the grounds that the flood of loose-moraled wartime pictures had made judgment more selective. But Masterson and McClafferty could destroy this sophism in a sentence. There were the eternal and absolute principles of Catholic morality. In a time of weakness and moral amnesia, one institution had shown its vigilance. There might be no authority in Hollywood that the clean-living and God-fearing could trust absolutely, but there was the Legion. That trust was to be put to the test at war's end with one of the most sensational issues in American film censorship history involving the fate of a mediocre western.

NOTES

1. Leff and Simmons found the title for their book *The Dame in the Kimono* in the suppression of the 1931 version of *The Maltese Falcon*, withdrawn in 1934 because of perceived immoral activities by Sam Spade. Myrna Loy was twice-victimized: her role as the mistress in *Arrowhead* (1931) was reduced to incomprehensibility by Breen cuts in 1934, and her only number in *Love Me Tonight* (1932) was removed because she sang in a diaphanous costume showing her navel.

2. Leff and Simmons, p. 57.

3. De Grazia and Newman, p. 49.

4. The exploitation of sex hygiene and nudist films in those years is related in Dave F. Friedman, *A Youth in Babylon: Confessions of a Trash-Film King* (Buffalo: Prometheus, 1990), p. 35 et seq.

5. *Motion Picture Daily*, April 12, 1938.

6. NLOD file, "Birth of a Baby," Irwin Esmond to Sam Citron, July 13, 1937.

7. De Grazia and Newman, pp. 219–20.

8. NLOD file, "Birth of a Baby," McClafferty to Groves, January 4, 1938; also NLOD press release, March 29, 1938.

9. *America*, January 1, 1938.

10. *Brooklyn Tablet*, April 23, 1938.

11. *New York Sun*, April 9, 1938. Mrs. Looram personally pleaded with news vendors in Manhattan not to sell the offensive copy.

12. NLOD file, "Birth of a Baby" contains a copy of Armstrong's letter.

13. *New York Evening Post*, March 11, 1938.

14. *Daily Worker*, March 14, 1938.

15. *New York Times*, March 17, 1938.

16. NLOD file, "Birth of a Baby," March 19, 1938.

17. Federal Council of Churches Newsletter, April 16, 1938.

18. Notice in *Variety*, May 4, 1938.

19. *Motion Picture Daily*, March 21, 1938. Despite the Legion rating, Archbishop McNicholas urged a boycott and expressed the hope that the city of Cincinnati would appeal the decision of Judge Charles S. Bell to grant an injunction against interference by the city manager who had threatened to ban it unless the birth scenes were deleted and attendance limited to those eighteen and over (*Motion Picture Daily*, June 1, 1938).

20. NLOD Film Classifications, 1936–64.

21. *Tidings*, June 5, 1953.

22. NLOD file, "Martin Luther," Mary Scott to Little, May 31, 1953.

23. NLOD file, "Martin Luther," Little to Mooring, August 24, 1953.

24. NLOD, *Annual Report*, 1939, p. 2.

25. In addition to those dealt with here, the list included *Strange Cargo* (1939, revised 1940) where, in the Legion's view, "one of the characters is a humanistic, Christ-like

figure" and *White Cargo* (1942) with a "lascivious" Hedy Lamarr as Tondelayo, a jungle goddess. These, too, were re-rated B, after excisions. NLOD Annual Report, 1942, p. 8.

26. NLOD file, "Yes My Darling Daughter," McClafferty memorandum, December 8, 1938.

27. Ibid., Memorandum, December 10, 1938.

28. *New York Sunday News*, February 25, 1939.

29. NLOD file, "This Thing Called Love," McClafferty, memorandum, February 13, 1941.

30. Ibid., Looram to Marie Lauck, IFCA chairman, Indianapolis, February 27, 1941.

31. Ibid., Harmon to Looram, January 27, 1941.

32. Ibid., Quigley to McClafferty, February 2, 1941.

33. Ibid., McClafferty press release, February 8, 1941.

34. Ibid., W. S. van Schmus to the Rev. Joseph R. McLaughlin, Church of Our Lady, Queen of Martyrs, New York, February 17, 1941.

35. Ibid., Springold to McClafferty, February 10, 1941.

36. This letter is reproduced extensively in Richard C. Gannon, *The Cardinal Spellman Story* (New York: Doubleday, 1962), pp. 331–32. McClafferty had appealed to the New York office of MGM with little result.

37. NLOD file, "Lady of Burlesque," Masterson memorandum, May 1, 1943.

38. Ibid., Masterson to the Rev. T. Gerald Mulqueen, June 10, 1943. Quigley's intervention was significant. He reminded United Artists that the Quebec censorship board that had earlier passed the film had "ordered 250 cuts as a result of the Legion's decision." Also, Masterson memorandum, May 18, 1943.

39. *New York Mirror*, May 15, 1943.

Chapter 5

Heyday and Hegemony

THE OUTLAW

A persistent image of Howard Hughes remains that of a shrivelled recluse grasping a Kleenex to ward off the germs that obsessed him in the last years of self-imposed seclusion. It was a different picture half a century ago. With a Clark Gable moustache and youthful good looks, he appeared as a sexier version of Charles Lindbergh; and, like the Lone Eagle, he had impressed America with his record-breaking round-the-world flight in 1938. Wealth acquired from aviation and a mining tool company enabled him to dabble at his hobby of moviemaking. In 1929 he produced *Hell's Angels*, with a striking blonde newcomer, Jean Harlow, as the female lead—one of the most visually interesting early talkies. Three years later the Hays Office had demanded that a social warning accompany his gangster yarn, *Scarface*, with its thinly veiled allusions to the incestuous lust of brother Paul Muni for his sister.

Never far, geographically, from Hollywood's bright lights and frequently caught by photographers in the company of a beautiful starlet, Hughes impulsively decided to return to the film scene while talk in the movie capital was of the phenomenal success of *Gone with the Wind*.[1] The publicity genius behind the Civil War epic was Russell Birdwell, who had turned the search for the actress to play Scarlet O'Hara into something of a national obsession. Hughes offered Birdwell $1,500 a week to stir up interest in his project, an episode in the life of Billy the Kid. Unlike the majority of westerns of the day, which featured hard-riding, clean-cut cowboys and equally pristine heroines, his would be that rarity—a sexy horse opera. Birdwell could do little to burnish the image of baby-faced Jack Buetel chosen to play the title role, but he saw unlimited possibilities in Jane Russell, the nineteen year old, part-time model and dental receptionist whom Hughes had chosen for the part of Rio on the strength of a collection of professionally made stills.[2] The stunts and stories concocted by Birdwell were to become the stuff of legend. Most notorious was the one of a cantilevered bra that would enable Miss Russell's main attributes to be displayed at their best whatever her posture. There was the whispered story that Hughes had had a film loop made of a steamy, semi-nude love scene between Buetel and Russell, which he replayed endlessly in the privacy of his home. And once the country was at war, Russell was to become a pin-up par excellence, and be voted by the Marines (with scant regard for syntax), "the girl we would most like to be marooned on a desert island with."

The actual production of the film was a catalogue of snafus, to use the phraseology of the time. The title was changed to *The Outlaw* after MGM preempted *Billy the Kid* for a western of its own with Robert Taylor. Hughes decided to assume personal responsibility for directing after a falling out with the experienced Howard Hawks. Gregg Toland, of *Citizen Kane* fame, agreed to remain in charge of photography. Since he was fully occupied with his nonfilm business during the daytime, Hughes was obliged to fly to the Moncapi, Arizona, location in the evening and shoot scenes far into the night. Thomas Mitchell and Walter Huston became exasperated with his quirky ways and more than once threatened to walk out.[3]

In its completed form, *The Outlaw* was a triangle drama of lust and jealousy. Billy and Doc Holliday have a long-standing feud over a horse. Sheriff Pat Garrett sees the Kid as a lawbreaker to be dealt with accordingly. Doc and the sheriff are old friends, but a bullet fired by Garrett and intended for Billy kills Doc instead. To this hackneyed plot is added Rio, the half-breed. She attempts to shoot Billy early in the plot, in revenge for his having killed her brother in a saloon duel; instead she ends up being raped by her intended victim. Later, in a remarkably quick change of heart, she climbs into bed to keep him warm when he has a fever. In the final sequence, they ride off into the sunset.

Incredibly, although the movie was completed in the fall of 1940, it would not be exhibited nationally for another six years. The first two of those were taken up with a series of fights between Hughes and Breen's office. Mostly they centered on the visuals and, specifically, the large breasts of Miss Russell which, as Breen complained to Hughes "were quite large and prominent . . . shockingly emphasized and, in almost every instance . . . very substantially uncovered." Ever a law unto himself, Hughes had ignored Production Code warnings and commanded cameraman Gregg Toland to fill the screen with them. Rio always seemed to find some excuse to lean over when wearing a peasant blouse, whether to mop Billy's feverish brow or to change her stockings. Besides the inadequately covered Miss Russell, there was dialogue filled with sexual innuendo and a bedroom scene that could be interpreted as a mockery of the marital state. When Doc discovers that Billy and Rio have become lovers, Billy reminds him that Doc had borrowed his horse—"tit for tat!" Doc later refuses to swap Rio for the horse with the tart observation that "Cattle don't graze after sheep."

Breen and his associates, Geoffrey Shurlock and Al Lynch, realized that, pious promises to the contrary, Hughes had ignored their strictures.[4] Approval would require at least thirty-seven cuts, most of them in scenes featuring Russell's partially covered breasts. It was soon clear, however, that Hughes was not open to traditional forms of PCA persuasion. With a gritty determination he had already evidenced in the business world, he prepared for confrontation. The route he chose was the Appeals Board, to which Birdwell was sent in May, 1941 with a collection of stills from current releases of the major studios that purported to show that the acreage of unadorned flesh in his boss's western was no greater than that revealed elsewhere.[5] While Breen snorted with indignation, the Appeals Board ordered cuts amounting to only one minute. That Breen accepted the decision with surly acquiescence may have had something to do with his imminent move to RKO, were he would be rid of these troublesome types.[6] Perhaps he hoped that collectively the Legion and state and local censors would achieve the requisite amount of bowdlerization.

Any hopes of a swift victory from that quarter were dashed by the decision of the enigmatic Hughes to shelve the picture for eighteen months while he concentrated on the ever-increasing demands of wartime arms contracts. Jane Russell kept the film's reputation alive. Birdwell released the infamous shot of her reclining in a haystack in an off-the-shoulder blouse—a dress she does not wear in the film—with the caption, "Mean, Moody and Magnificent." Eventually San Francisco, then as now America's most liberal city, was chosen for the premiere on February 5, 1943, a grand affair in those austerity-ridden times. Dozens of critics were brought from Los Angeles by special train to the Geary Theater, a first-run house. Still, not even all of Hughes's largesse could prevent lukewarm reviews, and for the remainder of its six-week run, audiences tittered or laughed in the wrong places, giving credence to a rumor that it was intended as a comedy.[7] All the same, curiosity and word of mouth kept the customers coming and, had he persisted with additional locales, Hughes probably could have recouped the $2,500,000 cost in that one city by the end of the year. That he tried unavailingly to change the picture's character by some frantic cutting may have been a contributing factor in his decision to withdraw it in April. Just before it disappeared, the Legion's San Francisco branch saw it and unhesitatingly recommended a C rating.[8]

The twelve-month period from the end of the Second World War was a happy time for the American movie industry. It coincided with the last great surge in attendance that would see more seats filled than at any time before or since. Jane Russell, still with only one unreleased movie to her credit and bored by enforced inactivity, had signed up with an independent company to make *Young Widow*. Hughes, determined to have his protégé appear in his creation first, dusted off the print of *The Outlaw* and prepared for an assault on the box office. The new publicity campaign dwarfed all of Birdwell's previous efforts. In addition to distributing thousands of copies of the haystack photograph, billboards carrying posters of the reclining Russell asked rhetorically, "What Are the Two Great Reasons for Jane Russell's Rise to Stardom?" The nadir of taste was plumbed when a skywriting plane flew over Los Angeles, drew two circles in the sky and neatly inscribed a dot in the center of each. Even that home of family entertainment, Radio City Music Hall, was not spared. For the New York premiere the marquee proclaimed, "The Music Hall Gets the Big Ones."

With a PCA seal of approval in its pocket, *The Outlaw* might have been immune from persecution, but there was another string to Breen's bow. The Production Code provided that "salacious, indecent or obscene titles should not be used in publicizing pictures." Advertising material was supposed to be submitted in triplicate and remain unused until a judgment had been given. Hughes had obviously ignored the procedure. After a brief hearing on April 23, 1946, the board voted to revoke the seal, whereupon Hughes retaliated by launching a million-dollar lawsuit.[9] To substantiate his claim that his ads were no worse than others, his lawyers presented stills and posters for Columbia's newest release, *Gilda*, with Rita Hayworth in a tight, strapless dress. There was more than a grain of truth in his assertion that the Motion Picture Association was biased against independents. *Harrison's Reports*, their trade journal, agreed that "by failing to apply to its major company members the same standards of decency it is demanding of Mr. Hughes and other independent producers, it has forfeited the right to demand of them strict observance of the provisions of the Code."[10] A voice from the past, that of Mary Pickford, gave added support to Hughes's contention that there was one law for the powerful majors and another for the rest.[11]

Hughes's protestations about the First Amendment and the curtailment of freedom of speech availed him not at all with the Hollywood establishment nor with the judge who ruled that he had accepted the authority of the PCA by submitting his film to it in the first place and was bound by its regulations. The judge also hinted that this challenge was a flippant exercise to draw attention to the picture. Whether Hughes was prepared to consider an accommodation with Breen is open to doubt. He certainly understood that, without a seal of approval, *The Outlaw* would be excluded from the majority of the country's movie theaters. But, if he knuckled under, it would be robbed of its biggest selling point, its salaciousness. The decision in the summer of 1946 was full speed ahead and damn the torpedoes.

These nautical weapons were also being readied by the Legion after it belatedly caught up with the picture in New York. Even as the decision over Hughes's appeal was being rendered, McClafferty was conferring with clerics as far apart as Wilmington, Delaware and San Diego to warn them of the approaching menace and asking them to work in collusion with the local police when they came, as come they surely would, to close the theaters showing it. The Bishop of Springfield, Illinois directed his parishioners to stay away, until further notice, from two local theaters that had had the effrontery to show the film.[12] And what the Legion had left undone, local censorship boards hastened to do. In New York officials threatened to withdraw the licenses of any cinema that played it. All of which whetted the public's appetite. Where it was allowed to be shown, attendance was invariably heavy. In Atlanta it outgrossed *Gone with the Wind*, and business abroad was spectacular.

Hughes's anger with the Legion led him to warn Martin Quigley that it was his intention, if his picture were not removed from the Condemned category, to publish attacks on the Legion in major newspapers throughout the country as an extra-legal agency seeking to override the law, and to demand a stop to picketing of theaters and the harassment of patrons.[13] Still, Hughes must have known that there was a law of diminishing returns for movies. Sooner or later he would exhaust the number of venues whose managements were willing to risk clerical and legal wrath. Not even a lurid reputation would compensate for so many closed doors. Legion strictures in Illinois, for example, had left the bewildered management wondering how they would survive once *The Outlaw* had completed its run and a lesser drawing card took its place. At best, Hughes could hope to play his picture in no more more than 3,000 theaters, or 25 percent of possible sites. With this in mind he approached Quigley. Quigley had earned a reputation as an intermediary between producers in trouble and the PCA or the Legion. Like McClafferty, he was so aghast at what unfolded during a private screening that he warned Hughes it might be unsalvageable. The Legion would certainly not budge over two elements—the implications t Billy rapes Rio in the stable and the vast amount of breast on display. dditionally, he drew Hughes's attention to the implications of the plot's con-lusion where the Kid, an acknowledged outlaw, rake, liar, cheat and fugitive is allowed to ride off with a woman he has violated to continue his criminal career unhindered. The Legion would demand retribution, perhaps a sequence in which Rio plunges a knife into her seducer's back. "As the film stands," warned Quigley, "it is a gross libel on you and your public reputation. Its influence is evil and reflects on your enviable reputation as citizen, industrialist, financier and notable contributor to aviation. You are the idol of youth. The time has come to think about the harm this picture has done."[14]

Quigley, if anything, had underestimated the mood in New York. Father Masterson felt that Hughes was making any kind of rapprochement impossible not only by continuing to exhibit his film but by deriding the Legion strictures over advertising that boasted, "They said it could never be shown. Now you can see it all, uncut!" However, in the remote possibility that *The Outlaw* could be sanitized, he had prepared a list of objections under nine separate headings. The scene in which Rio gets into bed to succor the trembling Billy is witnessed by her disapproving aunt. In attempting to justify her conduct Rio shouts, "You can bring a minister in the morning if it'll make you feel better about it. Now, get out! (To Billy): You're not going to die. I'll get you warm!" The implication, said Masterson, was that she was in a position to have carnal relations with the man should he revive sufficiently. Then, as Quigley had prophesized, severe exception was taken to the lack of any expressed disapprobation for the Kid's lifestyle. Some epilogue was required that would wag a stern, admonitory finger at him.[15]

While events seemed to indicate that Hughes might be brought to heel, the battle was not as one-sided as it appeared. For months, rumors had been cir-culating that the eccentric moviemaker, hugely wealthy as a result of his war contracts, was contemplating filmmaking as a full-time occupation by buying a studio and its accompanying chain of theaters. Such a move would provide hundreds if not a thousand locations for showing his western. Confirmation came from Quigley, who told Archbishop Scully that Hughes was negotiating with the Atlas Investment Company for control of RKO, a financial basket case that would become even more so under his stewardship, but with a chain of theaters coast to coast. Even if the deal fell through, he threatened to establish a major studio of his own and release as many as thirty features yearly, all of which he ominously intended "to defend in the name of justice and fair play."[16] Masterson had to consider some additional hard facts. Another screening of The Outlaw on May 17 had resulted in a hung jury, with fifteen voting for a B and fifteen for a C.[17] After some internal bickering, the Legion had just given its B to Duel in the Sun, David O. Selznick's sex-drenched western with Jennifer Jones exuding a carnality that was marginally more sophisticated but no less reprehensible than Miss Russell's. Invidious comparisons and allegations of favoritism to a Hollywood institution like Selznick were bound to resurface if nothing was done. Besides, The Outlaw was an old picture and destined to die soon of its own ineptitude.

Negotiations were resumed in the summer of 1948 and Hughes, weary of impasse, spent an inordinate amount of time in the cutting room. The barn scene was so truncated as to leave the spectator in doubt as to whether Billy did anything to Rio beyond wrestling her to the ground. Gone, too, was the bed-warming scene and most shots of Rio bending over to fix her clothes. To achieve a new modesty, Hughes was forced to reprint every foot of negative and use what substitution shots were available, taken from different and less revealing camera angles. As for moral condemnation of the outlaw, an off-screen voice concludes the drama with: "History is vague concerning Billy the Kid. Some people say he was a cold-blooded killer. But there are other legendary stories which describe him as a young boy who was a victim of circumstance and the wild, lawless surroundings of the untamed West. The Outlaw is based on one of these legends." The cumulative effects of the cuts demanded by the Legion (totalling 147) reduced the running time from 116 minutes to 96.[18] There was one battle left that the Legion declined to join, probably out of a feeling of lassitude. The advertising campaign continued on the same indecorous note, with stills of scenes that did not exist in the picture, including a fanciful recreation of the barn sequences with Billy dragging Rio by the hand to the proverbial fate worse than death over her protest, "Billy, let me go!"[19] But the Legion was happy to see the malodorous western performing ever more feebly at the box office until it was permanently withdrawn on Hughes's orders in 1952.

MOM AND DAD

It would be hard to imagine two men more different from each other than Howard Hughes and Kroger Babb. The one, immensely rich, enigmatic and secretive, flirted with show business for most of his life. Babb, conversely, was an expansive, uncomplicated showman for whom movies were a dominating passion. What they shared in common was their harassment of the Legion of Decency over a period of years.

Flamboyant is scarcely a sufficient adjective to describe Kroger Babb. Attired in inexpensive, off-the-rack suits that never quite seemed to fit his large frame, he exuded an aura of impudent confidence. After an uneventful boyhood in Wilmington, Ohio, he became the advertising and publicity officer for a mid-western theater chain where he whetted the talents that were to make him, as he modestly put it, "America's Fearless Showman." His early exploits had included burying a man alive in a casket under the main street of Wilmington for a week to boost the tourist trade in the city during the Depression. His career as a promoter of others' films began to pall in the early forties, at which time he was traveling with a print of *Dust to Dust*, a sex hygiene film owned by two of the so-called Forty Thieves, ex-carnival showmen who had turned their attention from gaudy midway shows to screen exploitation while preserving the same barker-style techniques. Their methods of reaping benefits from utterly trashy material were well honed, but Babb was to raise them to the *n*th degree of perfection.[20]

By 1944 he had amassed enough money to lure veteran director William Beaudine into making *Mom and Dad*, a cautionary tale of sexual ignorance and its awful consequences, to which he added a birth of a baby scene from a medical film shown at the Golden Gate Exposition in 1939 and lurid footage of the ravages of venereal disease purloined from some U.S. Armed Forces educational shorts. A piquant irony of the project was the employment of his newly wedded wife, Mildred Horn, whom he had wooed and won when she came at her church's behest to protest the screening of *Dust to Dust* in Indianapolis. She was to author the two booklets, *What Every Woman and Girl Should Know* and *What Every Man and Boy Should Know*, that were hawked at every performance for one dollar or fifty cents, depending on what the market would bear.

The publicity circus customarily began a week before *Mom and Dad* arrived at its venue. Radio spots and newspaper ads would extol its educational value while hinting at daring of unparalleled magnitude. A four-page tabloid printed in scarlet with photographs of sellout crowds and little vignettes such as the unavailing efforts of a youth to impersonate a female in order to gain access to the sexually segregated show was distributed door to door. Babb insisted on separate performances, not out of deference to feminine sensibilities, but rather to convince the waiting males that they were about to see material at the late show that was far too explicit for the weaker sex. Another addition to the pseudo-medical atmosphere was a lecture by Elliot Forbes, an "Eminent Hygiene Commentator," delivered during a break in the film. His strictures on self-abuse, promiscuity and birth control (he advocated only the rhythm method) were followed by the hawking of the booklets by "nurses"—local women paid five dollars a night to dress in uniform, whose subsidiary task, according to the blurbs, was to minister to even the stout-hearted who might succumb to the graphic on-screen images.[21]

At any one time Hygienic Productions had as many as twenty-five road shows playing simultaneously, each with its Elliot Forbes and phalanx of ladies in white. Of course these hygiene specialists were nothing of the sort, being, in the main, actors down on their luck and willing to read the cautionary messages and take a cut from booklet sales in lieu of salary. The name had been chosen for its brevity, resonance and Anglo-Saxon dependability. To cap the edifice, so to speak, local dignitaries were canvassed for recommendations of the show, with prizes for the most enthusiastic. Even if these individuals were numerous and fulsome in their praise, Babb would not hesitate to gild the lily. A typical letter to the editor would read:

Dear Mr. Babb,

I must confess. As Mayor of this town, I opposed the showing of *Mom and Dad* here. Now I am writing to thank you for bringing your wonderful, educational film to our city.

Let me tell you the happy ending of what could have been a tragic story. A beautiful, 17 year-old high school senior girl, the only child of a prominent, church-going local couple, had gotten herself into trouble.

She was afraid to tell her parents, who had raised her lovingly but strictly. The boy responsible for her condition left town, leaving the poor child alone and hopeless. She had no one to whom she could turn. She even contemplated suicide.

With one of her girl friends, she went to see your fine show. When she came home from the theater, she courageously told her mother and father the whole story. They were shocked; but being good Christians, they forgave her. They made arrangements for the girl to go live with relatives in a not-too-distant city, where, when the time came, she entered a hospital and gave birth to a healthy baby boy. Church people arranged for an adoption by a childless couple, and the baby was given a name and a caring home. The girl returned to her hometown, graduated from high school, and is now engaged to a fine young man from a good family.

Thank you Mr. Babb, for having the courage and wisdom to tell your people what their parents didn't.

Sincerely yours, Signed.

P.S. That girl was my daughter.

Babb was particularly proud of having composed that one.[22]

Initially, the very elusiveness of *Mom and Dad* for all the lubricious gossip about it, delayed Legion classification for three years after its release. It would seldom play for more than three days in any one locale, and Babb was careful to keep it out of the hands of city censors by exhibiting it in rural or suburban areas where their writ did not run large. What alarmed McClafferty and Masterson was a series of clerics' names being featured in the scarlet-inked tabloid. Prominently displayed in December 1946 was the slightly bewildered face of Msgr. B. Hilgenburg of St. Mary's, Carlyle, Illinois, juxtaposed with the new Chevrolet he had won "for the outstanding testimonial letter and endorsement given during the past year." The monsignor had called it "the most outstanding educational movie and the furthest step towards educating the masses in his entire religious and teaching experience." Checks from a few dollars to a thousand were flowing from Wilmington to priests all over the country for their boosterism.[23]

The Legion office spent much of January and February 1947 writing to all those who had been so honored by Babb, demanding to know why they had lent their support to a picture that would almost certainly be condemned if it would end its will-o'-the-wisp existence and remain in one location long enough to be rated.[24] The fine hand of the master showman was clearly behind it all. Misguided compassion and gullibility for an Eliot Forbes plea had motivated Father Edward Malloy of Rogers, Arkansas to aid an eminent hygiene commentator when he paid a late-night visit one Christmas eve. Mr. Forbes had implored him to give a commendation for his talk; failure to do so would mean his losing his job and spending the New Year in the cold with a wife and four children. How could the priest have known that a few words of encouragement would win him fifteen dollars and a place on page two of the tabloid? Father Stephen Rosetti of Hammond, Louisiana had been given a free ticket to the theater and asked to give his impressions as a spokesman for the Roman Catholic Church in the entire state.[25] There was even a kindly word from Msgr. Joseph Zeyen of Dubuque, Iowa, who had expired shortly after uttering his testimonial of praise and gone to greener pastures, too late, alas, to collect his winnings.

That these were connections of the most compromising kind was only slowly grasped by the majority of clergymen. The image of a priest driving around in a car he had received for recommending a smutty movie was not one to be relished. Even without Legion prodding, they attempted to have their names stricken from the roll of dishonor and to decline the prizes. A more amenable showman might have acquiesced, but Babb had no intention of eating humble pie. He suspected that the Legion was behind the campaign of coercion and accordingly levelled both barrels of his vituperative shotgun at what he persisted in calling "CLOD." He asked Masterson for an assurance that priests would be treated as human beings capable of thinking for themselves and expressing personal opinions without fear of being reprimanded, and that high-handed methods of attempting to control the movie industry be limited "to that 20 percent of the nation who prefer to be enslaved and dictated to by your church."[26] There was more in this vein when doubts were cast on Father Zeyen's endorsement. He had written not one but two letters of support, said Babb, dictated from the heart and not by any bishop, cardinal or pope. The Legion had gone so far beyond the boundary of good taste in its frantic effort for dictatorial powers that it was slowly leading the nation to another war of religious hatred.[27]

Now that the gauntlet had been thrown down, the Church struck back with severity where it could. Sex hygiene pictures were like crab grass, a perpetual nuisance that only tedious, diligent weeding could eradicate. Archbishop McNicholas, one of the Legion's fathers, had found it necessary to make periodical national pleas in the press to the industry for their extirpation. Since

Mom and Dad had not ventured near New York, it fell to a member of the Oakland branch to write the definitive report. His impressions confirmed the Legion's worst fears. Besides the content of the film itself, there was the unsavory atmosphere created by its very presence. At the performance he had attended half the audience was "colored" and of the remainder, three quarters were under seventeen. Prominent in the audience were "zoot suiters," "siderow characters" and "queers," some of whom directed lewd remarks at women exiting the earlier show despite police warnings to "cut the rough stuff." The screening itself had been punctuated by ribaldry, which Elliot Forbes's remonstrances had failed to quell. Altogether it had been a night when virtue was ridiculed and depravity applauded.[28]

It was clear that the reasoned discussion the Legion engaged in with the mainstream of the movie industry was out of the question. Only draconian punishment would suffice for exhibitors brazen enough to cooperate with the Babb circus. Theater owners were contacted in advance of playdates, not always an easy task despite the hoopla that heralded the approaching monster, and urged to reconsider their decision in the light of what might occur were they to persist. Bishops were encouraged to decree harsh punishments for recalcitrant movie theaters. Local chapters of the Knights of Columbus dusted off their regalia and prepared to picket on the sidewalk. And, above all, priests in the hinterland were warned to abjure the company of anyone remotely connected with Hygiene Productions and hard luck stories.[29]

Babb countered in a variety of ways. Like all good showmen, he knew that any publicity was good publicity. Waving a red rag at the clerical bull was one way to ensure good business. When *Mom and Dad* was faced by a Knights demonstration in Baltimore, he called on the local Masonic Temple to send in its troops to counter the display of medieval intellectual repression. The altercation that ensued between the two organizations was duly recorded by the media with commendable financial results the following day. He was always available to reporters who wanted his opinion on the Catholic Church's agenda, leaving them in no doubt that it was part of a monstrous plot to limit freedom of expression and end the separation of church and state, the very cornerstone of American democracy. The scurrilous tone of his *Newsletter* was reminiscent of priest-baiting at its worst. One issue, headed "The Pay-Off," is typical:

Two years ago when 20th Century Fox released "Forever Amber," the Catholic Church organization led by Cardinal Spellman threw 28 fits. Every Catholic was threatened with ex-communication if he dared so much as look at the front of a theater playing this "terrible" picture. The hullabaloo made the front pages for weeks and Catholic priests damned the Skouros brothers as being America's filthiest citizens—stooping to anything for the almighty dollar. But Mr. Skouros soon fixed this up with a tidy (reportedly) $250,000 check to Mr. Big and then by placing a mere 5 cent special "card" on the front end of "Forever Amber" saying that the film was fictional and not to be taken seriously by good little boys and girls. Time marches on and today it is interesting to note that Cardinal Spellman has again become a bed-fellow with these "filthiest citizens," since thru his blessing they obtained permission to shoot and are now releasing "Holy Year, 1950"—a propaganda film based on the current pilgrimage of mooches from throughout the world to see Rome, the Italian headquarters city of prostitution and racketeers. American exhibitors are being duly threatened in whispered tones to put "Holy Year, 1950" on their A-houses and kick in that film rental without a beef—or else! It would seem to the average observer . . . that if the same company that produced and released "Forever Amber" is good enough to make and release "Holy Year, 1950," that there should be no further bellyaching from the C.P.'s because "Mom and Dad" is on the same list of successes with "Prince of Peace." Excepting for the fact H.P. Inc. has been so busy it hasn't gotten around to making any $250 grand [*sic*] donations to Mr. Big or his Highness Almighty Dollar.[30]

Time and changing morality would eventually blunt the appeal of *Mom and Dad*. The advent of the Playboy centerfold and her imitators robbed female anatomy of its mystery. Natural childbirth would be discussed and illustrated in family magazines. When the movie finally made it to New York City in 1958 no amount of Babbian legerdemain could fill the theater and he was left to conclude sadly that by then the average citizen knew more than any Elliot Forbes.

FOREVER AMBER

The imminent departure of Monsignor McClafferty in 1947 for the more tranquil pastures of academe meant the elevation of the Rev. Patrick Masterson. Though he retained the title of assistant until McClafferty had taken up his new duties in Washington, D.C., he wielded a new broom with vigor during the transitional period and gave the industry fair warning that a Legion "forward policy" was being implemented to challenge both the studios and the Hays Office for perceived moral laxity. 1947 saw battle engaged on several fronts, against Hughes and *The Outlaw*, Selznick and *Duel in the Sun* and, no less tenaciously, against the potentially more formidable obstacle of Twentieth Century Fox and its president, Spyros Skouras.

The cause célèbre in this instance was *Forever Amber*. Like Margaret Mitchell before her, Kathleen Winsor had taken the publishing world by storm in 1944 with her first novel, a historical romance set in Restoration England that vied in length with *Gone with the Wind* at 956 pages. In best bodice-ripping tradition, its heroine, Amber St. Clair, bedded an even score of lovers in her climb from pig-keeper to mistress of Charles II, causing wags to suggest that a more apt title for this "breast-seller" might have been "Forever Under."[31] When Darryl Zanuck, production head at Fox, first evinced an interest in the book, the venerable Will Hays had warned him that it was probably unfilmable under the Code. Still he pressed ahead and paid the then-enormous sum of $200,000 for the screen rights, thereby ensuring that *Amber* would be a major production. The final cost, at $6,500,000, made it only slightly less expensive than *Duel in the Sun*.

It has been suggested that it was a relaxing of morals during the Second World War and the euphoria created by its satisfactory conclusion that induced Breen to dilute his hitherto rigid standards and jettison some of the previous decade's proscriptions against adultery and other forms of illicit sex. His nod of assent for James M. Cain's steamy, adulterous *The Postman Always Rings Twice* was a case in point. As far as the Winsor novel went, he may have been reassured by the appointment as producer-in-charge of William Perlberg, who had the wholesome *State Fair* and the dutifully reverential *Song of Bernadette* to his credit. By reducing Amber's tally of lovers to seven and emphasizing period detail at the expense of the constant bedding that had been the novels' fixation, Fox encountered little in the way of interference, and a Code seal was approved in September 1947. However, convivial feelings toward the company were at a premium in the Legion office, where Masterson had just viewed *Nightmare Alley*, the story of a carnival and its "geeks," which he found "offensive in the extreme." He had also scrutinized Fox's list of forthcoming projects with a distinct lack of enthusiasm. In a memorandum to Cardinal Spellman, he listed half a dozen potentially dangerous titles including *The Snake Pit* (on mental illness in a career-driven female) and *Gentleman's Agreement* (on antisemitism and divorce), on which Catholic opinion "was well-nigh unanimous that these were grossly immoral."[32]

The studio's reluctance to make available a print of *Forever Amber* until ten days before it was due to go into general release roused suspicions that an unsavory piece of celluloid was about to be foisted on an unsuspecting American public. These were confirmed when Fox, without consultation, announced a Legion screening for Friday, October 10, the start of a holiday weekend, which made it difficult for Masterson to round up more than eighteen reviewers and consultors.[33] It may be doubted whether a larger number would have influenced the outcome differently, since Masterson was determined to impose his authority and kill what he considered must be a salacious picture. Although there was only one vote out of eight for a C, with an even division of the remainder between A-II and B, the new Legion chief intended his action to be construed as a warning to those studios that might be tempted to imitate Fox and indulge in browbeating. Spyros Skouras, Fox president, was accustomed to settling contentious matters at his palatial country estate, a short drive from New York, over lunch, golf and dinner.[34] Masterson icily refused his invitation and suggested the cold formality of his office. Skouras then tried to load the blame on producer Darryl Zanuck's shoulders, adding, by way of mitigation, that if the company had not acted, one of its competitors would have picked up the hot property. When a company executive tried to calm the waters by suggesting that "treatment was decent, on the whole," Masterson responded that "good taste and good morals are not the same." *Forever Amber*, in Legion eyes, was "nothing but a glorification of immorality."[35]

Rebuffed, Skouras next entered on a course of action he was to regret. An inspired leak to Louella Parsons, doyen of Hollywood gossip columnists—at least in her own mind—was duly relayed to the nation via her weekly radio broadcast. By threatening to condemn poor *Amber*, she said the Legion was attacking the book, not the picture, and did not seem to realize that the two were very different. In any case, she had heard there was so much dissension in clerical ranks over the decision that local priests were to be allowed to decide individually whether or not to heed it.[36] A few days later, Charles White, vice-president of the Fox theater chain, told reporters sheer vindictiveness was at the root of the action. It was muscle-flexing of the worst sort. The Church would fulfill its proper function if it confined itself to ministering to the poor and the sick and left its membership free to attend whatever movies took their fancy. Then, treading on a particularly sensitive tiger's tail, he hinted that Cardinal Spellman was the *eminence grise* behind the Legion and the one consulted whenever doubt existed over ratings.[37] Perlberg kept the pot boiling with a statement in *Variety* on November 8, 1947 insisting that since the company had obeyed the letter of the Hays Office law throughout *Amber*'s making, there should be an end to bellyaching.

Now that the gauntlet had been thrown down, Masterson rolled out every weapon in his armory. Following announcement of the C rating for a picture that was "a glorification of immorality and licentiousness," a circular was sent to every diocesan director in the country giving the green light to any and all action each considered effective.[38] The picture had opened at over seventy locales nationwide and its notoriety enabled some theaters to boost admission prices by as much as 30 percent and still report record grosses. The November 1, 1947 edition of the *New York Times* reported that the Roxy in Manhattan had had its biggest day in history with gross receipts of $25,308. But the success was short-lived.

As often happens during wartime, signs of mutiny first appear among those in the front line of battle. In this instance it was theater managers who began to rue the day as an avalanche of clerically directed wrath descended on their heads. Taking Masterson's carte blanche to heart, Cardinal Dougherty of Philadelphia singled out the local Erlanger and Fox theaters as initial targets for a boycott if they did not remove the obscenity at once; otherwise he would pronounce a ban on attendance not only at those two theaters but at all other Fox locations attempting to show Fox movies for a year.[39] In Buffalo, nuns organized a letter-writing campaign by grade school children that resulted in six thousand complaints being delivered to a theater in five days. At one point it seemed as if dioceses were in competition with one another over which would mount the strongest campaign. Davenport, Iowa boasted four thousand signatures on a petition after just a weekend's canvassing, only to be outdone by Mobile, Alabama, which managed to collect five thousand. In Grand Rapids, Michigan the local chapter of the Legion joined forces with the nondenominational Better Film Council to have the city council impose a ban.[40]

With box office receipts showing a precipitous decline after the first week and showmen alarmed over the prospect of many empty seats far into 1948 long after the controversial picture had disappeared, the time had come to negotiate. Skouras would later admit that the Legion action had robbed the picture of $2 million in potential revenue. On October 27 Otto Preminger, Mrs. Looram, Masterson and Stephen S. Jackson, a former juvenile court judge and Quigley protégé from Breen's office, sat down to see if they could make an honest lady out of Amber. Masterson adamantly refused to enumerate the specific changes by which this might be achieved, since he felt that would be a no-win situation. If the alternations demanded were insignificant, they would have, practically speaking, the same picture. If substantial, the Legion would be charged with demanding the impossible. Rather, Skouras was told to make the revisions he felt were needed for approval and await a verdict.[41] Once more Quigley's invisible hand was behind an action that was to mollify the Church. A prologue emphasized that Amber did not succeed as a courtesan but ultimately met with frustration and tragedy because of her wicked ways. Dialogue cuts included her jibe at her husband, "Pride, I thought that had dried up in you a long time ago like all the rest of you!"—a subtle hint of his loss of sexual prowess. George Sanders, who had played the part of King Charles II, was brought back to emphasize the words, "for your journey" in the line, "I shall undertake to make provision for your journey," so as to leave no doubt in the audience's mind that he was not providing for her future as a monarch's mistress but simply supplying a carriage and horses for a specific trip. The most substantial alteration occurred in the final sequence. In the original, Amber had suffered something of a decline in society but still retained enough charm to seduce a male and be "forever Amber." As revised, she watched ashen-faced as her husband and son walked to a coach and out of her life, leaving her to face the prospect of bitter, lonely old age. As the prologue had predicted, "The wages of sin is death."[42] This last angered Preminger, who vehemently objected that the heroine had suffered enough. He refused to be associated with the change and so began a feud with the Legion that was to become a major controversy with a later film.[43]

The scrubbed version was screened on December 4 and rated B, since the movie's tendency to glorify sinful living in Legion eyes had been reduced but not obliterated. The announcement was accompanied by a statement from Skouras regretting his earlier petulance and promising to mend his ways.[44] The Legion's triumph was complete even if there were a few radical voices that felt no quarter should have been given and that *Forever Amber* should have been boycotted to death as an awful warning to others presumptuous enough to believe they could flout Catholic sensibilities. In any case, word of mouth that it was all talk and no action soon diminished its appeal and the studio recovered only half of its investment.[45]

DUEL IN THE SUN

The release of *Duel in the Sun* on New Year's Eve, 1946 brought in its wake a number of significant gains for the Legion of Decency. Prime among these was its ability to bring another of Hollywood's most powerful and respected figures to heel. Scarcely less notable was the contrition displayed by the Motion Picture Association of America (MPAA, the new name given the MPPDA by Eric Johnston who had succeeded to the presidency in September 1945), for its confessed negligence in failing to prevent the appearance of a salacious movie. The *Duel in the Sun* affair was also an earnest of Masterson's intransigent new leadership at 35 E. 51st Street.

David O. Selznick came from a movie family. His father had been one of the group that had invited Will Hays to Hollywood to clean house. Another relative was in the distribution business, and Irene Selznick, his wife, was the daughter of Louis B. Mayer. Selznick's reputation rested on a small number of expertly crafted, expensive-looking adaptations of the classics. These included *Anna Karenina, David Copperfield, The Adventures of Tom Sawyer* and *The Prisoner of Zenda*. There had been a contretemps with Breen during the making of *Gone with the Wind*, and the B rating it received from the Legion came as no surprise, considering suggestions of sexual promiscuity and a brothel scene. Nevertheless, he was to work cordially with the Legion during filming of *Joan of Arc*, sharply limiting the anticlericalism of the Maxwell Anderson stage original and taking care to mute the character of Cauchon, Joan's chief persecutor, so that he appeared in a far more favorable light than historians are apt to allow.[46]

Like *Gone with the Wind*, *Duel in the Sun* was filmed in the full glare of publicity. Its cost—$5.8 million—made it the most expensive feature in the United States to that time. The cast included two giants from the past in Lilian Gish and Lionel Barrymore and three bright, rising stars in Joseph Cotten, Gregory Peck and Jennifer Jones. Even the most casual observer might have noted ominous similarities between *Duel* and *The Outlaw*. Both eschewed the traditional elements of the horse opera, riding and shooting, in favor of a triangular love relationship between a heroine of easy virtue and two suitors. Jones as the half-breed Pearl has to choose between the decent Jesse McCanles (Cotten) and his ne'er-do-well brother, Lewt (Peck). The steamy relationship between Pearl and Lewt ends bloodily when they shoot and mortally wound each other. But carnal attraction will not be denied, and in the final sequence they painfully crawl across the desert to unite in death's embrace.

Breen was knowledgeable about *Duel in the Sun*, having bought the rights to the Niven Busch novel during his brief stewardship as production head at RKO. When he declined to go beyond the script stage, Selznick was able to get an option and begin shooting in 1946. Breen, by all accounts, paid close attention to its genesis, literally sitting behind the cameras on occasion and demanding that Jennifer Jones perform a new dance sequence to replace the too-erotic original. That he did not put his personal signature to the final, edited version was of no great consequence, since he had seen the rough cut two or three times. Geoffrey Shurlock, his deputy, was left to give the picture a clean bill of health, which he did with equanimity.[47]

Normally a print would have been run off and shipped to New York for showing to the trade and the Legion. The unexpected event that occasioned the Legion's displeasure at being denied that opportunity until after *Duel* had been exhibited commercially was a December 1946 strike at the Technicolor processing laboratories, which meant that only a handful of prints was available. To qualify for Academy Award nomination, a film must be shown for paid admission in Los Angeles during a specified period in the year prior to the ceremony. All available copies of *Duel* were rushed to theaters there on December 30 to meet the deadline.[48] There was nothing to prevent the Los Angeles chapter of the Legion from acting on New York's behalf, and this it did on January 3, 1947. The reaction was extremely hostile. Archbishop Cantwell led off with a pastoral letter requesting priests to advise parishioners not to attend a picture that was "morally and spiritually depressing," at least until the head office had handed down its verdict.[49] William Mooring of the *Tidings*, now a syndicated movie columnist for a number of Catholic magazines, lived up to his arch-conservative reputation. He saw it "as the beginning of a new and dangerous trend towards screen realism in which no regard is shown for reticence or appeals to reason."[50] This was vague and may simply have whetted the public's appetite. Soon, though, Protestant denominations joined in the rising chorus of negativism. There were objections to the irreverence shown to the cloth by the inclusion of a minor character, Sin Killer, a raving fundamentalist grossly overplayed by Walter Huston.

Selznick's expression of pained outrage at the reception given his picture would seem, in retrospect, to be naive. He could not have been unaware of the Legion's long-standing status as a revising mechanism for Code-approved films. The fate of *Forever Amber* was proof of that. Perhaps he may have felt that Breen's solicitude during *Duel*'s gestation period was sufficient to stifle most criticism. At any rate, the furor that developed highlighted a number of contentious issues surrounding the Code mechanism, not the least of which was occasional inconsistency between the Code and the Legion. While defending the MPAA's readiness to stand by its decision, Eric Johnston, who had replaced Will Hays, tacitly conceded that the Legion was a law unto itself. Equally, the Legion had been founded as the twin pillar to the Hays Office and regarded itself as a moral sieve for filtering out most of what was reprehensible. When the Legion's ire was raised, the victim was the individual film producer, not the Hays Office. Selznick was given to understand that if he chose to fight the Church, he would do so alone. Selznick also realized that with such a huge investment in the picture, it was necessary to have it play in as many theaters as possible. A C rating meant that it would not recoup a quarter of its cost. He turned in desperation to Martin Quigley, the "fixer upper."[51]

Quigley could offer no cast-iron guarantee that his intervention would disperse the clerical storm clouds that had gathered round *Duel*. Having seen a print early in January, he was of the opinion that the best to be hoped for was a B, which, while not ideal, would not seriously harm its potential at the box office. To that end he sent a list of proposed revisions that should be incorporated in any print destined for IFCA scrutiny.[52] Those Selznick hastened to execute, making thirty-two cuts and trims that varied in length from a few inches to sixty-five feet but reduced the running time by only two minutes. What Quigley and Selznick had wrought cut very little ice indeed with the reviewers. Father McClafferty was in his final months in office, having asked to be allowed to return to his first love, social work. His superiors granted his request by naming him director of the School of Social Work at the Catholic University in Washington, D.C. As a consequence, he gradually reduced his connection with the Legion, leaving the decision making to his assistant, Father Patrick Masterson.

According to one description, Pat Masterson had the face of an angel, the physique of a heavyweight boxer and a voice that could sound off like a traffic cop on Forty-Second Street during rush hour. His previous stint with the Legion had been interrupted by the war, when he had served as a Navy chaplain in the Marine Corps. There he had honed his talents as an affable but unbending leader of men. His prodigious energy and devotion to principle were to allow him to rise to the position of vice-president of the Pontifical Film Commission, a sort of Vatican watchdog for unsavory developments in motion pictures throughout the world. Sadly, he succumbed to a massive heart attack in 1953, of which his healthy frame had given no previous evidence.[53]

Masterson was so shocked after the Legion screening on February 7 that he wrote to Breen the same day to inquire how such a mistake in PCA policy could have been made. Enumerating violations of the Code chapter and verse, he feared that another lapse of this dimension "would injure the industry as a whole ... and strengthen groups in the country demanding that censor laws be passed."[54] Breen was mortified, stating that he regretted the "serious error" and hoped that some way might be found to soften what seemed to be "the serious offensiveness of this particular picture."[55] The vehemence of Masterson's attack dismayed Selznick, who was inwardly fuming that Eric Johnston and the MPAA had capitulated in quick order without a word in his defense. Meanwhile, the Legion had to be placated, presumably by the removal of scenes and dialogue. On one point Selznick was resolute. He would not change the finale of the bloodstained Gregory Peck cradling a dying Jennifer Jones, even if it was the scene which had shocked the most. His actual revisions, only a small portion of which are reproduced here, are a revelation of how, at least in the eyes of its creator, an inferior work resulted. Not only was there a forced change of emphasis on certain facets of the plot, but omissions and deletions sometimes had the unfortunate consequence of obscuring characterization with no concomitant elevation in the moral tone of the work. Selznick's alterations and the rationale for them were contained in a lengthy missive to Neil Agnew of Vanguard Films.

1. Senator's advice to Lewt: "But I have always told you—take your fun where you find it. . . . " Cut as suggested. (This represents a loss since it is practically the key line of the Senator's relationship with his son, and is the basis of this whole story thread—of the Senator being responsible for Lewt's behavior, and of his being the

product of a wrong-minded father's philosophy.) However, I am reconciled to the loss. . . .

3. Sin Killer Scene . . . Criticism of the line, "As nice and pretty as any padre of his own faith could have done," as being objectionable from the Catholic viewpoint. I am sure we have fixed this completely by cutting out the word "padre" so that the line reads, "As nice and pretty as any of his own faith could have done," thereby entirely eliminating the question of any religion.

4. The scene between Pearl and Lewt which has been referred to in the criticism as "the rape scene," although it is not rape at all. Have cut about half of this sequence, and perhaps more than this. Detailed list of cuts to follow but cuts include the shot of Pearl, her hips moving as she scrubs the floor; a cut of the succeeding shot; all of the shots of them moving back and forth across the room with the lamp being knocked over, etc.; the shot of Lewt putting his hand over Pearl's mouth; substantial cut of the kiss; substantial cut of Pearl's kiss; etc. Have left only the opening shots, the window shots, part of Lewt kissing Pearl and part of Pearl kissing Lewt in return. It is absolutely essential to leave this part of Pearl's kissing Lewt in return, as otherwise the scene becomes one of rape and in my opinion much more objectionable from the standpoint of audiences or censorship or anything else. In addition, it makes Lewt a rapist; which he certainly isn't. Lewt is never punished for this rape; Lewt would become an even more despicable character, thereby doing enormous damage to the film; Jesse would become an utter imbecile and an extremely unattractive character, for he would be turning on the girl and destroying her entire life, when she has been guilty of no wrong whatsoever and has simply been raped; the whole moral lesson of the picture would be destroyed; and the succeeding sequences would be silly because they are based entirely upon a girl's bitter remorse and punishment for having given in. . . . This represents a substantial loss which has been widely commented upon as one of the most brilliant scenes in the picture; and there has been particular comment on the artistry of the ballet-like moves of the people around the room. But I would rather take this loss, however bitterly, than lose the story point.

5. Mare sequence: We have cut entirely the objectionable lines, merely leaving the animal being brought it, and the line, "This here the one you meant, Lewt?", which is meaningless and certainly has nothing to do with the mare or anything else. It is also bad from a production and story-telling point of view, but unfortunately it is necessary for us to leave in this one line to establish our principals in the scene and also, secondarily, in order to avoid laboratory changes. We have cut the ranch hand's line, "She don't seem too happy to me"; Lewt's lines, "Aw, she's happy all right. You'd think she was going to her first dance," and Pearl's line, "If she throws a nice colt, I'd sure like to break it." . . . I think the idea of cutting out anything that has to do with animal breeding is somewhat pointless, especially since some pictures which have been designed particularly for children's audiences have made these same points, and have gone in great detail into the business of stallions and mares which I think most parents of today would tell you is part of the "birds and bees" routine with which children are taught the basic facts of life. However, I am reconciled to cutting them all, if it will help. . . .

9. Miss Jones wore a complete and modern bathing suit in the swimming scene, but in view of the disgraceful and slanderous attack upon her costume by a warped mind

(and I will guarantee that the loathsome creature responsible for this vicious attack has women relatives that wear every time they go the beach and every time they put on an evening gown, and also in their sport clothes, less clothing and clothing of a more revealing type than that worn by Miss Jones any place in this film), I have voluntarily trimmed still further one of the shots of Miss Jones in her bathing suit.

10. It is interesting to note that there has not been a single criticism of this booting (of Pearl by Lewt) scene from any source, or on a single preview card; and in a story of violence, and of crude Western people, and of primitive reactions and emotions, I regard it as a very serious loss to the picture that will do much to reduce its effectiveness. . . . I also regard it as inconsistent with the horror stories, war stories, gangster stories such as *The Killers*, mystery stories such as *The Lady in the Lake*, etc. all of which portray brutality in the extreme, to have this eliminated from a picture of this importance and stature and obvious sincerity. However, the cut has tentatively been made, and can permanently be made.[56]

On the contentious issue of the final sequence and that of Sin Killer, the two parties reached an impasse. At yet another Legion screening on March 8, the revision of the revised version split the reviewers and consultors neatly in half, with thirteen opting for a B and the rest for a C. It was McClafferty in one of his final acts for the Legion who suggested a way around the impasse. Reminding his bellicose assistant of Selznick's distinguished career in the industry and his reasonable assumption that his picture had met all the criteria for general release, he suggested a prologue and an epilogue. The former would establish that the Walter Huston character was "based upon a type of bogus, unordained evangelist who preyed upon the hungry need for spiritual guidance and who were [sic] recognized as charlatans by the intelligent and God-fearing." *Duel* would conclude with the same off-screen voice intoning: "Pearl Chavez, pursued, tortured by her own passions, whose moral weakness led to transgression against the law of God . . . Lewt McCanles, untamed, godless, whose unbridled reck-lessness brought havoc and destruction and brought down upon him in the end the frustration of all his hopes."[57]

The matter was finally resolved. *Duel in the Sun* went into general release in March, with a B rating and with only three minutes less of running time, the prelude and postlude compensating for many of the fifty-three cuts made.

But ill-feeling remained on both sides. Masterson was convinced that the Legion had acted out of a sense of misguided liberality and he counseled those clergy who wrote for advice on how to deal with the western when it came to their diocese that they would be doing their parishioners a favor by advocating nonattendance.[58] Selznick, for his part, bitterly castigated Johnson and one of his staff who had been rash enough to contrast *Duel* with *The Outlaw*. He was mortified to think that he was being compared to Howard Hughes, a "dilettante" who had used "every catchpenny attempt to sell tickets." There was a much larger issue, though, and that was the awesome, unbridled power of the Catholic Church in the United States. It was ridiculous to argue that the Legion was not a censorship body; it was far more powerful and active than any legally constituted organization. In bending opponents to its will it could not be more effective had it been legislated into existence by an act of Congress. To allude to criticisms of his film made by a few Protestant bodies was a red herring because the most they represented was unwelcome publicity that could be shrugged off without damage. On a prophetic note, Selznick warned that if the Code authority could not or would not defend its seal, the day was coming when producers would ignore it, with all the disastrous consequences their independence would bring.[59]

BITTER RICE AND *THE MIRACLE*

For the vast majority of the unilingual American public in the early forties, foreign language films were a curio, seldom discussed and even more rarely attended. In the whole of the United States there were probably fewer than two hundred bona fide art cinemas devoted entirely to classics, documentaries, the avant-garde and subtitled movies. A further three hundred or so occasionally screened the better-known English pictures that the major circuits did not pick up. This state of affairs began to change after World War II. Interest in the off-beat and Europeans films was fostered by a number of factors. Many returning ex-servicemen had spent some time in Europe. Even in the midst of fighting a war they often managed to pick up a smattering of the language and an interest in the culture of the country that was their temporary home. This interest did not evaporate when they returned to civilian life. A rapid increase in the numbers of those enrolled in higher education also had an effect. Some college campuses ran film programs where the entertainment was not always mainstream, and in the larger university centers, repertory theaters flourished as never before. Those who tested the strange waters often discovered to their delight and surprise that there was a reflection of real life in those pictures that the product of the Hollywood dream factory conspicuously lacked.

The immediate postwar era also saw the flowering of the Italian cinema. As a reaction against the vapid, sentimental "white telephone" dramas of the Mussolini era, a group of left-wing artists took the daily life of the working class as their theme and unconsciously launched the neorealist movement. Their dramas were set far from the tourist haunts. The slums of Rome, a remote Sicilian fishing village, the teeming apartment blocks of proletarian Milan were the venues where ordinary people wrestled with the harsh realities of postfascist reconstruction. It was taken as axiomatic that movie stars would rob these works of their authenticity, and so directors sought out individuals who had never before appeared on screen and whose ordinariness lent a verisimilitude to story lines that would not have rated a paragraph in a daily newspaper. Vittorio De Sica's *Umberto D*, for example, has at its center a retired civil servant whose concern is to find someone to care for his little dog before he goes into hospital, and the same director's *Bicycle Thief* hinges on the futile effort of an unemployed laborer to recover his stolen bike without which he cannot keep his new job as a billboard plasterer. At festivals, in the press and in film institutes honors were heaped on the heads of Roberto Rossellini, Luchino Visconti, Cesar Zavattini and others for these grim, low-budget, thought-provoking masterpieces that said something profound about the human condition.

It must be admitted that even in their native land the bulk of the corpus of neorealist work was never commercially successful. Italians, no less than their brethren elsewhere, were fascinated by American movies, regarding the cinema as a place for escapist entertainment, not for a gloomy reminder of the harsh reality outside. And so *Rome, Open City, La Terra Trema* and *Paisan* might come trailing their prizes behind them, but they were essentially only critical successes. When the average moviegoer in Rome was not lining up to gawk at Rita Hayworth's silk-encased figure in *Gilda* or Esther Williams in a variety of swim suits, he was looking for a home-grown equivalent. The commercial side of the Italian film industry provided pictures that aped the most extravagant of Hollywood escapism. Plots might be located in mountain hamlets or watery rice fields, but the protagonists would be handsome men and physically attractive women exuding a smoldering sexuality that was light years distant from the drab, proletarian characters of neorealism.

The Legion and Breen's office regarded developments across the Atlantic with suspicion and apprehension. Aside form the sexual content of European box office champions, there was, in at least some of neorealist works, implicit criticism of the Christian Democrat government and its close ties with the Vatican. A clause in the Lateran Agreements that the pontiff had signed with Mussolini in 1929 gave the central government power to ban or remove pictures found offensive by the Church, but either through clerical indifference or lethargy, the clause was rarely invoked. There was also an Italian equivalent of the Production Code administered by the government, but here, too, Latin permissiveness was in evidence. Examples of both types of Italian cinema began landing on American shores after 1945. Breen, in what is now generally regarded as a rank bad decision, refused to give a seal to *Bicycle Thief* because of two brief sequences. One sequence has the young boy preparing to answer a call of nature by standing against a wall only to be called away by an impatient father before he can relieve himself; the other is a brief scene in a house of ill repute on a Sunday morning, but there is no activity and the women are at breakfast. The PCA's rationale in refusing to license *Bicycle Thief* was that toilet humor was a low, disgusting subject according to Code definition, and to allow this innocuous incident would be to open the flood gates to imitators. Brothels were also proscribed and had been since early Code days. Again there was a question of precedent, which the Administration did not intend to set.[60] Despite its reservations about these scenes and a "leftist slant" to the social component of the film, the Legion nevertheless rated it B, to Breen's pained surprise.

In retrospect, the Legion's treatment of *Bicycle Thief* would be regretted as untoward generosity of a most compromising kind, since Italian imports were about to plunge it into the depths of controversy and lead to a fundamental change in American motion picture censorship. The permissiveness that Masterson and his new assistant, the Rev. Thomas Little found permeating pictures from that part of the world seemed to indicate that control was a dead letter. Distributors, including the largest, Lux Films, appeared to turn a deaf ear to requests that all titles should be submitted to Breen's office, just as they persisted in shipping only the more morally offensive and sensational examples from their stock. Behind curt refusals to accommodate the Legion was the unchallenged thesis that the only kind of foreign films that made money in the United States was the very sort to which the Legion objected. More, the lack of a seal could be publicized, giving the specific title added allure. Lux was under no illusion that any major company would ever pick up any of its titles. Better to play them in art theaters or even "grind houses" and realize quick profits than to conform to the dictates of decency with a bowdlerized product.

That might have been the tactic adopted with *Bitter Rice*, had it not caught the public imagination. Masterson's invitation to attend a preview on October 5, 1950 gave no indication as to what it might be beyond a drama of the Po Valley. It soon became apparent that the publicity campaign had not erred in describing its buxom young star, Silvana Mangano, as "a restless, glamor-mad, sensuous rice worker." Wearing a sweater that strains to contain her breasts and abbreviated shorts that outline every muscle and curve of her thighs, she is first seen performing a boogie-woogie dance for her fellow rice gatherers, all preparing to travel north for the harvest. Once in the Po Valley she encounters Walter, a thief and woman-beater, and his latest mistress, Francesca, both on the run from the police. She excites the criminal but also listens sympathetically to Francesca's tale of woe at having been forced into having an abortion by her callous lover. Another rice worker goes into premature labor in the fields and is delivered of a baby boy. Silvana receives a fake pearl necklace from Walter after she has agreed to help him rob the farm owner, but, remorseful at the misery she has wrought, she kills him and jumps to her death in the path of a speeding train.

In her summary of reviewers' opinions a week later, Mrs. Looram was at a loss to know where to begin with her summary of the film's moral transgressions. Indecent costuming and a low moral tone throughout were probably enough to put *Bitter Rice* beyond the hope of revision or redemption. Suggestive dancing, abortion—"a crime of murder morally unfit for inclusion in motion picture entertainment under any circumstance"—excessive realism in the childbirth scene, suicide as a plot resolution and insufficient moral compensation for the crimes of Walter and Francesca plunged the film deep into a morass of unacceptability. The whole was "a serious threat to Christian morality and decency."[61] William Mooring, always eager to find some evidence of an International Communist Conspiracy, declared that *Bitter Rice* was illustrative of a trend to mock traditional Christian belief coming from a country whose largest political party was brightest Red.[62]

Ordinarily, Lux Films might have been resigned to a C rating and played

Bitter Rice via the usual scandalous route of exploitation cinemas for a few weeks until it had exhausted its potential. However, the New York press had been unusually impressed and reviews were enthusiastic. "Mangano is XXXier than both Mae West and Jane Russell," proclaimed Walter Winchell in the *New York Mirror*. Bosley Crowther of the *New York Times* found her "nothing short of a sensation . . . full bodied and gracefully muscular. It is not too excessive to describe her as Anna Magnani minus fifteen years, Ingrid Bergman with a Latin disposition and Rita Hayworth plus twenty-five pounds." The *Times-Herald* critic said that she had "the robust proportions of the Venus de Milo and the personality of a Sherman tank." Such plaudits aroused interest nationwide. Lux was approached by Fox Theaters to play saturation bookings on the West Coast and Warner Brothers let it be known that they would not be averse to making some of their first-run cinemas available to house the formidable Mangano. Such success carried a price, of course. The forces of civil and clerical morality immediately went on the offensive. In Albany the police chief led a raid on the projection booth of the Ritz and bewildered customers were left staring at a blank screen at the point where Walter starts making eyes at Silvana.[63] Father John Metz was able to secure a promise from the manager of the Colonial in Harrisburg, Pennsylvania that he would end the run prematurely.[64] The Boston city censor let it be known that he cut C-rated films as a matter of course and *Bitter Rice*, undoubtedly headed in that direction, would not be spared if it were rash enough to appear.

It was evident to Lux, the Italian distributor, that runaway hit status would necessitate negotiations with the Legion. In agreeing to meet objections, it was to spend ten weary months of haggling, a period that was unavoidably prolonged by the necessity of having to convey all instructions to Rome, where changes in the negative had to be made. The problem of Mangano's costuming proved intractable, since she wore form-hugging outfits from first to last.[65] The by-now obligatory epilogue was applied to mitigate the suicide. An anonymous hand drops rice on the ground while a voice intones: "Ashes to ashes, dust to dust and rice back whence it came. Each handful of these hard-gotten grains guiltily falling on the poor clay—a token of forgiveness from those who had known her." The childbirth sequence had its character changed by the substitution of a single line. "Gabriella is seized with labor pains!" became "Gabriella needs help!" and it was now possible to interpret her cries of anguish as "originating from gallstones, appendicitis or some other non-maternal ailment." Francesca's reminiscence on her abortion, a major stumbling block, had to be resolved by a subterfuge that only those proficient in lip reading in Italian could divine. The dubbed dialogue was changed, while the actress continued to mouth the original words. American audience heard:

"They sent me away. I was going to have a child."
"Tell me, what about the baby?"
"He was stillborn. I wanted it, too, but he didn't care. He said children are a nuisance."

The attentive lip reader would have picked up the following:

"They sent me away. I was going to have a child."
"Tell me, what about the baby?"
"He wasn't born. I was happy about it but he said no. He said children would be a nuisance."

Those and other cuts had reduced the running time by ten minutes, but the Legion was not yet satisfied. At a reviewer's meeting on June 7, 1951 the majority felt that it was still a C-ish picture with a sensuality of motivation that all the cutting in the world could not correct.[66] Lux's patience and specifically that of its New York representative, Clare Catalano, was beginning to wear thin. She told Father Little, Masterson's assistant, that her job was in jeopardy if an accommodation could not be reached. She was under pressure to bring in American dollars even if it meant "cutting the picture to ribbons."[67] Little may have felt some compassion for the woman who was widowed the day following their conversation or he may have been swayed by her tearful plea that as it now stood, *Bitter Rice* was just a forthright story about a group of average migratory workers battling with the earth, the elements and their own simple natures. The Legion was not prepared to capitulate completely, but he kindly advised that what was required now was in the nature of cosmetic changes, not wholesale revisions. The removal of close-ups of bare legs and partially covered breasts seen through tattered clothing sheared another three minutes from the final, approved B version, which went into general circulation on September 13.[68] Little was glad to be rid of the story, not because of the protracted negotiations but rather to be able to devote more time to another Italian film, *The Ways of Love*, for whatever furor had arisen over Mangano and her earthy rice workers was but a storm in a teacup compared to the hurricane that was already blowing about the Legion and the Church.

It would be untrue to say that *The Miracle* came as a bolt from the blue. In August 1948 Mrs. Looram had seen it at the Venice Film Festival as a companion piece to Jean Cocteau's *La Voix Humaine* in a double bill. Simultaneously she learned that Joseph Burstyn, the Polish-American, New York–based distributor of art movies was at the resort bidding for the U.S. rights. Burstyn and his partner, Arthur Mayer, were no strangers to censorship battles. It was they who had fought Breen over his refusal to license *Bicycle Thief* and complained to the police about the sympathetic picket lines that the Knights of Columbus had thrown around the theater despite a B from the Legion. Unlike their commercial counterparts, art film distributors lead a schizophrenic existence, dealing with what they feel ought to be the presentation of pure cinematic art and having to give the public what it wants in order to survive. Glowing success alternated with abysmal failure. Thus Rosselini's widely admired *Open City* had not saved his *Germany, Year Zero* from oblivion, nor were the plaudits for De Sica's *Bicycle Thief* to rub off on *Umberto D.* Still Burstyn persisted, even after Mayer had given up in despair of ever breaking out of what was cruelly but not inaccurately called the "egg-head market." Success depended on a number of variables, but of inestimable value were a catchy title and cooperation from the popular media, since independents did not have a Hollywood-style publicity machine at their disposal. Feature articles and publicity blurbs might reach beyond the coterie of the faithful to the vast, untapped mainstream audience. Burstyn's strategy with *The Miracle* was dictated, in part, by its awkward length—forty-two minutes—which meant it had to be double- or even triple-billed. He decided to attach it to Marcel Pagnol's *Jofroi* and Jean Renoir's *A Day in the Country* and call the trilogy *The Ways of Love*.

Rather than wait for an official viewing, Masterson decided to attend the premiere privately at the Paris Theater on December 12, 1950. The souvenir program with its pen and ink drawing of a male ogling a couple locked in a passionate embrace and another female spread-eagled on the grass was a presentiment of the evil to come. When the lights went up, the Legion secretary sat stunned momentarily. *The Miracle* was far, far worse than Mary Looram had described. Its sacrilegious and blasphemous mockery of Catholic religious belief, never mind its condonation of illicit sex, put it beyond the pale. No amount of excision nor any recourse to mitigating prologues or epilogues could possibly save it. He immediately went to the manager's office to demand the abomination be taken off the screen immediately and permanently. The response was a shrug of the shoulders and something to the effect that each was entitled to his own opinion.[69]

What had appalled Father Masterson was a grim anecdote about human cruelty and religious intolerance in a remote community. Anna Magnani plays a simple-minded goat herder despised by the local villagers as she passes by, mumbling incomprehensibly. On a hillside she encounters a bearded stranger clad in flowing garb and carrying a staff, who seems to have the aspect of a saint. He first makes her drunk and then seduces her. Because of her befuddled condition, she thinks she has conceived a child of miraculous origin, whom she addresses as "Blessed One." When the villagers learn of her condition, they hold a mock procession and crown her with a basin as the "Blessed Virgin." Jeered and ridiculed, she flees to the local church where she gives birth to a male child sired by "St. Joseph."

The IFCA screening on December 30 was a mere formality, with a unanimous recommendation for the Condemned rating. In the interim, Masterson had begun to galvanize the opposition. He knew that Burstyn stood behind the Paris management's decision to continue playing the film. It was also art-house fodder, which meant that a Legion threat of a boycott of theater chains would have scant impact. Moreover, there was the awkward fact that it had been publicly exhibited in Italy without Vatican intervention. The *New York Herald Tribune* added fuel to the flames by pointing out that there was a Papal representative on the Venice Festival selection committee to screen out blasphemy who had obviously not felt it necessary to use his clout in 1948. Was it not true, asked the paper, that Mr. Rossellini, the director of *The Miracle*, was sufficiently persona grata with the Holy Father to have had his cooperation in making his recently completed film of the life of St. Francis of Assisi? Beyond this, again, was the knowledge that it had been admitted to the United States by customs and had been given a license by the Board of Regents of the State of New York a good month before its opening. Legislation passed the previous year in the state legislature had forbidden criminal prosecution of a motion picture previously licensed.[70]

Masterson's persistence in the face of these potential setbacks was characteristic of the tough, uncompromising executive secretary the bishops had chosen. The business of papal acquiescence was soon cleared up. A letter from the Centro Cattolico Cinematographico, the Italian equivalent of the PCA, confirmed that it had condemned *Il Miracolo* as "a parody of a sublime evangelical story which stands as the basis of very Christian belief." Turning to the obtuseness of the Paris Theater, Masterson invited the head of the State Board of Censors and Edward T. McCaffrey, Commissioner of Licenses for the city, to accompany him to the den of iniquity on 58th Street on December 21 to see for themselves. For good measure the police commissioner was given a three-page memorandum of Legion objections.[71] With McCaffrey it was a case of preaching to the converted. He was a National Commander of the Catholic War Veterans and delighted in dressing up in a uniform, which reminded some of the young Captain Ernest Rohm of Brownshirt fame. Victory seemed assured when the Paris Theater was ordered to close and Burstyn was warned not to attempt to show his picture elsewhere in the city.

These matters might have ended had not Burstyn been as tenacious a pit bull as his clerical opponent. Heartened, perhaps, by the news that New York movie critics had voted *The Miracle* Best Foreign Language Picture of the Year, he appealed to the New York Supreme Court on the grounds that the City License Commissioner had exceeded his authority as he was not a duly constituted film censor. The court agreed, and on New Year's Eve Anna Magnani's anguished cries once more reverberated around the walls of the Paris. Preparations also went ahead for a ceremony to honor the picture at Radio City Music Hall.[72] Now it became a fight without quarter asked or given. Masterson went to the top, asking Cardinal Spellman to do what he could to support the Legion. He obliged with a statement to be read at all masses advising not only New Yorkers but all thirty million Catholics in the nation to stay away altogether "from places of amusement that are showing it now or may show it henceforth."[73] At the theater itself most evenings saw as much drama off-screen as on. The fire commissioner, George F. Monoghan, a Catholic and Legion member, closed it one night for a perceived infraction of safety regulations when a customer waiting in line to enter briefly stepped into the exit lobby. The place was evacuated twice for bomb threats. Customers brave or brazen enough to buy tickets had to run a gauntlet of pickets and had two pamphlets thrust into their hands, one from the Knights of Columbus and another from the Holy Names Society, comparing *The Miracle*, by some convoluted logic, to *Birth of a Nation* and *Oliver Twist* as detrimental to freedom of speech and racial tolerance.[74]

January was a bad month for Burstyn and his little picture. The trade papers, in their separate ways, lambasted him for his obduracy. Quigley rode the fashionable hobby horse of the International Communist Conspiracy in his *Motion Picture Herald*: "An essential bulwark of the Western World against Communism is religious belief and practice. The Reds and their friends at home must be smiling."[75] On a more practical note, the *Independent Film Journal* wondered aloud who was brainless enough to show the antisemitic *Oliver Twist* and *The Miracle* when they set the industry's public relations back ten years. Determined to keep Radio City's unsullied reputation intact, the Archdiocese of New York urged Nelson Rockefeller to veto the planned function for a sacrilegious and revolting picture.[76] The journalists decided to go to the Rainbow Room of the Rockefeller Center instead. While all of this was heartening to the Legion, the fact remained that *The Miracle* was still playing. Moreover, the enemy was not vanquished. Rossellini cabled Spellman, charging that the Church had completely misinterpreted his intentions:

In *The Miracle* men are still without pity because they have not come back to God, but God is already in the faith, however confused, of that poor, persecuted woman; and since God is wherever a human being suffers and is misunderstood. The Miracle occurs when at the birth of the child the poor, demented woman regains sanity in her eternal love.

Successful politicians and their appointees ignore public opinion at their peril. Having opened a Pandora's box by their original action of granting an exhibition license, the Board of Regents thought it imperative to have another look at the film. Conscience played a secondary role to expediency. Numerically, there were more Catholics who had been galvanized to attack than there were partisans of freedom of expression to defend it. The city officials now repented of their decision and asked Burstyn to show cause why the license for his sacrilegious movie should not be canceled. Burstyn had a reply—the First Amendment—but he was careful not to mention it at this point. The Regents justified their about-face by raising the specter of civil insurrection in Manhattan, a reference to the nightly ruckus outside the Paris Theater that was "a menace to peace and order."[77]

If anything was required to unite the disparate groups in defense of *The Miracle*, it was this reneging on the Regents' part. Even within the hitherto secure citadel of the Church, dissenting voices made themselves heard. The *Commonweal*, with conscious and devastating precision, editorialized: "It seems as if we American Catholics reduce the struggle for the hearts and minds of men to a contest between picket lines and pressure groups and in doing so slight the emphasis which Catholic doctrine puts on free consent and reasoned morality." William Clancy, a highly respected English professor at Notre Dame, deplored "this semi-ecclesiastical McCarthyism accompanied by some of the odious methods which this now implies, its 'guilt by association,' its appeal to prejudice and non-intelligence, its hysteria."[78] How sad, said the *Catholic Messenger*, that a diocesan editor should fail to distinguish between the Thomistic notion of individual moral freedom and civil liberty guaranteed by the Constitution by asserting that the latter does not guarantee anyone any rights to do what is wrong. That kind of oversimplification offered genuine reason for the fears of non-Catholics.[79]

The decision of the New York Court of Appeals to uphold the Regents' action sent *The Miracle* affair to the highest court in the land. In the context of shifting public sympathy for the underdog (the Supreme Court's decision to strike down the separate-but-equal doctrine in schools was imminent), the justices' decision in favor of Burstyn was not altogether surprising. Rossellini's motion picture came at the tail end of four decades of discrimination against the genre as an art form and as a means of propagating ideas. With devastating accuracy Felix Frankfurter dismissed the shibboleth of "sacrilege" as an age-old excuse to crush dissent by whoever or whatever happened to be the dominant religious power structure of the moment. In England, to attack the Mass was once blasphemous; after the Reformation, to perform it became so. Blasphemy was a chameleon phrase that meant the suppression of whatever went against what the prevailing authority established as orthodoxy. With a thinly veiled swipe at the Church and the Legion, the Chief Justice observed that the New York censors tended to ban only that to which objection was taken by a religious group. But it was the Court's dismissal of the 1915 decision treating motion pictures as different from the printed word that has been termed the first, great defeat of Catholic motion picture pressure. It exposed the fallacy that because films were a business conducted for profit they fell outside the protection of the First Amendment whereas books, newspapers and magazines were means of expression whose liberty had to be guarded. These, too, were enterprises no less beholden to the profit motive. Further, even if one were to accept the dubious hypothesis that motion pictures possessed a greater capacity for evil than the printed word or other modes of expression, it did not follow that they should be denied constitutional protection or be subject to unbridled censorship.[80]

The explosion that the Court had detonated temporarily stunned the Legion. Cardinal Spellman's hasty poll of leading clerics elicited the response that a dignified silence was the most prudent course. There were a few scraps of comfort. The Court had not attempted to extend constitutional protection to obscene material per se, nor had it abrogated the legality of precensorship by state and city boards. Still, there were clouds on the horizon that boded ill. The American Civil Liberties Union was in the process of taking up cudgels to "combat pressure groups aimed at censorship," a crusade whose very vagueness spelled danger.[81] In Ohio a bill had been introduced in the legislature to abolish the state censorship board, and *La Ronde*, a wittily wicked merry-go-round of extramarital affairs from France, was going the same court appeal route as *The Miracle*. Few clergymen were prepared to admit that the struggle to keep the Rossellini film off the screen had been an ignoble failure, but an even tinier minority probably questioned whether Anna Magnani's sexual encounter with a bogus St. Joseph threatened American civilization. Still, a new approach, focusing on the positive, educational aspects of a motion picture rather than exposing the negative, lay in the future.

NOTES

1. For Birdwell's association with *Gone with the Wind*, see Roland Flamini, *Scarlett, Rhett and a Cast of Thousands* (New York: Macmillan, 1975), p. 88 et seq.

2. There are conflicting stories as to how Hughes chose Russell. Hawks claimed he found her as a five dollar-a-week dental receptionist in Los Angeles (interview in *Take One*, December 1971, pp. 23–25); Ballard claimed that he made a portfolio of photographs for her professional use.

3. PCA file, "The Outlaw." The Margaret Herrick Library of the Academy of Motion Picture Arts and Sciences contains various press reports on difficulties encountered.

4. Ibid., March 28, 1941.

5. Leff and Simmons, p. 118.

6. Ibid., p. 119.

7. It was so regarded by a majority of the British press. After the San Francisco premiere, *Time* called it "a strong candidate for floperoo of all time" (February 22, 1943).

8. NLOD file, "The Outlaw," McClafferty memorandum, February 26, 1943. The condemnation was announced on February 25.

9. *Hughes Tool Company v. Motion Picture Association of America*, 66 F. Supp. 1006 (S.D.N.Y., 1946).

10. *Harrison's Reports*, May 11, 1946.

11. As told to *Variety*, September 25, 1946.

12. NLOD file, "The Outlaw." Mrs. Looram and Father Brendan Larnen, Legion assistant secretary, met informally with Hughes and United Artists representatives on October 3. Hughes requested the Legion "call off its war dogs" (i.e., pickets) even if it would not remove the C rating. McClafferty had visited Hughes in Los Angeles and was invited to inspect the Spruce Goose plane.

13. Ibid., McClafferty memorandum, October 14, 1946.

14. Ibid., Quigley to Hughes, October 3, 1947.

15. Ibid., Masterson to Quigley, October 1, 1947. A Senate committee then investigating Hughes's wartime military contracts heard Bennett E. Myers, a retired major-general, confess that Hughes had authorized him to offer the Legion $150,000 and Mayor William O'Dwyer of New York $100,000 to permit screenings. Needless to say, the Legion and Hughes denied all knowledge of this. *Motion Picture Daily*, November 13, 1947.

16. NLOD file, "The Outlaw," Quigley to Scully, February 19, 1948. Hughes insisted he was being victimized because of his Protestantism.

17. Ibid., Masterson to Scully, undated. By the time the verdict was reached some reviewers had seen it twenty times.

18. Ibid., Harry L. Gold to Masterson, April 27 and May 28, 1948 contain progress reports on cutting.

19. Ibid., Masterson to Monsignor R. Murphy, October 1, 1948.

20. The only account of Babb's career is in Friedman, *A Youth in Babylon, passim.*

21. Finding it difficult to do business on the black theater circuit, Babb hired former Olympic gold medalist Jesse Owens to hawk the booklets.

22. Friedman, pp. 49–50.

23. NLOD file, "Mom and Dad," All American Showmanship Contest Winners (1946).

24. Ibid., Masterson to the Rev. Charles J. Planche, February 11, 1947.

25. Ibid., the Rev. Edward R. Maloy to Masterson, August 28, 1947.

26. Ibid., Babb, "Open Letter" to *Michigan Catholic*, November 5, 1946.

27. Ibid., Babb to the Rev. Richard R. Krapfl, July 31, 1947. According to Babb, "the late Monsignor added greater eulogies regarding the super-educational value to the general public of the film in a second letter."

28. Ibid., E. V. McCoy to Masterson, undated.

29. Ibid., J. F. Tucker, diocesan director, Wilmington, Delaware Legion of Decency, circular letter, October 15, 1948.

30. Hygienic Productions, *Newsletter*, vol. 5, no. 28, July 15, 1950.

31. Fox's press kit noted its seventy-seven weeks on the best-seller list and its cast of three-hundred characters.

32. NLOD file, "Forever Amber," "Memorandum for the Information of Diocesan Directors of the National Legion of Decency," October 20, 1947.

33. Ibid., Masterson to Daly, October 23, 1947.

34. Ibid., Skouras to Masterson, October 16, 1947.

35. Ibid., Memorandum to Scully, October 16, 1947.

36. Louella Parson's husband was a Fox employee.

37. NLOD file, "Forever Amber," Charles W. Neill to Masterson, December 6, 1947.

38. Ibid., Edward J. Gorman to Masterson, October 23, 1947.

39. Ibid., Dougherty to Howard Minsky, November 1, 1947.

40. Ibid., Gorman, diocesan director, Fall Rapids, Massachusetts Legion of Decency, sat in his car opposite the theater, counting 902 admissions to three screenings.

41. Ibid., Masterson to Scully, October 29, 1947. Masterson had had conversations with Ulric Bell, "a kind of commissar for movies . . . and a definite leftist."

42. Ibid., Skouras to Masterson, undated but probably late November, contains a detailed description of all cuts and changes.

43. Ibid., Masterson memorandum. Preminger's major battle with the Legion would occur over *The Moon Is Blue.*

44. Ibid., Scully to Masterson, December 2, 1947. "I communicated the idea that a repudiation of box office success as a standard of morality plus a regret that such an issue had been raised be included in the statement."

45. Production, negative and publicity costs totalled $7.3 million; grosses at December 31, 1948 were put at $4.1 million.

46. Masterson prevailed on Devlin to supervise the production, guard the Church's reputation of innocence in her death and keep an eye on Father Doncoeur, whom Selznick had brought from France as technical advisor. See NLOD file, "Joan of Arc," Masterson to Devlin, September 4, 1947.

47. QP Box 2, David O. Selznick to Neil Agnew, Vanguard Films, January 10, 1947.

48. *New York Times*, January 18, 1947.

49. NLOD file, "Duel in the Sun," January 4, 1947.

50. *Tidings*, January 23, 1947.

51. QP Box 2, Quigley to Selznick, January 10, 1947.

52. Ibid., Quigley to Masterson, February 22, 1947.

53. Masterson's vigilance was apocryphal. He threatened to award the thriller, *Panic in the Streets*, a C rating for this exchange between husband and wife: "Reed—It could happen to me, too. Just like having another baby. Nancy—One of these days, huh?" "(It) implies the wife practiced birth control and openly discussed it with her husband." NLOD file, "Panic in the Streets," Masterson memorandum, June 6, 1950.

54. NLOD file, "Duel in the Sun," Masterson to Breen, February 18, 1947.

55. Ibid., Breen to Masterson, February 22, 1947.

56. Ibid., Quigley to Masterson (enclosure), February 24, 1947.

57. Ibid., McClafferty memorandum, March 13, 1947.

58. Ibid., Masterson to the Rev. C. P. McGiffin, November 26, 1947. It was "a particularly bad 'B'. If you discourage showing of the film, you will be doing the people of the community a distinct favor."

59. Ibid., Arthur De Bra (MPAA) to Masterson, August 21, 1947.

60. The controversy is examined in Leff and Simmons, Chapter 7.

61. NLOD file, "Bitter Rice," Looram to Masterson, October 20, 1950.

62. *Tidings*, March 16, 1951.

63. *New York Times*, February 8, 1951.

64. NLOD file, "Bitter Rice," Metz to Masterson, March 5, 1951.

65. Ibid., Clare Catalano to Little, June 29, 1951.

66. Ibid., Little memorandum, June 7, 1951.

67. Ibid., Little memorandum, June 14, 1951.

68. The Legion demanded and received Lux's permission to scrutinize press releases and assorted publicity materials.

69. NLOD file, "The Miracle," Masterson memorandum, December 2, 1950.

70. This and other evidence was forthcoming at the court hearing in *Burstyn v. Lewis Wilson, Commissioner of Education, State of New York*, May 25, 1952.

71. NLOD file, "The Miracle," Masterson to Spellman, December 20, 1950.

72. De Grazia and Newman, p. 80.

73. NLOD file, "The Miracle," Masterson memorandum titled "*The Miracle*—why it is blasphemous and sacrilegious," January 1951.

74. The publicity campaign protesting exhibition was organized by the Committee of Catholic Lay Organizations of the Archdiocese of New York.

75. *Motion Picture Herald*, January 22, 1951, p. 1.

76. NLOD file, "The Miracle," Albert Muller to Nelson Rockefeller, January 15, 1951.

77. De Grazia and Newman, pp. 79–80.

78. *Commonweal*, March 2, 1951.

79. *Catholic Messenger*, March 4, 1951.

80. *Burstyn v. Wilson*, 343 U.S. 495 (1952).

81. NLOD file, "The Miracle," Internal memorandum, Chancery Office of the Diocese of New York, May 27, 1952.

1. Archbishop John T. McNicholas of Cincinnati, first president of the Episcopal Committee for Motion Pictures, from which the Legion emerged in 1933. Courtesy Religious News Service.

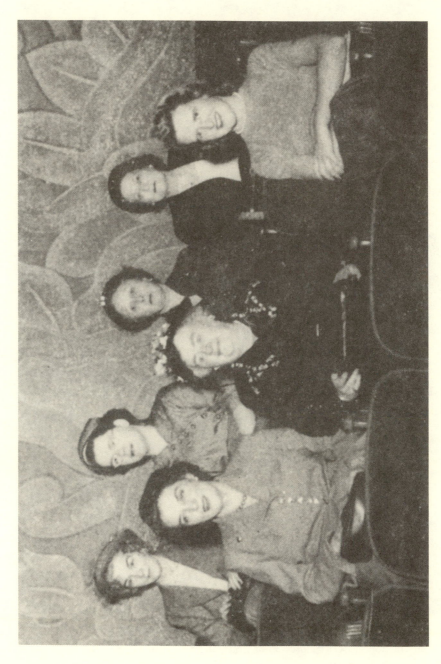

2. Members of the IFCA scrutinize a picture. Courtesy Religious News Service.

3. "Mrs. Looram's Ladies" discuss a verdict with their chief and mentor. Mary Looram is seated center. Courtesy Religious News Service.

4. A final decision is made. Fathers Patrick Masterson and Thomas Little with reviewers from the IFCA. Courtesy Religious News Service.

5. *Lady of Burlesque*. Vaudeville was an unsuitable theme for decent movies in the Legion's eyes. Michael O'Shea's ogling of Barbara Stanwyck's thigh was symptomatic of the picture's general offensiveness. Courtesy Museum of Modern Art/Film Stills Archive.

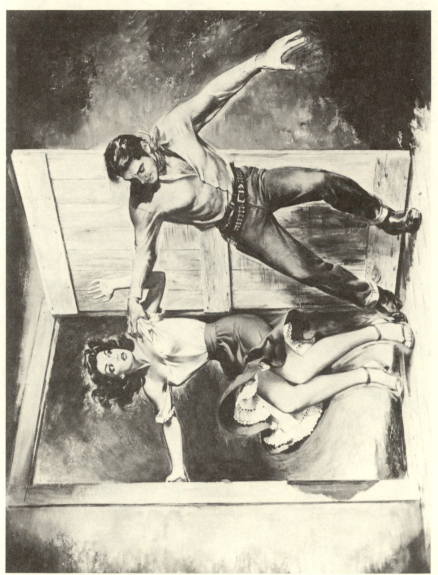

6. "Don't, Billy, don't!" read the caption on this advertisement for Howard Hughes's *The Outlaw*. Neither this, nor the off-the-shoulder blouse portrait of Jane Russell in a haystack, appeared in the actual picture. Courtesy Museum of Modern Art/Film Stills Archive.

7. Illusion versus reality. Though Hughes's publicity for *The Outlaw* included the famous photograph of Jane Russell in a low-cut, off-the-shoulder blouse, the dress actually worn, as seen here, was much more modest. Courtesy Museum of Modern Art/Film Stills Archive.

8. The girl with the impact of a Sherman tank. Silvana Mangano's figure-hugging costume was only one of many objectionable elements in the Italian drama, *Bitter Rice*. Courtesy Museum of Modern Art/Film Stills Archive.

9. Anna Magnani and her seducer, "St. Joseph," in *The Miracle*. No film aroused as much Legion wrath as this forty-four-minute episode of a simple goat herder who believes she has been impregnated by a saint. Courtesy Museum of Modern Art/Film Stills Archive.

10. Jane Russell again, and as big a headache as ever to the Legion. She appears here in a torrid dance scene from *The French Line*, another piece of sensationalism from Howard Hughes. Courtesy Museum of Modern Art/Film Stills Archive.

11. The wages of sin is a boycott. Prospective patrons for *The French Line* are given due warning at this Union City, New Jersey, theater in 1953. Courtesy Religious News Service.

12. In *Kiss Me, Stupid!*, Polly the Pistol's antics, not to mention her neckline, struck the Legion as distasteful. Courtesy Museum of Modern Art/Film Stills Archive.

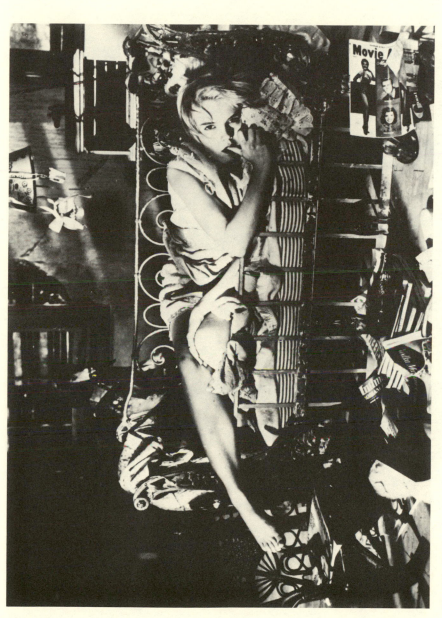

13. Baby-Doll—the thumb sucking title character with the body of a woman and the emotional maturity of a child. The screen version of the Tennessee Williams short play was to bring the Legion into conflict with a major studio. Courtesy Museum of Modern Art/Film Stills Archive.

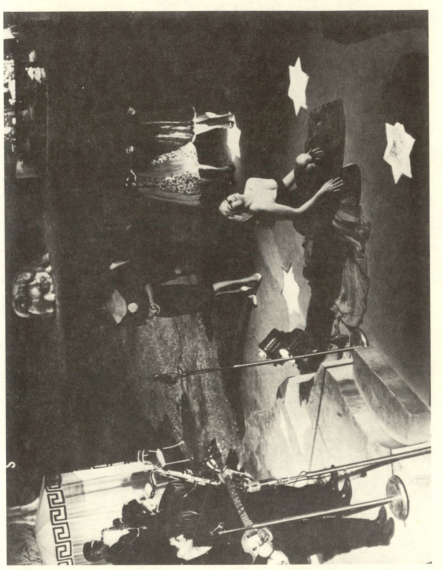

14. Anita Ekberg reveals her impressive bosom in *La Dolce Vita*. Fellini's deeply felt work divided the Legion's old and new guards, and the verdict dismayed those who had always looked to it as a bulwark against "filth." Courtesy Museum of Modern Art/Film Stills Archive.

15. The old order changeth. Mrs. Looram and Msgr. Little with Father Patrick Sullivan. Sullivan's hiring, as Assistant Secretary, would coincide with the publication of *Miranda Prorsus* and herald a new philosophy. Courtesy Religious News Service.

16. Cooperation rather than confrontation. Archbishop John J. Krol of Philadelphia, Msgr. Little and Barney Balaban of Paramount Pictures at the First Annual Film Awards ceremony of NCOMP in February 1966. Courtesy Religious News Service.

_____ Chapter 6 _____

Cracks in the System

The record of the Catholic Church in America during the Senator Joseph McCarthy era is a checkered one that still awaits full-length examination. While much light has been shed on the politician from Wisconsin, himself an adherent to the faith, the behavior of the Church hierarchy was not without blemish. Certainly there is much from the times that those involved would prefer to forget. The Church's official silence during the persecution of individuals for their political beliefs and its tacit approval of loyalty oaths demanded of public and private employees are rightly seen as blots on its escutcheon. As for the Legion's role, it is difficult to conclude that it was other than a wholehearted supporter of some of the worst excesses of the period, when a hysterical anti-Red crusade impacted on the motion picture industry, bringing in its wake charges of witch-hunts.[1]

That there should be hostility to the propagators of the shibboleth that religion is the opiate of the masses is understandable. The heinous philosophy of atheistic Communism so intimately associated with the Soviet Union and its canonized leader, Joseph Stalin, was an intellectual challenge that could not be ignored. That the Holy Mother Church in its various guises continued to suffer persecution behind the Iron Curtain was also indisputable and equally distressing. Less forgivable was the Church's egregious equation of left-wing thought with outright subversion of minds and the body politic in fifties America.

A number of Soviet films had been brought to the United States before the outbreak of the Second World War. The Legion had regarded them with suspicion but preferred to ignore them as sleeping dogs in the hope that lack of publicity would confine their exposure to the handful of radical theaters bold enough to import them. For the motion picture business, a more positive, ideological stance became imperative after Hitler's surprise attack on the U.S.S.R. in the summer of 1941. Not only was it necessary to reevaluate the hitherto reviled Bolshevik regime in terms of a freedom-loving ally, but cognizance also had to be taken of Hollywood's initiative. Movie audiences had been amused and regaled with condescending tales of stolid commissars and their cringing inferiors in *Ninotchka* and others of its kind. Now a bond was to be forged between the two peoples with a common aim of defeating Germany. The film capital rose nobly to the cause.

Much of this the Legion regarded with profound misgivings. Since early in 1940 it had kept a file of left-wing activities in the entertainment industry. As compiled by Blanche Cunningham, a reporter hired for the specific task, it was a weekly communique on topics as diverse as Woody Guthrie's promotion of John Ford's *The Grapes of Wrath*—that "slanderous attack on agricultural free enterprise," American Communist Party sponsorship of "Red Movies" at a San Francisco art theater and the *Daily Worker*'s plaudits for *His Favorite Wife*, "because Garson Kanin, their fellow traveler directed it."[2] But, by 1942, the problem of how to treat pro-Russian movies had become acute in face of productions such as *North Star*, which portrays the Ukraine as a pastoral paradise peopled by lusty-voiced collective farmers and their rosy-cheeked girlfriends. An idyllic existence is shattered by the arrival of the German army, which first occupies the Ruritanian village and then proceeds to impose a region of terror. The arch-villain of the piece is a Prussian doctor, played by a bullet-headed Eric von Stroheim at his sneering, supercilious best. His solution to the shortage of blood for soldiers of the master race is to drain all of it from the bodies of hapless children. He gets his comeuppance at the hands of an elderly bolshevik doctor who also happens to have been one of his students. With much conscience-searching this gnarled medic cannot tolerate the perversion of the Hippocratic Oath, and shoots him dead.

The Legion frowned on such racial stereotyping and saw it as an evil portent for the hopes of toleration and forgiveness at war's end.[3] But the stream of pro-Russian pictures kept coming. The appearance of *Mission to Moscow* and *Song of Russia* in 1943 marked the high water mark of movie adulation for the Stalinist regime. *Mission to Moscow* was based on reminiscences of Joseph E. Davies, America's prewar ambassador to the country. There was some truth to Father Masterson's jibe that it should more properly have been titled "Submission to Moscow" for its adulatory tone and blithe acceptance of the official Soviet version of contemporary history. The Moscow show trials of 1936–38 were presented as models of judicial fairness with earnest Bolshevik prosecutors politely eliciting confessions of treason from a succession of shifty-eyed Trotskyites, all in the pay of Hitler. As with *Spain Fights On* and *Spain in Flames*, it landed the Legion in a quandary. In one respect it might have received the highest rating since it contained nothing offensive to decency as the term was customarily understood. Still, Mrs. Looram was at pains to remind her ladies that it required a mature mind to recognize the film for what it was—unadulterated Red propaganda of the most insidious kind. Like Masterson, she was inclined to have it renamed, her choice being "Lend Lease to Communism." She wondered what the "thousands of religious martyrs, the millions who had died in the planned starvation of the Ukraine, the Russians who now languish in concentration camps would say about it." Though the Legion would have preferred to give *Mission* the same rating it had applied to *Blockade*, now there were other sensibilities to consider. The Office of War Information, the government's liaison between Washington and the film industry, had been hastily created on the morrow of Pearl Harbor. It quickly became a gigantic promotional-cum-censorship machine that looked askance at any action potentially injurious to an ally. It would almost certainly have seen that manifestation in an S.C. classification. Grudgingly, and after lengthy deliberation, the Legion chose A-II, though it insisted on an accompanying notation: "This film in its sympathetic portrayal of the governing regime in Russia makes no reference to anti-religious philosophy and policy of said regime."[4] The image of a benevolent Uncle Joe Stalin was safe for another three years.

The conclusion of World War II, followed immediately by the Cold War, saw a rapid deterioration in relations between the two superpowers. Russia was once again the Land of Godless Bolsheviks bent on world domination. The House Committee on Un-American Activities (HUAC), which had made sporadic forays into the film capital in the late thirties, was rejuvenated under the chairmanship of J. Parnell Thomas, a pint-sized ex-insurance salesman and, in 1947, it returned. This second excursion was altogether more fruitful in rooting out home-grown Communists and fellow travelers. For all the inquisitorial excesses of HUAC, its session in Los Angeles proved the old adage that there is never smoke without fire. Members (and an ever larger number of ex-members) of the American Communist Party (ACP) had been active in Hollywood in the Depression years, drawn, some insisted, to the cause through idealism and a sense of justice for the disadvantaged; seduced, said others, by the slogans and facile solutions that were two-dimensional appeals to a two-dimensional community. Nowhere was the gap between haves and have-nots greater than in the city. A number of highly paid movie people with feelings of guilt to assuage and a determination to use at least some of their wealth to expose the shortcomings of capitalist society had gravitated toward the ACP. They, and others, found the party the only vocal forum where the issues of racial segregation and persecution of minorities were openly condemned. On a more mundane level, it had become tangentially involved in the battle over unionization of actors and craftsmen. There, the employers had attempted to subvert the process by methods as ruthless as firing dissidents and setting up rival unions run by gangsters who guaranteed industrial peace at a price. A bitter struggle to counter the company unions brought some Hollywood socialists into prominence, among them John Howard Lawson, first president of the Screen Writers' Guild. Though industrial peace reigned by war's end, old hatreds died hard. The HUAC investigations breathed new life into charges of subversion and gave the movie moguls a chance to even the score. The Waldorf Declaration of 1947 was a collective decision by film companies not to employ known or suspected Reds and to ease out those suspected of harboring subversive intentions. Innocents,

no less than troublemakers, found themselves unemployed and blacklisted over-
night. The charge, though often not publicly stated, was past or present political
affiliation or a lack of patriotism, as perceived by HUAC. The Hollywood Ten
who were cited for contempt of Congress and imprisoned were only the most
visible of thousands on the blacklist. For the most part they were driven to
sever their connection with the movie industry or seek employment abroad. As
with all classic witch-hunts, there was an alternative to ostracism. Salvation
for those willing to confess lay in cooperation with the FBI and HUAC in
naming names of those not already ferreted out, and in some public confession
of contrition for their own sins. By way of penance for being associated with
North Star and *Song of Russia* and their sort, Hollywood began producing anti-
Red pictures from 1947 onward. Initially, the Communist was some way from
American shores, as in *The Red Danube* (1948) and *The Iron Curtain* (1948).
By 1949, however, the foe had become, literally, *The Enemy Within*, having
easily penetrated the arsenal of democracy. He was in San Francisco (*The Woman
on Pier 13*, 1950), Pittsburgh (*I Was a Communist for the F.B.I.*, 1951) and even
Hawaii (*Big Jim McClain*, 1952). In its zeal to alert citizens to the ever-increasing
menace, the Legion made one of the most remarkable classification decisions
in its history by turning a blind eye to several violent episodes in the otherwise
unmemorable *Guilty of Treason* (1950). Despite the adult theme of political and
religious persecution and two graphic torture sequences, it was awarded an A-
I rating, putting it in the same category as the most innocuous of children's
entertainment.

Guilty of Treason was the work of a shadowy corporation, Freedom Productions, that made nothing else of significance in its brief existence. Though billed
as an action thriller, no attempt was made to conceal its ulterior motive—to
vilify an East European government and to capitalize on flourishing anti-Red
sentiment in a manner that would be eminently acceptable to the official Catholic viewpoint. Based on a true story, the central character is Joseph Cardinal
Mindszenty who had been arrested, allegedly brainwashed, tried and imprisoned
by the Hungarian authorities for dealing in foreign currency and plotting against
the state. That he had been an outspoken critic of the educational system and
demanded compulsory Catholic religious instruction in schools are nowhere
mentioned in the film. Having been administered drugs and forced to undergo
hypnosis, the primate is tricked into signing a false confession. An equally
contentious aspect of the plot concerns a Hungarian woman who fought against
the Nazis only to discover that what had replaced them is worse. Her treasonable
thoughts are confided to a Russian lover who, as a matter of course, betrays her
to the authorities. Arrested, she is tortured, first mentally and then physically,
but dies rather than confess to nonexistent crimes before her sadistic interro-
gators. Those sequences where she is hoisted off the ground by ropes attached
to her wrists and then immersed in scalding water were described as "gruesome"
and "appalling" by Gerald Pratley, a respected film critic for the Canadian
Broadcasting Corporation,[5] a view echoed by the Canadian *United Church Ob-*

server, which found the film's crude stereotyping contained the worst excesses of racist propaganda seen in any movie since the end of the Second World War.[6]

The Legion noted these derogatory comments with displeasure, hailing *Guilty of Treason* as "worthy of every commendation," and it threw itself enthusiastically into the campaign to make it a success.[7] This capsule comment was a rare deviation from normal procedure, of course, since only negative aspects of a picture were customarily highlighted. The Church's imprimatur was further emphasized at a special presentation in the Waldorf Astoria hotel in New York on December 27, 1949. Five hundred members of the press and assorted dignitaries were treated to lobster thermidor and champagne, followed by ringing endorsements for the picture from Cardinal Spellman and Clare Booth Luce prior to screening. Just who was responsible for this largesse added an aura of mystery to an already mysterious production, since the Overseas Press Club, under whose auspices it was held, was a modest operation with funds as befitted its status.[8] The evening ended with Bishop Scully of the Episcopal Committee urging the faithful to make every use of the film in their parishes "to alert public opinion to the dangers and methods used by the anti-God forces arrayed against us." A full-color, twenty-page comic book presenting Mindszenty's ordeal, intended for juveniles, was hurried into publication and made available to churches at cost, nine cents a copy, by the Catechical Guild.[9]

For all the money and energy expended in promoting *Guilty of Treason* (Freedom Productions budgeted $50,000 on publicity in the Boston area alone), the returns were disappointing, as the public remained indifferent. Even a revamped publicity campaign playing down the religious angle and featuring a lightly clad Bonita Granville in bondage dangling over a cauldron of boiling water had little impact other than embarrassing Martin Quigley, who had been one of the film's enthusiastic sponsors.[10] By the summer of 1950 it was decided to cut losses and consign the ordeal of the cardinal to the vaults.[11]

Undismayed, the Legion continued its enthusiastic advocacy of "Red-baiting" movies, although the Legion naturally viewed them in a more positive light than that. The Legion's esteem owed something to a favorite standby of the genre, the inclusion of an understanding priest. An omniscient father was ever ready with a word of consolation for the disillusioned atheist or the lapsed Catholic who, in *The Red Menace*, had sold her body to lure hot-blooded but unwary males into the Communist party. Elsewhere, he might have a homily to refute dogmas and disconcert the rabid Marxist. Among other conventions of the series was the conceit that if one really wished to escape from the Communist snare, the FBI and the Catholic Church were the Tweedledum and Tweedledee of confessionals. Both were ready and eager to listen to the outpourings of disillusioned Reds. A Barry Fitzgerald type sometimes acted as a link between the undercover agent and the government, dispensing blarney and encouragement in sizable dollops.

As well as bestowing unstinting praise on the movies themselves, the Legion subscribed to the dictum that eternal vigilance is the price paid for eternal freedom, scrutinizing those few fellow travelers and Red sympathizers who had not been caught up in HUAC's net. In his *Annual Report* for 1952, Masterson cautioned against intemperate haste in forgiving those who had declared their apostasy in public. Elia Kazan and actress Judy Holliday were among several claiming to have seen the light, but Masterson felt that their reliability could only be gauged by proof of future good behavior. For those who had taken the Fifth Amendment when asked to admit to treachery, there could be no sympathy. Their deviousness in manipulating the Constitution for base ends put them beyond the pale. To allow them to remain, or return, as popular screen entertainers where they could surreptitiously continue to poison the public mind was unthinkable, and if they had to choose between the Scylla of public obloquy and the Charybdis of exile abroad, so be it. America would be well rid of them. The report contained a note of resignation over the failure of these laudable, ostentatiously anti-Communist pictures to reap their merited reward at the box office. Semi-documentary accounts of brave men forced underground to live the lives of "slimy Reds" in order to thwart Moscow-orchestrated plans for the ruination of the American economy (as Matt Cvetic had done in *I Was a Communist for the F.B.I.*) left the theatergoing public cold. Not even John Wayne's dispensation of justice to Hawaiian traitors in his own, inimitable, two-fisted manner could energize a complacent public. There was a prickly aggressiveness about Masterson's interpretation of the situation. The willful refusal of the average citizen to absorb the lessons of these movies he attributed, in part, to the lack of enthusiasm on the part of the studios.[12] To have had to produce these films at all was regarded as sufficient penance by Warners et al., without their having to embark on a publicity campaign for them as well. Much blame also accrued to lukewarm and even hostile press reviews, which the Legion chief felt were yet another manifestation of "leftist pressures in the media."[13] Masterson failed to note one irony in his stance. While the Legion had always been quick to denigrate sex hygiene and anthropological documentaries for their purported educational value, holding that motion pictures were essentially an entertainment medium, right-wing indoctrination was apparently exempt.

It was a measure of the meteoric rise and fall of Senator McCarthy that the spate of anti-Red movies dried to a trickle within a year of his public humiliation. Science fiction had already replaced them with beings from outer space seeking to dominate the planet as the allegorical Communists, though how many moviegoers made the connection is hard to calculate. There were even a few glimmers of recognition of the excesses of the era and of the need to make amends. One of the first was *Storm Center* (1956). Its realization, even three years before, would have been inconceivable. Its positive reception in the press was an indication that the tide of reaction was ebbing.

Storm Center deals with a middle-aged, spinsterish, small-town librarian who defends the right of a pro-Communist book to remain on the shelves in the teeth of opposition from the city council and other dignitaries. When faced with the choice of removing the polluted volume or losing her job, she elects to resign. A mentally troubled child then proceeds to torch the library, at which point a chastened citizenry, recalling Nazi-era book burnings, rallies behind her to rebuild and restock the book in question, *The Communist Dream*. The original idea came from two well-known scriptwriters, Daniel Taradash and Julian Blaustein, and dated from the darkest days of the Hollywood Inquisition. It would surely have been one of the most intriguing comebacks in the annals of screen entertainment if Mary Pickford had acted on impulse and taken the part. Stanley Kramer, Hollywood's most liberal producer in that era, got as far as casting Barbara Stanwyck, but could not obtain financing. Not until Taradash and Blaustein formed their own company, Phoenix, with Bette Davis as the librarian, was the project brought to fruition.

Truth to tell, there was precious little that was daring in *Storm Center*. Even the volume at the center of the controversy is described by the librarian as so laughingly inept that a cursory reading by the most gullible would expose the follies and contradictions of Marxist philosophy. Nevertheless, the Legion was most unhappy at the news of its release and determined to launch an attack. Others might have been feeling remorse for their silence during the excesses of the McCarthy era; it, on the other hand, was prepared to stay on guard against manifestations of unregenerate liberalism on the screen. In mounting its offensive, it began by exhuming the past indiscretions of Blaustein. Some judicious research by the indefatigable William Mooring revealed that he had been cited in the 1948 Tenney Report of the California Senate Inquiry on Community Influences for "association with Leftist causes."[14] When Paul J. Hayes, the Legion's new executive assistant, contacted Columbia, which had agreed to distribute the picture with some reluctance, as to why it had made this unpatriotic gesture, he was given a guarded explanation. Top-flight writers were a precious commodity. Harry Cohn, the studio chief, had allowed the duo to "get the picture out of their system" in return for completing more conventional scripts.[15] Little was not placated and determined to give it the lowest rating possible. As was customary with political films, sex, nudity, bad language and kindred elements were conspicuously absent, thus ruling out a B or C. The best the Legion could do was to impose the Separate Classification, with the rider that "the highly propagandistic nature of the film (book burning, anti-Communism, civil liberties) offers a warped, oversimplified and strongly emotional solution to a complex problem of American life. Its specious arguments tend seriously to be misleading and misrepresentative by reason of an inept and distorted presentation."[16]

This was strong medicine, but right-wing elements of the Catholic press rallied to the cause, providing equally scathing analyses. The *Sign* called it "pure hokum, badly written, acted in harried style and about as convincing as a 1956 repudiation of Stalin. The left-wing apologists can do better than this."[17] Mooring questioned whether any sympathy should be spared for the librarian character, a city employee who countermands the orders of duly elected city fathers to remove a subversive book from a public, tax-supported institution. The answer was obviously a negative, but it could spur real-life imitators to commit similar infractions. Father John B. Sheerin in *New World* mused as to whether the picture was really about freedom of expression, as Bette Davis had insisted in one of her rare public appearances in Washington to defend it, or whether it was "a cunning argument to allow the state to countenance printed filth and treason."[18] For the Legion, a depressing feature of the debate was the relative indifference of the public. There were condemnatory letters in the columns of several right-wing journals. But *Storm Center* remained a curio of the fifties with no sequel.

Only among the old guard did suspicions of liberal domination of the medium die hard. When Stanley Kramer's *On the Beach* debuted in 1959, some Legion members grumbled that its antiwar message about the fate of a handful of survivors of World War III was potentially damaging to the morale of the American people and the fine reputation of the military by equating the consequences of nuclear warfare with racial suicide.

THE MOON IS BLUE

The Broadway stage in 1950 was busy, self-confident and prosperous. A substantial number of straight plays competed for the audience's dollar with some memorable musicals. F. Hugh Herbert's *The Moon Is Blue* was typical. It was a comedy of manners with charming, stylishly clothed, middle-class characters exchanging witticisms amid nice furniture. The plot spoofed seduction and virginity but in an ever-so-genteel manner. A successful architect picks up a girl atop the Empire State Building and finds a way to lure her back to his apartment. There she enunciates her views on romance, sex and marriage in a frank but disarming manner with lines like "Lots of girls don't mind being seduced," "Men are usually bored with virgins," and "Most bachelors have mistresses. Have you?" Despite her candor, she remains in the virginal state herself and eventually elicits a marriage proposal from the captivated architect. His friend, a seedy, middle-aged wolf, is also reformed in the process.

Herbert, and stage director Otto Preminger, tried to interest first Warners and then Paramount in a screen version, only to be turned down because both perceived that the cavalier approach to sex and marriage would raise major issues with the Production Code Administration. Undaunted, the two formed their own production company and made an agreement with United Artists for distribution.[19] As those in the know had predicted, a seal of approval was denied because of the use of the words "virgin," "seduce," and "pregnant." In blue-penciling the phrase "You are shallow, cynical, selfish, and immoral and I like you!" Breen had acidly noted that the Code did not permit someone to be simultaneously immoral and likable. In short, the picture promoted "low forms of sex relationship," as prohibited by the Code. A more pliant director might have gone the well-worn route of compromise and revision. Preminger was not of that breed. An autocrat of the old school, a Viennese Fritz Lang, his imperiousness on-stage and off brooked no opposition. His screen adaptation had followed the stage version closely and to have complied with Breen would have meant major emasculation. He was adamant that the film version would stand except for a sop to moralists in the form of a closing remark by the roué on the shortcomings of leading an immoral life. Less, asserted Preminger, would rob it of "the outspoken freshness of the original."[20] After the PCA had given a categorical thumbs down, Preminger had his New York lawyer, Samuel Rosenman, plead its case before the Appeals Board. The argument would be that the story was essentially a moral one since the heroine remains unsullied throughout and wins a husband for her stance. Rosenman was an ironic choice for the mission since it was he who had opposed Howard Hughes over the withholding of a seal for *The Outlaw*, but he felt that justice and changing morality were on his side on this occasion. The rationale failed to convince. Nicholas Schenck of Loews voiced one collective opinion: "I wouldn't let my daughter see it. It's true that the girl is not seduced in the time she spends with the boy, but other girls in a similar situation might get closer to the flame." Another held that the heroine's lack of a chaperon when she visits the apartment was a signal to youth that trysts were morally permissible. Nor was virginity a laughing matter in the eyes of millions of respectable mothers of daughters. The appeal was denied.

Some commentators on Legion policy in the *The Moon Is Blue* affair have professed to see its support of Breen as a gesture of solidarity in unstable times rather than springing from any deeply held conviction that the picture was irremediably corrupt. This interpretation is based on a sentence in a confidential memorandum sent to diocesan directors on July 11, 1953 announcing the Condemned classification. The wording intimates that the film's commercial success could be fatal to the Production Code's future position as a bulwark against the rising tide of screen immorality. It is also suggested that the Legion would have been quite prepared to grant a B, which a small majority of reviewers had recommended after a June 9 viewing. However, there is evidence that leaves room for doubt, starting with Quigley's appeal to United Artists' president Arthur Krim to alter the movie despite Preminger's objections. This was made while *Moon* was still in the production stage. Quigley's objection was based on the conviction that it advocated "free love."[21] In a lengthy missive that Little penned a few days after Masterson's sudden death on June 9, he excoriated the film both for its dialogue and, far more dangerously, for its clever exposition of a morally degenerate plot by superficially sympathetic characters. "The pattern of living and behavior" wrote the new executive secretary, "is so attractively portrayed as to arouse in the mind of the viewer an acceptance of what might easily lead to a breakdown in public and private morality." As such, it constituted "an overthrow of the religious and moral training of youths and adults alike."[22]

The Legion's customary artillery was pressed into service to destroy *The Moon Is Blue*'s chance of success. Cardinal Spellman gave what now seemed like his obligatory injunction against attending on pain of sin while Legion chapters throughout the country were urged to organize letter-writing campaigns in schools. Picketing of theaters, noting the names and addresses of Catholics daring to attend and delivering them to the local priest, and the plethora of miscellaneous protests that the ingeniously minded could devise were all utilized. Unfortunately from the Legion's standpoint, some of its guns were spiked from the outset by a combination of circumstances, some unforeseen, others antici-pated but difficult to control.

Of immediate concern was a review of the picture in the July issue of the Oregon-based *St. Joseph's Magazine*, whose comparative obscurity did not prevent it from grandly billing itself as "America's Catholic Family Monthly." The young critic, Richard Hayes, had been embarrassingly fulsome in his praise of the picture, predicting that this "delicious adaptation . . . will surely figure in any moviegoer's list of the brightest and most originally charming comedies of the year, with its impudent wit and some wise common sense concealed beneath a candied surface."[23] Too, there was the awkward fact that the by-then defunct Catholic Theater Movement, a play-classifying equivalent of the Legion that borrowed its nomenclature, had given Herbert's comedy a B rating. Oversha-dowing both of these was the consequence of the so-called Divorcement decree. First announced by the Supreme Court in 1948 but implemented tardily by the major film companies, it forced them to divest themselves of their theater chains, thus ending the vertical combination of production, distribution and exhibition that had constituted a cartel since the early twenties. Now that these exhibitors were no longer in thrall to the big studios, they were in a position to show non-seal pictures if they had hit potential. While this freedom had been assumed since 1942, a sort of gentleman's agreement operated, whereby only Code-approved pictures were screened. But in an era of diminishing attendance, exclusion was a luxury that many could no longer afford. United Artists had also broken away from the ranks of the MPPA. That raised the possibility of *Moon* receiving exposure greater than that accorded to any previous seal-less picture. A perusal of the hundred-plus C-rated titles on the Legion's roll of dishonor to that date would have revealed that it contained not a single product of a major studio, a situation that was about to change. Finally, and perhaps most troubling of all, through word of mouth there was a perception among the rank and file of Legion members that they were being denied access to a harmless little comedy whose content paled in comparison with that of an ever-increasing number of sex dramas coming from overseas.

The most pressing issue demanding attention was the intemperate notice in *St. Joseph's Magazine* that might cause public confusion if allowed to stand. Indeed, an eagle-eyes advertising executive with United Artists had spotted the accolade and ordered existing publicity materials withdrawn and revamped to include the flattering quote. The obscure Oregonian critic now found himself in the august company of kindred spirits from *Life*, *Newsweek*, and *Variety*, all of whom had given positive reviews, though his fame was to be short-lived. A request came from Cardinal Spellman to the archbishop of Portland requesting that this independent spirit be disciplined.[24] There were extenuating circumstances. Hays had to submit his copy three weeks in advance of the magazine's publication date and so had been forced to review the picture prior to announcement of the Legion rating. He was also aware of the Catholic Theater Movement's less censorious classification of the play which, he assumed, would be mirrored in the Legion appraisal. His expression of remorse duly appeared in the August issue, carrying some of the hallmarks of a purge trial confession. He admitted to "insensitivity" and "misjudgment" and deferred "with great respect to those who have disagreed with me and disputed my estimation."[25] Even so, Little felt that there was a touch of proud humility in the apology and that this errant son's self-abasement could have been more complete had he recognized the harm he had done the Legion.[26]

For all the energy expended in keeping *The Moon Is Blue* off American screens, the specter of the Supreme Court decision in the *The Miracle* case hung heavily over the scene. A challenge to a Maryland censorship board ban was successfully upheld by a Baltimore judge who called the action "arbitrary and capricious" and found the picture "neither obscene, indecent or immoral but a story of virtue triumphant." In a coda he hinted that too many boards were inclined to take their cue from "pressure groups." Only three days after this blow, a Hudson grand jury declined to accept a charge of obscenity brought by the Jersey City police department, which had seized a print from the Stanley Theater and forced its closure. In Kansas City, Judge Harry G. Miller, Jr. struck down a 1917 ordinance that gave the local board of review the power to ban films without reason, thereby allowing *Moon* to play after a year's delay.

By the fall of 1954 Little had to admit that the Legion had gone down to resounding defeat for the first time in its existence. By then, Maggie McNamara's spunky behavior had been seen in 8,813 movie houses, with an additional 3,928 still awaiting the pleasure. In the process, she had earned around $4 million for the Herbert-Preminger company, or ten times the production cost, making it a hugely profitable enterprise. What these statistics implied was even bleaker on close examination. Receipts in areas with a heavily Catholic population were proportionately as large as elsewhere. All the protestations and admonitions had failed to keep a significant number of Legion members from ignoring their pledge on this occasion. For the first time, too, letters protesting the classification outnumbered those approving.[27] The thinking common to most was that Preminger's little picture was harmless even in relation to many higher-rated domestic titles, including Marilyn Monroe's *Niagara*, a portrait of postmarital restlessness at its most scandalous. A thought crossing many minds was expressed by Msgr. Ferdinand Falque of Minneapolis, for whom *The Moon Is Blue* was "a marvellous argument against promiscuity in sex enunciated by a girl who has a clean and natural attitude towards marriage." Every argument against it seemed to prove how wrong millions of Americans were in their hypocritical, double-standard attitude toward the male-female relationship.[28]

Little was unrepentant, insisting that his decision was the correct one. The time had not yet come when dissident voices were able to impose their will.[29] Meanwhile, there was battle to be done with that perpetual thorn in Legion flesh, Howard Hughes.

THE FRENCH LINE

In its fight to retain its share of an increasingly fragmented audience for entertainment, Hollywood seized on any gimmick. The early part of the fifties saw a frantic clutching at straws to arrest the downward trend in attendance and lure the lost millions from their still temperamental black-and-white television sets. A less partisan advocate of innovation than those who clustered around worried studio heads could have warned boosters of Odorama or "the smellies" that it was doomed. The idea of flooding a theater with the odor of whatever happened to appear on screen at the moment, be it sizzling bacon or a garden of roses, created impossible logistical problems for theaters, never mind its limited application. Cinerama, with a gigantic, curved screen that almost encompassed those sitting near it was horrendously expensive to install and profitability depended on a steady stream of visual spectaculars in a format that, as it turned out, could not be supplied. CinemaScope, a Twentieth Century Fox patent of a French invention, had a mailbox-shaped screen and was the poor man's Cinerama. It did, however, have the advantage of greater versatility and lower cost, lending itself to the portrayal of full-color spectacles that television could not offer. But from 1951 to 1954 many bets were on three-dimensional pictures or "3D," which gave the illusion of depth. The first full-length picture in the format, a dim white-hunter-versus-lion tale, *B'wana Devil*, was a surprise hit that triggered a rush by the major studios to adopt the format. The dramatic potential of the process was never explored with any intelligence. Instead, audiences were bombarded by blazing arrows, hypodermic needles, swords and, in the nadir of taste, a stream of tobacco juice expectorated by a cowboy. Moviegoers also objected to having to wear the tinted glasses without which the images were just a blur. By 1954 the craze was declining as rapidly as it had risen. The films themselves were unexceptional, and a decade later it would be hard to recall a single 3D title. The possible exception was *The French Line*, a comedy with musical numbers interjected. Its notoriety stemmed not from its technical format but from its salaciousness.

The French Line was a Howard Hughes production made in the RKO studio he had bought in 1947. Under his erratic stewardship RKO had lurched from crisis to financial crisis pretty much as in the past. By 1952 it was averaging losses of $5 million annually.[30] Much of the blame could be laid at the door of Hughes himself. There had been no diminution of idiosyncratic methods employed by this eccentric Texas millionaire in producing movies. He had tinkered interminably with *Jet Pilot*, an absurd Cold War drama about a defecting female Russian pilot, Janet Leigh, and her U.S. Air Force interlocutor, John Wayne, delaying its release for three years, by which time most of the interest had dissipated. The director of *Where Danger Lives*, John Farrow, was driven to distraction because of Hughes's constant interference in the scenes in which his latest discovery, Faith Domergue, appeared. By 1953 disgruntled stockholders were beginning to ask awkward questions. Hughes turned to the woman who had brought him his greatest commercial success, *The Outlaw*. Jane Russell was to be cast as Mary, a Texas oil millionairess, whose wealth scares off potential suitors. Told that France is the land of romance, she takes a transatlantic trip, pretending to be a poor fashion model on her way to Paris to look for work. The ploy succeeds. On board ship she meets a Latin smoothie, Gilbert Roland, and true love wins out an enervating hour and half and a dozen musical numbers later. The slim plot and generally banal aspect of the picture gave no indication of the torrent of wrath it was about to unleash.

A procedural flaw in the Production Code gave primacy to script rather than visuals. Most PCA staff time was spent minutely analyzing dialogue, leaving the pictorial aspect to be dealt with at a later stage or even on completion of the picture. The plot synopsis that Hughes submitted gave every indication of an innocuous entertainment, and the number of deletions requested was small—a few double entendres and a running joke centered on the homosexual proclivities of a minor character. But when Breen watched *The French Line* in its entirety in November 1953, he was forcibly reminded of Hughes's breast fetishism. The female cast had been chosen for its collective ability to sustain the extremes of décolletage costuming. As for Russell, the outfits she wore made her peasant blouses in *The Outlaw* seem positively decorous by comparison. When she was not threatening to spill out of a low-cut swimsuit, she was executing a striptease on the run behind assorted pieces of furniture or splashing provocatively in a bathtub. And, for good measure, the whole was served up in the 3D format, which projected Russell's bust in astonishing fashion. As the *Motion Picture Daily* remarked,

Whatever you may have imagined the three dimensional camera might be made to do with subject matter like this has been done—at long range, in middle distance and closeup. Miss Russell's is by no means the only bosom explored to the utmost by the cinematographer's roving lens, but it is she alone who performs down near the close of the picture a dance of declared desire which as hasn't been seen on any unrestrictedly public screen in all those 50-odd years.[31]

The accompanying publicity kits were hardly less objectionable, with a poster of Russell learning forward to expose as much of her torso as possible, with captions that read "J. R. in 3-D. That's all!" and "Jane Russell in Three Dimension—and What Dimensions!"

When Breen and his staff agreed that a seal of approval was out of the question without drastic revisions, Hughes's response was to emulate Preminger and release the picture without it. He, too, was undoubtedly drawing comfort from the instability of the censorship scene attendant upon the *The Miracle* and *La*

Ronde decisions. Perhaps he anticipated some general relaxation of standards that would severely weaken the PCA and cause large parts of the Code to become redundant. At the same time, one should not underestimate Hughes's perception of his own strength in the existing order. With his unlimited funds, he could launch a publicity campaign based on the forbidden fruit aspect of his movie, since there was little else to commend it, as most reviewers were at pains to impress on their readerships. The Legion certainly presented a stumbling block, but Hughes saw it as an aging ship that was beginning to spring a dozen leaks. To plug each hole was an exhausting business. Father Little had not had a single day's relaxation since Masterson's death and was busy coping with *The Moon Is Blue*. As more and more "unsuitable" pictures kept appearing, the Legion might die of its own exertions, or—and this was an equally rosy prospect—fail to deter a new generation less in thrall to the Church than its parents had been.

His optimism was rewarded initially when *The French Line* debuted at the Fox Theater in St. Louis on December 29, 1953, without having been rated by the Legion. The choice of venue was a brazen one: the city had a Catholic population of over four hundred thousand. The first day's receipts were $6,924, the largest grossed by any RKO film in its history and its best opening day in six years. If enough venues could be found, the $1.4 million cost would be recouped in the domestic market by the end of the following summer, and there was still the overseas market, where its lurid reputation would precede it. The most that the PCA seemed able to do was to call for a $25,000 fine, a paltry amount to a multimillionaire with a hit on his hands. Even Jane Russell's public act of self-abasement was helping in a perverse way. She told the press that she had "beefed and argued" over certain scenes. As for the skimpy clothes, she had had "an awful time with the dance costumes they wanted me to wear. They were really bad . . . hardly anything at all."[32] Hughes exulted that every time his star opened her mouth, receipts grew at the box office.

It was clear that the Catholic Church was the main bulwark between decent screen entertainment and a renegade motion picture. The first salvo in the war was an announcement read in all St. Louis churches urging ostracism. Archbishop Joseph E. Ritter's pastoral letter went further than usual in forbidding attendance under penalty of mortal sin.[33] So far the center of agitation had been in the one city. Whether Hughes would bow to such pressure if implemented on a nationwide scale was not clear, but the Legion was willing to proffer the olive branch before it enjoined the faithful to choose between Jane Russell and eternal damnation. There was a visible Catholic presence among the higher echelons of RKO. James Grainger, its president (Hughes was chairman), was prominent in Church circles while his son, Edward, who had produced *The French Line*, was a graduate of St. Francis Xavier and Fordham Universities—a sad example of the permissiveness that had overtaken these institutions of higher learning, lamented one cleric.[34] During an extended conversation with the senior Grainger, Little was appraised of the situation from the other side of the barricades. Hughes firmly believed that he was being persecuted by the Catholic Church as much for past sins as for authorship of *The French Line*, and that Ritter's injunction had been composed in advance of the picture's appearance. The edict was "a violation of Christian charity towards someone who had donated over one hundred million dollars of his own fortune to needy causes." As for the refusal to grant a seal, that had been the petty, vindictive action of Breen, "a sick man ready to retire" and "his underpaid assistants who compensated for their poverty by throwing their weight around with moneyed people." Grainger was far from sanguine over the chance of a requested revision in the torrid dance sequence which, he calculated, would cost over a quarter of a million dollars to reshoot. Little acidly observed that since RKO had already reaped "a billion dollars' worth of publicity," this would be but a minimal concession to propriety.[35]

Hopes of a reconciliation between the two parties continued to flicker for a few weeks longer. A company press release announced that the film would be withdrawn from St. Louis—so far its only venue—on January 18, 1954, and that plans were afoot to submit a reconstituted version to the PCA. Then, with the typical quirkiness he had shown in the past, Hughes reneged on both promises. His decision may have had something to do with the product shortage that was facing exhibitors. Output in Hollywood was sharply lower in response to declining attendance, making the theaters scramble for anything that had staying power. Sam Goldwyn had just detonated a verbal bomb by questioning the relevance of the twenty-year-old Code, advocating its updating at the very least. Breen was plainly seen to be in ill health from a persistent back ailment and lung disease. In combination, all of these portents might bring the rickety edifice that was American film censorship tumbling down. Attractive through the prospect seemed, it ignored sour reality. *The French Line* was not the stuff of a libertarian crusade. Compared to those deeply felt Italian neorealist works that had encountered similar opposition, it was an overblown peep show, not worth defending on artistic or any other grounds. It did not even possess the minimal wit of *The Moon Is Blue*. Desperation to survive would someday galvanize the exhibition side of the industry to rise against Breen's successor and the Legion, but that day was not yet at hand.

Meanwhile, the Legion had just begun to fight. When news reached New York that Russell was still packing them in at the Fox and was about to go nationwide, Little announced the C rating with a pointed reminder of the mortal sin injunction from St. Louis the previous fall. On Scully's recommendation, the high and mighty of the land were canvassed.[36] These included Senator Edwin C. Johnson of Colorado, whose bill to license all actors, directors and producers had chilled the industry, and J. Edgar Hoover of the FBI. Hoover expressed sympathy for the Church's aims but regretted that movie censorship lay outside his jurisdiction. Johnson praised the Legion for being the only effective body in the land that could stem the tide of filth that the *The Miracle* decision had allowed to flow freely. Local dioceses were given another carte blanche to adopt whatever tactics they thought would work. In Buffalo the Legion branch inundated the Lafayette Theater with so many phone calls and letters of complaint that extra help had to be brought in. The content of some of the material, much of it anonymous, was abusive. None were more alarming than those that treated staff to lurid descriptions of what awaited them in hell for allowing *The French Line* to defile the city and one in particular which prophesied that God would visit cancer on the projectionist for his sins. In Pittsburgh the Holy Names Society targeted Gerald McShea, manager of the Fulton, who was warned that he would be refused the sacraments if he persisted in showing the film. Priests in Greenwich, Connecticut formed a procession and marched three abreast before the Pickwick with placards reading "Save Your Children from Moral Polio" and "Help Save America from Moral Filth."[37] A cartoon syndicated in much of the Catholic press showed a disheveled, unshaven Howard Hughes leading two skunks by a leash down a deserted street past doors marked "decency" that had been slammed in his face.[38]

Too late, Hughes began to cut his picture according to its destination. In states notorious for the severity of their censorship he actually removed more than Breen had asked for. When word of mouth revealed that the spicy bits had disappeared, the crowds began to thin. Not even the RKO chain would book it. What public reaction failed to achieve, indifferent and hostile reviews completed. In what had been a dismal year for the forces of public morality not only in movies but in literature and magazines, there could be some satisfaction with a job well done.

Illness finally took its toll on the veteran chief of the PCA. There was a distinct feeling of trepidation within Legion ranks at the passing of the torch from the hands of the physically ailing Breen to Geoffrey Shurlock in February 1954. Shurlock's Anglicanism was not exactly held against him but it was nonetheless deemed significant enough for inclusion and comment in Little's generally disquieting *Annual Report* for 1955. It deplored the rapid lowering of standards that seemed to have followed this changing of the guard and left a nagging doubt that differences between Code and Legion might not have widened to the same degree had someone of the Catholic faith still been in charge. Faced with a mounting number of objectionable titles, Little went to Hollywood in February 1954 to acquaint the new head of the Production Code as well as studio heads with his concerns. In private conversations and press statements he intimated that the Church and, by definition, his organization, would be forced to take a serious stand reminiscent of its position in the early thirties unless evidence were forthcoming of a willingness on the industry's part "to ameliorate film fare from a moral point of view."[39] Skeptical of claims that television was making serious inroads and balkanizing audiences to the extent claimed by the companies, he continued to harp on the need for family-oriented pictures as of yore, for which the Legion and Breen had rightly taken credit. To doomsayers who talked of days that would never return, Little's response was direct though ingenuously wrapped in statistics purporting to show that wholesome, uplifting A-rated fare consistently out-performed the rest. In 1954, he pointed out, fifteen of eighteen pictures grossing $4 million and upwards had been so classified, and if one really wanted to delve into the past, it would be to discover that eighteen of twenty-six Oscar winners since 1928 had been so favorably viewed by the Legion.[40]

This sanguine assessment of what would continue to attract customers was not shared by the moviemakers or by the trade press. Instead of the ninety million weekly admissions recorded in 1947, only thirty million had bought tickets in any equivalent period in 1954, and the situation was deteriorating. Box office receipts were stagnant or, at best, marginally higher, but only because admission prices continued their inexorable and necessary upward climb. With the abject failure of Odorama, 3D and similar forgettable gimmicks, the search for a winning formula continued. Historical epics in color, with stars, crowds and other lavish production values gave audiences spectacles that the black-and-white television set, still limited to showing B features, could not provide. But the "idiot box" in the living room seemed to have a hypnotic effect in confining people to their chairs for many and varied types of entertainment, to which the skyrocketing advertising revenues of the three networks bore witness. Furthermore, epics were expensive to make and a single failure could have calamitous consequences for the studio—as *Cleopatra* was shortly to prove for Twentieth Century Fox. If, as surveys tended to verify, the shrunken movie theater audience was no longer family-oriented but rather composed primarily of teens and young adults in their twenties, the Code and the Legion with their inflexible standards and outmoded attitudes were dangerous obstacles in the way of supplying this market with more mature movie themes. Utterances in the recent past of Sam Goldwyn and Eric Johnston, head of the MPAA and successor to Hays, to the effect that the Code had stayed still while the world moved on, underlined the notion. The press eagerly seized on the possibility of a potential rift between Legion and Code, former allies in the decency wars.

Shurlock was in a paradoxical situation. On the one hand he had a great deal of sympathy for those chafing under a set of regulations that a quarter of a century and two major wars had possibly rendered anachronistic. He privately indicated his willingness to go out on a limb for the worthy title that broke moth-eaten taboos. On the other hand, he was unwilling to let his office be used by tasteless Young Turks as a magic wand, one wave of which would sweep away all vestiges of the Hays era. Equally, and out of a sense of self-respect, he could not allow himself to be regarded as an ineffectual successor to the formidable Breen, to be bypassed by contemptuous studio executives on their way to deal with the real power in the censorship stakes, the Legion. In private he assured Little that his attacks on declining moral values in contemporary American filmmaking were appreciated because they would provide him with a strong weapon in negotiations with producers and directors. Recalcitrant filmmakers could still be threatened with the bogeyman in New York if they thought they could bully or bypass the Production Code Administration.[41]

The inescapable perception that the balance had tilted in the Legion's direction was made apparent in a plea to Little from the *Hollywood Reporter* that it change the procedure under which it vetted films. Prefaced with a suggestion for "a meeting of the minds" between the Legion and the PCA, the editorial went on to suggest that the existing situation by which only completed pictures were judged in New York was frustrating and costly to the studios. Recourse should be had to Msgr. Devlin and the Los Angeles branch to watch an answer print and make an on-site decision before hundreds of copies were struck and shipped to exchanges for release.[42] *Variety* reported that it was mention of the Legion, not Shurlock, that brought pained expressions to the faces of studio executives. It ran from the anonymously subservient, "If they want to cut one of our pictures in half, and if I feel it'll make more money that way simply because Catholics will then go to see it, I'm all for cutting it," to Robert Aldrich who feared that, with a weakened Code, the virus of religious interference might become contagious. "Sooner or later," he affirmed, "some other organized camp is going to catch on to the idea that by loud threats they'll get Hollywood to toe their particular line."[43] Aldrich spoke from recent bitter experience, having been forced to make major cuts in his Mickey Spillane thriller, *Kiss Me Deadly*, including a complete change in the ending, in order to earn it a B. Yet if the Legion was a threat to the mice, no one seemed brave enough to bell the cat. In 1954, a Screen Producers Guild plan to establish a committee to assess Legion influence and recommend possible steps for its diminution had failed to find more than one member of the film community with enough temerity to serve and risk possible retribution. The project had been abandoned. And, as if that were not confession enough of impotence, the action of two of the mightiest studios put the issue beyond doubt. In the summer of 1955 MGM inserted a clause in its distribution contract with independent producers making it mandatory that they deliver their finished product to the parent company with nothing in it that would merit worse than a B rating. Under the regulation, a maverick filmmaker was to be held liable for all expenses incurred in making the necessary changes. This, and a similar move by United Artists giving it the right to call bank loans on a filmmaker who would not alter a C picture, created an ominous precedent whereby producers would now face financial penalties if they failed to meet censorial standards as well as those imposed by the Production Code. It made doubly urgent the implementation of a mechanism for preclearance since the same court-decreed freedom that had been accorded to motion pictures such as *The Miracle* and *La Ronde*, had been applied to literature. There were several book titles, such as Norman Mailer's 1948 novel, *The Naked and the Dead*, awaiting screen adaptation, but any film version of a controversial book carried a huge risk for the buyer of rights unless he was prepared to bowdlerize it heavily.

Little refused to move or be moved. The mountain would continue to come to Mohammed: The center of gravity would remain in New York, for it was there that pictures would continue to be judged. As he saw it, there were enough old heads in charge in Hollywood to know what would pass muster and parameters of acceptability were in abundance to serve as guides to those newcomers not yet familiar with Legion dictates. While the Production Code Administration might be in a temporary state of flux, it could regain the respect it had enjoyed of yore simply by flexing its muscles and returning to the precepts of the recently departed Breen. The fencing game of how much to ask for and how much to give would continue to be played. There were lots of projects on the drawing board that everyone knew, in advance, would merit no better than a B rating. It was up to Hollywood to tailor its cloth accordingly and up to Shurlock to prove his mettle by wielding the right amount of scissors.[44]

TEA AND SYMPATHY

One manifestation of the loosening of Code strictures in response to changing social attitudes was a slight concession in regarding adultery as a necessary, and not wholly reprehensible, vehicle for plot resolution. Another was the theme of homosexuality (or the "pansy flavor" as it was unofficially referred to in the censors' vocabulary), which could now be vaguely alluded to although it still could not be condoned under any circumstance.

These grudgingly given relaxations permitted MGM to film Robert Anderson's stage play, *Tea and Sympathy*, in 1955 after a considerable effort on the author's part to adjust the original to meet PCA requirements. The Broadway success dealt with a prep-school student, Tom, whose sensitivity and aversion to manly sports like football are the despair of his father and cause the lad to question his sexuality. He is reportedly seen sunbathing in the nude with a teacher suspected of harboring homosexual desires, and he confesses to a love of poetry. A visit to a "cheap waitress" ends in disaster when he finds himself unable to consummate the sex act. It is not until the sympathetic and unhappily married wife of his housemaster, Mrs. Reynolds, offers herself to him that his problem is resolved. The curtain rings down dramatically on the two about to go to bed together.[45]

Metro knew only too well that, as it stood, the plot would never pass muster even with a liberated PCA and, having paid Anderson $200,000 for the screen rights, it set him to work on a revision. His solution to the one issue was to equate the boy's behavior with effeminacy rather than homosexuality, dropping all reference to the nude sunbathing incident and having him, instead, sew a button on his shirt in the company of wives of the teaching staff. Mrs. Reynolds' adulterous act posed as great a problem, requiring some compensatory value. This was ingeniously achieved with a flashback. The movie begins with the now-adult Tom returning to school ten years later as a successful novelist, husband and father of three. He is handed a letter by the embittered housemaster written by his wife, now long gone and living alone "somewhere outside of Chicago." In a voice-over she tells him of "the wrong we did" and of how it ruined her marriage without bringing any happiness. She confesses that she erred in being unfaithful instead of allowing Tom to find another way out of his sexual predicament.

For Anderson and the studio this seemed penance enough, since the woman had paid for her transgression with a life of misery and loneliness. Shurlock concurred.[46] Not so the Legion. In an unusual break with precedent, Little had written Nicholas Schenck, MGM's president, while filming was still in progress, voicing concern over the story changes. By tradition, the Legion confined itself to the scrutiny of completed pictures awaiting general release. The alterations to *Tea and Sympathy*, as the Legion understood them, appeared to be "only a coloration of the incidents and hence no elimination of the grounds for serious moral objection."[47] For good measure, a copy of this was sent to Shurlock to alert him to the potential gravity of the situation. The move both delighted and vindicated Martin Quigley who, as part-time advisor to MGM, had adamantly opposed buying the property. For all the scrubbing of the original, the odor of homosexuality must still, of necessity, cling to the plot as a pivotal mechanism. Though it was difficult to object to the housemaster's wife denouncing the cruelty of Tom's schoolmates in calling him "Sister Boy," said Quigley, this was exactly the line of reasoning used in ultraliberal circles to defend homosexuals as victims of society, and it was beyond him to fathom how the picture, no matter how tastefully done, could fail to encourage "sexual deviants."[48]

Unlike RKO under Hughes or even the occasionally belligerent United Artists, MGM was not the sort of studio to challenge the Legion to a jackets-off fight. It realized it had a picture with appeal to a minority taste—substantially the same middle-class audience that had appreciated the play on the New York stage. If given a C rating, anything less than enthusiastic reviews would make exhibitors loath to book it in a period of abysmal attendance, especially since neither of its stars, Deborah Kerr and John Kerr (no relation), was a major box office attraction. Metro also hoped to boost its chances by having the premiere in Radio City Music Hall, which still adhered to its policy of excluding C-rated pictures. And so, when the majority of Legion reviewers gave a thumbs down verdict on August 7, 1956, the studio scampered to comply with suggestions for improvement. Unlike Quigley, the IFCA had been far less concerned with the homosexual angle than with adultery. It felt that the letter had pointed no accusatory finger at Tom in agreeing to consummate sex with a married woman. Little suggested that if some lines of dialogue could be inserted that would "point up the immorality and repercussions that dawned on the young man as a result of Miss Kerr's so-called 'heroic act,' the Condemned rating might be reconsidered."[49] While Anderson busied himself redrafting the woman's confessionary letter, a flurry of phone calls and telegrams flew between Los Angeles and England. Deborah Kerr was persuaded to cut short a European vacation and return to London to record the revised version, which now included the sentence, "You have romanticized the wrong we did, you have evaded the unpleasant reality."[50]

To the company's dismay, Little gave this effort a thumbs down. He had been peeved at not being consulted on the actual wording of the corrected form and he considered the word "wrong" too elastic and insufficiently strong "to indicate the seriousness of the moral infraction." In his opinion, MGM ought to search the dictionary for a replacement that would "pinpoint the gravity of the adultery."[51] With time running out, since nationwide bookings of *Tea and Sympathy* had been taken for mid-September, there were only two courses of action left. Dore Schary, MGM's production chief, was inclined to ignore the Legion, release the Condemned product and reap the fruits of the added publicity that the label would carry, just as had happened with *The Moon Is Blue*. When informed of this, Little warned the company that it would be a foolish move. He had been told in confidence by United Artists executives that exhibitors' ill-will arising from screening the Preminger film had not been worth the price of box office success. Moreover, if the studio persisted in this attitude, it was his intention to publicize the classification in advance of release, pressure Radio City not to accept the picture under any circumstance and lodge an official complaint with Eric Johnston.[52] The alternative was compliance. Cooler heads than Schary's prevailed. Anderson was sent to New York to await what amounted to clerical instructions on how to cleanse his movie.

The playwright was in a testy mood on arrival, convinced that he had already gone too far in compromising his artistic integrity to appease bluenoses on both coasts. He had asked several friends what they thought of the adultery sequence and their response had been, "What adultery?" Quigley got things off to a bad start by reviving the homosexual element and the extreme moral danger the film posed to impressionable youth because of it. Few recognized its "insidious position" in the plot because "the evil is so smoked up that it is not recognized as evil." Leaving that matter unresolved, discussion then turned to the letter. Anderson insisted that to revise the revision and harp on the guilt and sin of the parties would give it a preachy tone that audiences would rightly dismiss as artificial. As it now read, sufficient moral retribution had surely been visited on Mrs. Reynolds. Tempers gradually rose until the author suddenly stood up and stalked out but not before advising the astonished clerics that he washed his hands of the whole affair. It was now up to MGM.[53]

In truth, the ball was back in the Legion's court, since the IFCA and reviewers had not yet seen the reconstituted version. The omission was repaired on September 9, when forty-two attended a screening of the one that differed from the original only in the rerecording of the letter-reading, which Deborah Kerr had made three weeks previously. The vote split evenly, fourteen each for A-II, B and C, and settled nothing, of course. Mrs. Looram termed it the most divisive verdict she had experienced in her twenty-year connection with the Legion. It was at this juncture that Bishop Scully decided to pull rank and adopt a papal conclave approach to the dilemma. The Legion executive, Quigley and those consultants and reviewers who could spare the time were sequestered in an office with instructions that none should leave until a majority decision had been reached. The bishop and Quigley came to verbal blows over the latter's unswerving conviction that the story dealt with sexual perversion. Scully pointed out that, while the boy had been charged in the play with homosexuality, in the film his only "crime" was an interest in poetry and classical music rather than physical sports. Unable to convince the others, Quigley left in high dudgeon and so began a gradual parting of the ways with the body that he regarded as largely his creation.[54] After ten hours' discussion of the pros and cons of a Condemned classification, a vote was taken for a compromise B. The outcome of the previous evening's split undoubtedly influenced the decision. The varied impact of *Tea and Sympathy* on those assembled would no doubt be mirrored in its reception by the general public. Justice, too, demanded that a company as prestigious and as cooperative in the past as MGM should be given every consideration. But looming like the Ghost of Christmas Past over the proceedings was the example of *The Moon Is Blue*. A C rating that was ignored by the rank and file because they felt the film was essentially harmless robbed it of its force. In the event it was applied with similar results, the success of the picture would be in direct proportion to the weakening of the Legion.

The B was announced on September 11. The accompanying explanation carried a truculent tone: "This film, based on a stage play of the same name, which was highly controversial because of theme and treatment, has been adapted to the screen with certain changes that repair, in a limited manner, the original moral offenses. However, the solution of the plot still tends to arouse undue sympathy for and to condone immoral actions. In addition, it contains suggestive sequences."[55] For Hollywood, homosexuality was still, by Oscar Wilde's definition, "the love that dare not speak its name." More than a decade would pass before it was treated with anything approaching honesty. Adultery, on the other hand, was regarded as a much less heinous crime and imminent changes to the Code were to reflect as much. Unfortunately for MGM, *Tea and Sympathy* was unable to benefit from the controversy. Youths stayed away in droves and, having played to that middle-aged, middle-income segment of the movie audience that was fast diminishing, it disappeared from view, barely recouping its production costs in the process.

BABY DOLL

Of all domestic playrights to raise censorial ire at this time, none did so more frequently and vexaciously than Tennessee Williams. His *A Streetcar Named Desire* (1952) had been shorn of four minutes at the request of the Legion after cuts had been made to placate the Hays Office. The Legion, through Quigley, had raised particular objection to expressions of carnal desire on Stella's face for her brutish husband, Stanley Kowalski. It had also forced a significant alteration in the plays' conclusion by having Stella leave him after the rape of Blanche. The director, Elia Kazan, made a bitter attack on both the Church and the pusillanimity of Warners in the face of clerical objections. The necessity of avoiding the dreaded C had caused the film company to ignore the entire question of artistic integrity.[56]

Kazan's frustrating experience with *Streetcar* had been followed by another encounter with the PCA that was only slightly less acrimonious over aspects of *The Rose Tattoo*. Heeding the adage that to be forewarned is to be forearmed, he formed his own company, Newton Productions, where he would have complete control over the final cut. This plan was designed to accommodate another Tennessee Williams adaptation that the author composed from a 1940s vignette, *Unsatisfactory Supper*, and *27 Wagons Full of Cotton*, a one-act drama that had been staged in New York in 1955. The combination, *Baby Doll*, was a study of decadence among poor white trash in the Deep South, centering on an ill-matched couple, he a tormented forty-year-old married in name only to an emotionally immature but sexually precocious teen who, to symbolize her lack of readiness for marriage, sleeps in a child's cot and sucks her thumb, surrounded by nursery paraphernalia. His preoccupation with this frustrating marital state causes him to neglect his cotton business. In a fit of temper, he burns down the cotton mill of his nearest competitor. This individual is a self-satisfied Sicilian whose suspicions lead him to Baby Doll, from whom he extracts a signed confession of her husband's guilt. He achieves the confession through a mixture of intimidation and sexual cajolery. When the husband returns and finds them together, he suspects the worst and runs amok, fires off his rifle and is hauled off to the local asylum by the police.

To obtain a seal, Williams had toned down parts of the stage version in the very first draft, most importantly the seduction scene, which was only to be inferred in the film. Though Warners made a print available to the Legion far in advance of its planned release in December 1956, it was with the caveat that Kazan was neither disposed to make any changes nor to enter into any discussion of its moral content. A grim-faced Little watched it in silence. Here, if proof were needed, was a deplorable example of what had befallen the Hays Office in the space of barely two years. His outrage reached the boiling point when Warners let it be known that *Baby Doll* would open just before Christmas to catch the holiday trade. "An effrontery not merely to Catholics but to all Christians and decent thinking people, especially in the festive season!" fumed the Legion chief.[57] There was no doubt in Church circles that *Baby Doll* was a test case, "the most important subject matter which we faced during recent times," said the *Annual Report* for 1957.[58] Kazan's intransigence, if allowed to succeed, would encourage other directors to demand contracts leaving their work inviolate. In the Legion's response there was a return to first principles, of hitting Hollywood where it mattered most—in the pocketbook. Once again Cardinal Spellman was prevailed upon to ascend the pulpit of St. Patrick's on December 16 and warn all Catholics to avoid *Baby Doll* under pain of sin. This made attendance a far more heinous crime than the customary "occasion of sin," since it would involve deliberate disobedience of a Church superior. The large congregation was told that it was "astonishing and deplorable" that such immorality masquerading as entertainment had received a seal "under the so-called regulatory system of the Motion Picture Association of America." What raised the eyebrows of some assembled was the Cardinal's insinuation, in language that still smacked of the McCarthy era, that Williams and Kazan were being delinquent in their allegiance to the United States in producing such filth. It was the moral and patriotic duty of every loyal citizen to defend America not only from the dangers that confronted it from beyond its borders but no less from moral danger within. "The conscienceless, venal attitude of the sponsors of this picture and of all immoral pictures," Spellman declared, "constitutes a definite, corruptive moral influence." These utterances were rendered even more incongruous by Spellman's prefatory remarks voicing dismay over the Hungarian government's treatment of Catholics during the recent uprising. As the *New York Post* angrily editorialized two days later, it would be hard for the impartial observer to see how the ruthless enslavement of Hungarian freedom fighters could be even remotely equated with the appearance of a movie, even if it were generally agreed that the movie was certain to exert a corrupting influence. Surely few would support the notion that Kazan, Williams and Warner Brothers had committed a crime against humanity even vaguely comparable to the Red Terror now stalking Budapest. Indeed, "it might be said quite contrarily that the terror to which the Legion of Decency has intermittently reduced Hollywood bears some authentic, if minimal resemblance to the suppression against which Hungarians have rebelled. They have had enough of cultural commissars and every other kind of ideological bully."[59]

Kazan also expressed outrage at the sermon, and told the press he was willing to take his chances in the court of public opinion. More in sorrow than anger, he found it hard to believe that "an august branch of the Christian faith is not larger in heart and mind."[60] A notably discordant clerical note came from the Anglican Dean James Pike of St. John the Divine in New York, who had purposely attended with his wife and a rabbi. He called it "a religious statement" and questioned whether its sensuality was as blatant or as pernicious as that flaunted in deMille's *Ten Commandments*, which the Legion had awarded its highest rating. But Little was not about to back down over a matter of prestige and principle, nor could he. Spellman's voice was now the most authoritative in the American Church and it behooved lesser lights to listen and follow suit. If Shurlock lay bound by permissive chains, the Legion would show the movie world where the center of morality lay. Within two weeks of the denunciation, bishops in eleven dioceses issued an unprecedented joint statement advising Catholics they had an obligation in conscience to heed the cardinal and avoid *Baby Doll* under pain of sin. Scully took the first opportunity that presented itself to flex clerical muscle by imposing a six-month interdict on the Strand Theater in Albany for its audacity in opening the picture on New Year's Eve.

Other boycotts followed. Joseph P. Kennedy, perhaps with half an eye on his son's future career as president of the United States, refused to book it into his New England chain, calling it "the worst thing that has ever been done to the people and the industry. I think it should be banned everywhere."[61] Help even came from unexpected but welcome quarters abroad. The British Catholic Film Institute protested to the *New York Times* that its spokesman had been misquoted and that, far from praising the picture, it had found *Baby Doll*'s "repellant character deprived it of all vestiges of entertainment." The director of the French Centrale Catholique du Cinéma, the Legion's Gallic equivalent, ordered an initial decision in favor of the movie, for adults with reservations, but then changed to condemned.[62] Two Canadian film boards, those of Quebec and British Columbia, obliged by banning it completely. Even the press was luke-warm. Bosley Crowther was disturbed by its "foreignness" and *Time* bluntly accused it of being "the dirtiest American motion picture that has ever been exhibited."[63]

When the furor eventually died down, the Legion congratulated itself on a job well done. It boasted that its objections had been heard, considered and reasonably honored. This estimation has to be tempered by considering conflicting evidence. In those cities where protest was muted, attendance was very good and accounted for the bulk of the $5 million *Baby Doll* grossed. But results of a Legion survey taken after the picture had spent itself showed that it had played fewer than half of its potential engagements, considering its authorship, casting and story appeal. Some movie exhibitors were sufficiently weary of bomb threats and Knight of Columbus picketing to plead with Warners not to involve them in future screenings of C-rated films.[64] Warners itself refused to divulge an exact figure of earnings but admitted that it ended up a break-even proposition at best. The decision to withdraw it from circulation in 1957 was, perhaps, an admission of defeat. Thereafter rumor circulated that the company had destroyed it to the last copy in hopes of placating the Legion on future, controversial releases. In fact, the rights reverted to Kazan after ten years. In 1969 he made a deal with Cinemation for a rerelease mainly in drive-ins with a Restricted rating from the Motion Picture Association of America.[65] At that time the Legion's successor, NCOMP, chose to be very reticent, and it played without incident.

To the uninformed, asked to compare the American film censorship scene on New Year's Eve, 1956, with that of a decade earlier, little would appear to have changed. The Code was still in place, although Eric Johnston had promised late in the year that four absolute taboos—against drug-taking, abortion, prostitution and kidnapping—would be lifted. Even so, the MPAA intended to police their use closely. Furthermore, as a kind of quid pro quo, or as some viewed it, a sop to the Legion, Johnston agreed to tighten up many other Code provisions by enlarging on their injunctions and by substituting more explicit language for the vague definitions used in the past. Tougher standards were to apply to, among other items, open-mouthed kissing, profanity and the negative depiction of religious personages. Even in those pictures where they were revealed as poseurs, great care had to be taken not to bring the institution of religion *per se* into disrepute as a direct consequence of their actions. True, miscegenation had been dropped entirely but this was one change with which the Legion had never agreed, and it was doubtful whether any company would risk a fracas in the Deep South by a liberal application of the new freedom. As Father Little contemplated his past year's work, he could afford to take pride in the vigilance and dogged determination of his office in combatting and mitigating the evil effects of such productions as *Tea and Sympathy* and *Baby Doll.*[66] In reality, the status quo was about to be visited by an eruption of earthquake proportions. 1957 would see changes of such magnitude that the character of the organization would be changed beyond recognition.

While it is customary to see the fifties as the gray flannel suit era and to associate free love, free speech, casual sex and similar acts of societal defiance with the mid-sixties, initial rumblings against conformity were being heard while Eisenhower was still president. Religion itself was not immune.

The new era of clerical glasnost and perestroika was ushered in not by the Legion staff at 453 Madison Avenue but by Rome. Since the start of his pontificate in 1939, Pius XII had attempted, with some success, to make up for ground lost by his Vatican predecessors. They had immured themselves behind papal walls in dour, self-imposed imprisonment as a response to the loss of lands to the state during the final stages of the movement for Italian unification a century before. Using the media for innumerable addresses to the faithful and appearing in public whenever the opportunity presented itself, Pius made the pontiff a more approachable, less austere figure than any in living memory. The revelation that he received regular injections of sheep's glands to maintain his vitality (the media erroneously but persistently referred to them as monkey glands) was a human touch that further endeared him to Catholics worldwide. As he contemplated the cinema in what were to be the dying days of his pontificate, it struck him that the Church's attitude toward this most popular entertainment had been consistently negative. Films seemed to have become the eighth deadly sin of the twentieth century. The clerical approach approximated that of Moses and the Ten Commandments, with an authority figure handing down immutable pronouncements, the majority of which prohibited rather than promoted behavior. Priests, by most accounts, were never hesitant to lash out at specific movies and to inaugurate or support demands for their banishment or to rally behind those boycotting theaters for screening the unsuitable. In the United States, the Legion pledge was a recital of disavowals and repudiations; its rating system was equally negative. The best assessment any picture could hope to achieve was "unobjectionable," and since 1935, no attempt had been made to single out and praise elements in an otherwise objectionable or condemned film.

Pius's thirteen thousand word encyclical, *Miranda Prorsus* ("Remarkable Technical Inventions") was an elaboration of a missive he had sent to the International Catholic Film Office's Study Days conference meeting in Havana in January 1957. In it he had commended the practice of classifying according to moral content but added that "this necessary action must be accompanied by an educational endeavor in the strictest sense." The cinema was "a privileged instrument put providentially at the disposal of man to make him participate in an authentic and specific culture." The encyclical stressed the ability of the medium, "this most noble art," to create "at least the flavor of understanding among nations, social classes and races" and to "champion the cause of justice." The "marvellous inventions" of radio, television and the cinema were God's gifts no less than man's creations, which the Church welcomed with great joy. Their principal aim should be "to serve truth and virtue," and from them, "very many benefits as well as very many dangers can arise, according as men make use of them."[67]

This reverberant pronouncement secured an immediate response from the Legion, though some might have wished a way could have been found to delay it until Shurlock, like the cowardly lion in *The Wizard of Oz*, had rediscovered his courage. Though he was in the midst of the campaign to keep *Baby Doll* off the screen, Bishop Scully hastened to signal the beginning of a new approach in "The Movies: A Positive Plan," an article that appeared in *America* on March 30, 1957. The initial step was to be the formation of study clubs—film appreciation groups—at Catholic colleges and universities. Pointedly, these would be under lay, not Legion, control, with the National Council of Catholic Men and Catholic Women doing the spade work to get them started. If successful, the idea would be developed nationwide into an educational program at the high school and parochial level.[68] A measure of cinematic literacy would be the happy result. This rosy assessment obviously depended on the willingness of the rank and file of laity to jettison its ingrained idea (which, as most Catholics could attest, the Legion had never disavowed) of the movies as a simple-minded entertainment and embrace the concept of cinema as an art form. But old habits died hard. In universities the motion picture was just beginning the struggle to gain respectability as an academic discipline in the teeth of entrenched conversatism. Students flocked into courses to obtain credit for an activity that had until then carried no reward, namely, watching movies. Interest at the parish level, however, was minimal from the outset because the laity was disconcerted at being told that much of what had been offered through the years was trash. They were even more disinclined to desert the artless pleasures of Hollywood at its most crassly commercial for the perceived obscurity of the French *nouvelle vague* or Italian neorealism. Elizabeth Taylor and Rock Hudson had nothing to fear from Jean Luc Godard and Vittorio De Sica. Corliss has speculated on whether the comparative failure of the study clubs was further evidence of "the Catholic mentality," which responds positively to specific moral imperatives but finds difficulty in practicing voluntary Christian counsels when the whip hand of discipline is absent.[69]

The September 1957 appointment of a Jesuit, Patrick J. Sullivan, to replace

Paul J. Hayes as Little's assistant was to be another indication of the way the wind of change was blowing, although this was not the intention of his sponsor. Sullivan, then teaching moral philosophy at Woodstock College, was the first nondiocesan priest on the Legion staff, having spent his career, to that point, in academe. Martin Quigley had requested Cardinal Spellman to use his good offices to obtain the release of Sullivan. *Miranda Prorsus*, as a portent of change, was ill-advised in Quigley's estimation, and his worst fears were confirmed when some eminent theologians took its promulgation as an occasion to add to comments in the Catholic press that the Legion was hopelessly archaic. Desperate to save his creation from revisionism, and conscious of the fact that hostility toward it emanated from Jesuit circles, Quigley decided to move deviously and, as events would prove, too cleverly. He knew that members of the Society of Jesus were famed for their mutual supportiveness to a degree not found elsewhere in the Church. He calculated that if he could control the young, inexperienced Sullivan, the rest of the order would fall in behind. The newcomer was to be treated early to an exhibition of the power and prestige of the editor of the *Motion Picture Herald*. Quigley had a specially raised table at one end of the Oak Room in the Plaza Hotel in Manhattan where movie executives regularly lunched. It was his custom to enter magisterially, the executive secretary on one arm and his assistant on the other, and proceed to his chair, graciously acknowledging the salutations of film men en route. Sullivan, far from being impressed by this monthly ceremony, saw it as an expression of Legion obeisance to a layman with no official connection to it. Within a year he had prevailed on Little to decline the invitation and thereafter have business with Quigley transacted in the office.[70]

If Quigley was in any doubt that the old order was changing, the way forward was further illuminated by a November decision to add a new ratings category, A-III. The action was a frank acknowledgement of the fact that the B had become the Achilles heel of the Legion, a catch-all classification for pictures ranging from those almost approved to those almost condemned. Reviewers had unconsciously indicated the need for an addition by referring in their reports to "light" and "heavy" Bs, the former unobjectionable for adults but not classified as A-II because of their unsuitability for adolescents. Behind the decision, too, was a tacit admission of failure to keep members from attending B pictures en masse. They were a growing category and it seemed self-evident to the Episcopal Committee that their success was injuring the Legion's effectiveness in imposing a heavy B. By redefining the A-II as "morally unobjectionable for adults and adolescents" and establishing the A-III as "morally unobjectionable for adults," the B would now stand for what it was supposed to signify, i.e., "objectionable in part for all," and not just unfit for adolescents.[71]

Quigley was incensed by the change (for which he had not been consulted) and saw behind it the ungrateful hand of his perfidious protégé. He took the occasion of its announcement to lament to Scully that his decision to recommend Sullivan had "misfired in a wholly unexpected manner." Rather than listen to the voice of experience, the young Jesuit had imposed his own mind set, "a mass of academic notions growing out of the theories of various of his colleagues in the Society." Here was a straw in the wind, "a course of disaster . . . set by persons with little knowledge and no experience." They were "driving upon the rocks an important achievement of the Church in the United States." The new rating would prove to be the thin edge of a thick wedge that would be driven into the body to allow immoral pictures. The whole business of "adult" and "mature" was nothing but a smokescreen by producers, because, in practice, those terms were "synonymous with sordidness, suggestiveness and cruelty." It is my view," he concluded, "that no picture however prudently it may be treated that deals with adultary [sic] fornication and possibly incest—no matter how socially acceptable the character may be—is not something for a Catholic agency under the direction of the Bishops to view as unobjectionable."[72]

Undeterred, Sullivan and a converted Little pressed ahead smartly with more reforms, dismissing Quigley's Jeremiah-like lamentations as overblown reaction to needed change. The IFCA was next to feel the cold breath of criticism. While Mrs. Looram's Ladies had long been considered sacrosanct by virtue of their long, unbroken connection with the Legion, they were increasingly being assailed in the press. An editorial in the *Motion Picture Exhibitor* referred to them as "a group of unskilled and untrained amateur 'Critics' who could not be relied upon to separate technical details from personal entertainment preferences," and it lumped them with "other smart ladies with no kids to meet after school, and with mink jackets and time on their hands."[73] Mrs. Looram fought back with a spirited defense of the training program, but Little and Sullivan could not ignore the collective effect of these barbs on the Legion's reputation.[74] The powers of the IFCA were to be limited in a nonconfrontational way. The method chosen meant, first, extending the number of consultors from around two dozen to sixty and then to over one hundred, giving them an overwhelming majority when it was necessary to deliberate over a problematic title. Just as significantly, the consultors' composition underwent profound change. Instead of reliance on clerics and business and professional men, recourse in the future would be to individuals with some knowledge of, or connection with, the motion picture as an art form. Movie critics, scriptwriters, program planners for repertory art cinemas and students and instructors from the nascent film departments that were starting to make their presence felt in college and university faculties in and around New York comprised a new breed of evaluator. They were liable to have less than complete sympathy for the strict enforcement of decades-old moral standards.

The new faces on the consultors' board were not at all chary about denigrating a system that had been in place before some of them were born. They converted some of the old guard in the process and gave new heart to others who had sometimes felt they were voices in the wilderness. When the Polish *Joan of the Angels* appeared in the city in 1962, trailing its Cannes Special Jury prize behind it, its equivocal portrait of a seventeenth-century convent where the sacred vied with the profane raised the old bogeyman of sacrilege among reviewers who voted for a Condemned rating.[75] Among the consultors, the distinguished, veteran movie columnist for *America* whose connection with the Legion spanned two decades, wearily commented:

I hate condemning any film that has some stature and seriousness of purpose. Each time we do this we get a worse black eye with the people, even well-disposed people, who take movies seriously. Yet, ironically, these "good C films" pose almost no moral threat to the people with the kind of mentality that would lead them to consult the Legion of Decency list in the first place. . . . I think it would help if we faced up to our own guilt in creating the predicament in which we find ourselves. We failed, along with many other opinion makers inside and outside the Church, to understand the nature and impact of mass entertainment. Out of this misunderstanding we formulated, with the best intentions in the world, a policy which, in actual practice, not only did not protect Catholics from moral harm in their choice of screen entertainment but even discouraged the formation within themselves of a sense of personal responsibility and a rational approach to entertainment which, in our democratic, pluralistic society, is the only effective protection an individual can have against adverse influences.

Now we know better. . . . We no longer think that superficiality is a virtue or that ticklish moral problems are unsuitable. . . . Yet, in our week-to-week decisions we constantly give the benefit of the doubt to the shrewdly gimmicked-up product of the Hollywood huckster which *is* degrading to the mass audience, and come down like a ton of brick on the artist whose work, however difficult, ambiguous, irritating, partial, unsatisfactory, etc. is a search for the truth and is no great threat to the mass audience because the last thing in the world they [sic] want from movies is the truth.[76]

Sentiments of this nature were to become ever more common in the evaluations of the consultors. Though it was to take a good ten years, Mrs. Looram would eventually be driven to the conclusion that her group had increasingly less to say to the organization, at which point they would part company.

LA DOLCE VITA

Respect for and appreciation of a controversial piece of film art was part of the *Miranda Prorsus* revolution. Federico Fellini's *La Dolce Vita* soon provided a textbook example of how old and new traditions warred in the bosom of the Legion.

By 1959, the Italian motion picture industry had changed almost beyond recognition from its poverty-stricken, immediate postwar aspect when De Sica, Rossellini and their neorealist contemporaries were fashioning their unglamorous works on shoestring budgets. Hollywood discovered postwar Italy as an alternative filmmaking venue in the late forties. In addition to having a variety of scenery and a benign climate not unlike that of Southern California, it had trained technicians from the Mussolini era and, not least, a cost-of-living index that made filming an attractive proposition. Within a decade Rome was bustling with U.S.–Italian coproductions. Sword-and-sandal epics became the rage, spawned by the runaway success of *Hercules*, a classical mish-mash that boasted the physique of a hitherto obscure actor, Steve Reeves. Since nothing succeeds like imitation in the movie business, the rush was on at Cine Centa, or "Hollywood-on-the-Tiber" as it came to be known, to plunder mythology for the world market. In 1960 it was possible to find Mickey Hargitay, Bob Mathias and Lex Barker, all Mr. Universe types, working simultaneously on variations of the same theme.

It was this Rome of white convertible Cadillacs, Renaissance villas, agents haggling over deals, paparazzi and wild parties in places the tourists never saw that Fellini used as the setting for *La Dolce Vita*, "The Sweet Life." The focus of the story is Marcello Rubini, a jaded newspaper columnist who wanders through a dozen or so sequences designed to expose the vacuity and rapacity of contemporary Roman society. Fellini had left rural Italy as a sixteen-year-old to work in Florence and Rome. He was shocked by the amorality and the temptation to pursue the superficially easy existence that these cities afforded. It left a profound impression that he vowed to commit to celluloid, "to take the temperature of a sick society," as he put it. Basking in the prestige that had followed reception of his early work, especially *The White Sheik*, *La Strada* and *Nights of Cabiria*, he was able to raise $1.5 million for this intensely personal project.

The film opens with a startling image: a huge, granite statue of Christ dangles from a helicopter on its way to installation in St. Peter's Square. Christ may be returning to earth but he is out of reach of the people. That same evening in a nightclub, Marcello is castigated by a playboy who has been the centerpiece of one of his muck-raking articles. In this same club Marcello meets the nymphomaniac daughter of a wealthy businessman, and their evening together terminates in the apartment of a prostitute. At dawn he returns to his house to find that his neglected mistress has tried to commit suicide. Though he rushes her to hospital, he cannot remain by her side since he has to meet a pea-brained Hollywood movie star renowned more for her bustline than her thespian abilities. She soothes her passion by splashing in the Trevi Fountains. Another woman celebrates her divorce in the company of drunks, lechers and homosexuals. A bored aristocrat opens his palace for an orgy. Two frightened children dishonestly tell of having seen an appearance by the Madonna. A decent, tormented intellectual who seeks in art the truth he cannot find in reality kills himself and his children in despair. The film ends with yet another party in a seaside villa, where sexual games among hedonists elicit more boredom than passion. At dawn the revelers find a monstrous fish dragged up on the beach in fisherman's nets. A symbol of innocence in the form of a young girl whom Marcello had befriended earlier beckons him, but it is too late.

Long before it reached the Legion's screening room, *La Dolce Vita* had caused a furor in its native land. Fellini found himself being variously reviled as an immoral nihilist, a Communist and a Catholic propagandizer. The Holy See was at the center of the turmoil when Archbishop Sir of Genoa, director of Catholic Action, hailed it as a moral portrait of a sinful society within a framework of bitterness, boredom and despair. Two leading Catholic papers, Il Popolo and Il Quotidiano, published favorable reviews. Then came an about-face, occasioned, according to Fellini, by a protest to the pope by Count Della Terra, a spokesperson for and member of the Roman aristocracy that had been so mercilessly vilified in the film. His denunciatory article, headlined "Basta!" appeared in the Vatican's own l'Osservatore Romano. Immediately the two Catholic journals hastened to retract their approval. The papacy then condemned the picture.[77]

It might be anticipated that Fellini's work would experience a rough reception at Legion hands. The director was, after all, partially responsible for The Miracle, having written the script and played the part of "St. Joseph" in that infamous opus. But it was a sign of changing times that a wait-and-see policy was adopted until it had been evaluated. The increase in the number of film-literate laity and liberally minded priests recently recruited into the ranks of the consultors was evident when a vote was taken after the April 15, 1961, screening. The old guard, 18 reviewers, had been swamped by 102 consultors. Though there was no neat division into two camps, an analysis of the voting indicated the liberalism of the latter. A minority of 22 (including 13 reviewers) voted for condemnation for a variety of reasons including "low moral tone," "a philosophy of despair" and that old moral chestnut that had been the undoing of The Miracle, "blasphemy." An almost equal number, 23, judged it acceptable enough to be permitted to mature audiences either through an A-III or Separate Classification, to which were joined a further 28 plus Little and Sullivan who were in favor of awarding the S.C. rating. The recommended safeguards were a recognition that there was a distinct audience for films of this type. These included awarding the rating to a subtitled print only, requiring tasteful advertising, excluding unaccompanied juveniles, and imposing first-run ticket prices in select theaters. Those precautions, it was averred, would discourage the mass audience one associated with sensationalism.[78]

The issue was no sooner settled than it was violently reopened by debate from traditional quarters. The intransigent attitude of opponents stemmed from a deeply held, unswerving opinion as to the role of the motion picture and its audience. While the Legion appeared to be forging ahead into unknown territory with the flag of Miranda Prorsus nailed to the mast, conservative Catholics viewed with dismay its acceptance of purportedly artistic pictures containing philosophies alien to and, in some cases, downright hostile toward the Church. Behind this were views on the composition of the movie audience. Was it, as the Legion had come to believe, fragmented with a segment of educated, aesthetically mature individuals, or was it still plebian, impressionable and vulnerable to moral subversion and political demagoguery? Martin Quigley was one of the first to enter the fray, with consequences that would permanently alienate him from the institution he had helped establish. He made two impassioned appeals to the Episcopal Committee and Bishop McNulty, an ex-chairman. For the editor of the *Motion Picture Herald*, the rut had set in long before Fellini's "obscenity" beached itself on American shores. Without mentioning Sullivan by name, he deplored "the tragic predicament into which the Legion of Decency has plunged the Catholic interest," not through lack of intelligence or conscientious responsibility but rather,

due to the pitfalls inherent in an ambitious scheme, from previously identified sources to demolish the structure that had, for 23 years, been the policies and procedures of the Legion, and in its place to establish a New Order—a new order which would bring the Legion to the respected attention and approval of the Civil Liberties Union, of advanced thinkers who quietly scoff at the Church's insistence upon moral disciplines and those who regard art and culture not in the sense of a means towards the moral perfection of man—but as a way of life.

Quigley scornfully dismissed the choice of the S.C. rating for *La Dolce Vita* as a willful misuse of the category. It had never been intended as a shield for morally degenerate pictures, and yet, as in the recent case of *Suddenly Last Summer*, whose plot hinged on a young woman successfully pimping for her homosexual brother, moral unacceptability had been ignored. Contrary to Legion assertions, the rating it applied to the Fellini picture would not be interpreted by Catholics as meaning it was unsuitable for certain age groups, but as some sort of commendation. Nor did he spare the hired hands of the new policy. The consultants, a collection of "academics keen in the pursuit of cultural maturation and from a background and experience far dissimilar from that of the mass of movie patrons," had subjectively injected into certain types of films "interpretations and implications which might convey meanings to them but certainly not to the typical moviegoer." The average man or woman would carry out of the theater "no sardonic commentary on society" but only "images of the practices of adultery, fornication, prostitution and striptease." In this group he lumped those who thought and spoke "a modernistic mumbo jumbo," including Bosley Crowther, who had praised the film as "licentious but moral."[79]

Quigley also enunciated a viewpoint on the age limitation, subtitling and a supervised publicity campaign. Limiting attendance to over-18-year-olds rested on the "futile assumption" that it was either possible or practical for exhibitors, even those who were willing to cooperate, to enforce any precise check. Like vendors of fish and vegetables, they were loath to pass up sales because of a perishable product. Anyone honestly seeking a truthful answer, and not just one that supported a hypothetical notion, would readily agree that ticket sellers were unable to judge the age of many prospective patrons. The Legion's reference to "a responsible policy of exhibition" was another red herring, for it brazenly suggested the full potential of moral harmfulness would be mitigated, that something less than maximum virulence would afflict the audience. The subtitles told the story and the screen image would remain the same whether the dialogue was in a foreign language or not. As for advertising, Astor Pictures's guarantee that its prim posters could not possibly appeal to prurient interest might well occasion the reply, "By whom?" It was one thing to control publicity for a handful of art theaters; no such supervision would be possible once *La Dolce Vita* went on general release to every nook and cranny of the land.[80]

Support also came from the *Wanderer*. Like its diocesan partner, the *Tidings*, it regarded the incursion of foreign films into neighborhood theaters as an unfortunate development. In particular, it considered sexually oriented European titles to be the work of political and intellectual opponents of the Church. Mostly socialists and Communists, their ulterior motive for shipping these tainted wares across the Atlantic was the moral destruction of the American people. It also viewed the career of the recently deceased Senator McCarthy in a different light from the liberal press. He was no alcohol-befuddled rabble-rouser who had latched onto a cause to save his sinking career but rather a true patriot driven to drink by the skepticism of the people and the stress of trying to unmask Reds. The Wisconsin hero might be gone, but his enemies had not been vanquished. One of the *Wanderer*'s investigations unearthed the "murky past" of Louis Folivot, the producer of *La Dolce Vita*, whom it characterized as "a very dangerous Stalinist agent and a member of the international Communist apparatus." His crimes seemed to be as numerous as the grains of sand on a beach, ranging from "the planning of Stalinist, so-called anti-Fascist fronts in the 1930s" to the editing of *United Nations World*, "a pro-Russian publication." The appearance of the Fellini film put spring into the step of *Wanderer* editorials. "The sinful and degenerate picture" fulfilled perfectly the "commandments of Red propaganda"—to take the name of the Lord in vain, to break down Christian traditions and to dishonor the father and mother so that bourgeois morality could ultimately be destroyed. Those who ought to have known better, like Moira Walsh of *America*, had played into the hands of subversives in praising the Italian film while simultaneously panning the ponderous but theologically correct *St. Francis of Assisi*. The Catholic press had a purpose other than teaching what was "arty" in the cinema and that was to point out the good, the moral and the spiritually uplifting.[81]

Quigley's doleful prediction that *La Dolce Vita* would eventually be seen in a more popular English-dubbed version did come to pass in 1965, when a somewhat abbreviated print was released by Columbia. A poster featuring the low-cut dress of Anita Ekberg replaced the staid original at that time.[82] But the picture remained a *succés d'estime* and never achieved much beyond art-house status. In any case, the morality of Fellini's movie hardly seemed worth worrying about by then, so far and so fast had the censorship scene moved in five years.

NOTES

1. The Catholic Church's role is touched on in Larry Ceplair and Steven Englund, *The Inquisition in Hollywood* (Garden City, N.Y.: Doubleday, 1980).

2. NLOD, miscellaneous files, 1934–49.

3. Mrs. James F. Looram, *Quarterly Bulletin*, vol. 18, no. 3, 1943, pp. 11–12.

4. *National Catholic Office for Motion Pictures, Film Ratings* (New York: NCOMP), p. 162; also NLOD file, "Mission to Moscow," Masterson to McNicholas, April 24, 1945.

5. Canadian Broadcasting Company, "This Week at the Movies," March 12, 1950. Some indifferent editing and an abrupt conclusion leave the heroine's fate in some doubt. She may have perished in a slave labor camp. Similarly, her Russian lover's death may have been suicide.

6. *United Church Observer*, March 15, 1950.

7. NLOD file, "Guilty of Treason," Quigley to Scully, September 6, 1949.

8. Editorial in the *Witness*, January 12, 1950, p. 1.

9. *The Truth Behind the Trial of Josef, Cardinal Mindszenty* (N.p.: n.p., n.d.) It purported to show "the true historical perspective against the backdrop of the Communist world-wide war against religion and its five part technique to stamp out the Church."

10. NLOD file, "Guilty of Treason," L. Brien to Field Representatives, Eagle-Lion Distributors, May 3, 1950.

11. Ibid., Ed Golding to Mooring, May 3, 1950.

12. Masterson paid tribute to the Catholic War Veterans for their unceasing vigilance. NLOD, *Annual Report*, 1951, p. 27.

13. Ibid., p. 8.

14. NLOD file, "Storm Center," Little memorandum, June 1, 1956.

15. Ibid., Hayes memorandum, July 11, 1956.

16. Ibid., Little to Nate Springold, June 4, 1956.

17. The *Sign*, July 1, 1956.

18. *Variety*, August 8, 1956.

19. Leff and Simmons, pp. 189–91.

20. De Grazia and Newman, pp. 86–87.

21. NLOD file, "The Moon Is Blue," Little to Diocesan Directors, June 11, 1953.

22. Ibid., June 18, 1953.

23. *St. Joseph's Magazine*, June 1953.

24. NLOD file, "The Moon Is Blue," Spellman to Archbishop Edward D. Howard, July 12, 1953.

25. *St. Joseph's Magazine*, August 1953.

26. NLOD file, "The Moon Is Blue," Little to the Rev. Michael Owen Driscoll, September 24, 1953.

27. Ibid., Mrs. W. C. Boughner to Legion of Decency, December 4, 1953. "We have a right to raise a voice but that does not include the right to use 'gangster methods' if the people do not wish to listen. It was not the people who spoke but a Roman Catholic priest."

28. Ibid., Ferdinand Falque to Little, December 4, 1953.

29. The NCOMP would re-rate it A-III in 1969. Ibid., Richard Hirsch to Martin Gang, September 25.

30. Leff and Simmons, pp. 203–4.

31. William R. Weaver, *Motion Picture Daily* editorial, December 30, 1953, p. 2.

32. *Life*, January 11, 1954.

33. NLOD file, 'The French Line," Little memorandum, January 14, 1954.

34. Ibid., text of a phone conversation between Looram and Breen, January 10, 1954.

35. Ibid., Little memorandum, January 18, 1954.

36. Ibid., Little to Scully, January 18, 1954. Also contacted were the heads of the American Legion, Jewish War Veterans and the Federation of Women's Clubs.

37. *Variety*, May 12, 1954 carried the headline: "French Line Turned into a Crusade."

38. See, for example, the *Monitor*, March 12, 1954.

39. NLOD, *Annual Report*, 1955, pp. 7–11.

40. NLOD, *Annual Report*, 1954, pp. 72–75.

41. Ibid., p. 7.

42. NLOD file, Legion of Decency, 1955, W. R. Wilkinson to Little, April 30, 1955.

43. *Variety*, July 6, 1955. Some studios had taken to giving the Legion rough cuts of prints to save expense should a specific scene fail to pass muster.

44. NLOD, *Annual Report*, 1955, pp. 23–25.

45. The play was banned from the London stage by the Lord Chamberlain.

46. NLOD file, "Tea and Sympathy," Howard Dietz to Little, October 4, 1955.

47. Ibid., Little to Nicholas Schenck, September 27, 1955.

48. Ibid., Little memorandum, October 1, 1955.

49. Ibid., Little to Haven Falconer, August 7, 1956.

50. Ibid., Little memorandum, August 9, 1956.

51. Ibid., Little to Falconer, August 23, 1956.

52. Ibid., Little to Charles Reagan, August 30, 1956.

53. Ibid., Little memorandum, September 7, 1956.

54. Ibid., Little memorandum, September 14, 1956. The marathon meeting began on September 11.

55. Ibid., Little to Bishop Hubert M. Newell, September 12, 1956. In one of its rare instances, the Legion executive (with Scully's support) cast its vote with the minority of IFCA reviewers where the vote had been 15–12 for a C.

56. Kazan's outburst against perceived Warner Brothers capitulation to the Legion was made public in his letter to the *New York Times*, October 12, 1951.

57. NLOD file, "Baby Doll," Little to Spellman, December 13, 1956.

58. NLOD *Annual Report*, 1957, p. 9.

59. *New York Post*, December 18, 1956, p. 8.

60. Kazan, letter to the *New York Times*, October 12, 1951.

61. *Showman's Trade Review*, December 22, 1956.

62. NLOD file, "Baby Doll," Jean Dewarin to Little, February 9, 1957.

63. *Time*, December 24, 1956.

64. NLOD, *Annual Report*, 1957, p. 9.

65. *Variety*, October 8, 1969.

66. NLOD, *Annual Report*, 1957, pp. 11–12.

67. Corliss, p. 48.

68. A further development was establishment of the National Center for Film Study in Chicago whose membership comprised those engaged in film education work in high schools and colleges. It was to participate on a very occasional basis in rating decisions of titles which the NCOMP judged particularly controversial. And so, somewhat belatedly, Chicago had some input in Legion affairs.

69. Ibid., p. 66.

70. Author's interview with Sullivan, Fordham University, May 1990.

71. NLOD file, "Pledges and campaigns," November 12, 1957.

72. QP Box 2, Quigley to Scully, May 16, 1961.

73. *Motion Picture Exhibitor*, June 22, 1955.

74. Ibid., July 13, 1955.

75. NLOD file, "Joan of the Angels," May 24, 1961.

76. Ibid., undated.

77. NLOD file, "La Dolce Vita," Little to David B. McGuire, September 16, 1961.

78. Ibid., Memorandum to Bishop McNulty, May 24, 1961.

79. Ibid., Quigley to McNulty, May 5, 1961.

80. Ibid., May 19, 1961.

81. *Wanderer*, August 24, 1961.

82. The television version was considerably bowdlerized. All references to God and the anti-Christ were deleted, as was Ekberg's striptease and her line, "I sleep with only two drops of perfume."

Chapter 7

Goodbye Legion, Welcome NCOMP

LOLITA

The pamphlet from the Committee Praying for the Body, Soul and Mind of Sue Lyon and Her Parents said it all:

> Where are the parents of Sue Lyon—or don't they care about selling the body of their little 14 year-old girl to be an object of international lust and sensuality? Aren't they concerned that after she lives through the role in this dirty, gutter book that she will end up debauched and depraved? (or do we have to mention Errol?)
>
> Are there no laws for contributing to the delinquency of a minor—where are the district attorney, chief of police?
>
> Can this teenager be released from school by her principal, the Board of Education for purposes of making this immoral movie of incest and fornication?
>
> Where are the United States attorneys, the State Department? Can our children be taken out of the country for the filming of these dirty sex scenes?
>
> God help the United States if we have to sink to the level of open debauchery and open lusting on our sweet innocent teenage girls.[1]

The cause of this outpouring of outrage (and others of a similar vein would follow) was the filming of *Lolita*, a novel by the Russian-born, American-naturalized Vladimir Nabokov. Written in 1954, it had bumped from one publisher to another without finding a taker. Simon & Schuster had rejected it on the advice of Mrs. Max L. Schuster, who flatly told her husband, "I won't have my name on that dirty book!" New Directions had passed because James Laughlin, its president, believed publication would leave a permanent stigma on the author's wife and family. In 1955 Nabokov sent it to the Olympia Press, a Parisian institution whose jungle-green-covered paperbacks were synonymous with hard-core pornography and eagerly stuffed in the suitcases of overseas visitors to the City of Light. Soon there were half a dozen pirated editions, including a Swedish version containing only the sex scenes and a Japanese version whose front cover portrayed the title character with Jane Russell–sized breasts.[2] Eventually, in 1958, G. P. Putnam brought it out in the United States to mixed reviews, with the balance tilting toward the *New York Times* verdict of "disgusting" and "repulsive." This was painful to the intellectual Nabokov, who had been married to the same woman for almost forty years, and enjoyed mathematical puzzles and classifying butterflies. He confessed to an interviewer that he rather disliked little girls and knew nothing about sexual aberrations.

Such statements struck nonliterary critics as hypocritical and mendacious. *Lolita* is cast in the form of a confessional by a sexual psychopath, Humbert Humbert, a French translator who relates a two-year-long encounter with a twelve-year-old girl. The description of his deviant compulsion begins with his decision to rent a room from an attractive and sexually starved widow, Charlotte Haze, in order to be near the object of his lust, a gum-chewing nymphet. When the mother is killed, Humbert spirits Lolita off to summer camp and consummates their affair in a motel, the Enchanted Huntress. Though initially afraid to leave his side, she eventually wearies of the fugitive existence with a man three times her age. She dumps him only to take up with another older male, Clare Quilty, a sex dilettante, alcoholic, bisexual and ex-Hollywood scenarist who is the author of the play in which she has appeared at school. Though he later marries an easy-going, childish woman, Humbert cannot banish thoughts of Lolita. When they meet again after three years, she is married to a Mr. Average American nonentity and expecting a child. Humbert convinces himself that Quilty was the architect to his misfortune, tracks him down and shoots him several times in a cold fury. The narration is concluded from the death cell.

Reaction to the novel in the Catholic press occasioned heated correspondence there as elsewhere. The *Commonweal* reviewer, Thomas Molnar, praised it as the confession of a civic and moral outcast who suffers from more than he delights in his predicament. In his own way Humbert repeats the Augustinian error of perceiving and approving good yet following evil as he spirals down the serpentine road of corruption. Molnar pleaded for an evaluation of Nabokov's work on literary, not moral grounds. Lolita could not be defended because she remains unknown to the reviewer, existing only through the lustful gaze of her stepfather. Only at the very end, married to a decent simpleton and comically serious in her anticipation of the maternal state does she become recognizably human.[3] This cut no ice with much of the journal's readership, which variously saw the novel as the logical continuation of a permissiveness that had allowed the Kinsey Report on male sexual behavior to see the light of day or as a literary landmark of the most pernicious sort, giving legitimacy to the hitherto taboo theme of pedophilia.

In the halcyon days of Hays and Breen, a screen version of *Lolita* would have been an utter impossibility; but in the words of the folk song of the period, the times they were a' changing. In 1956 the Code had dropped its strictures against a variety of themes including drug addiction and prostitution, though it had retained sexual perversion on the list, a rubric that surely applied to the Humbert-Lolita relationship. Too, Shurlock seemed to be more interested in the intention and treatment of controversial themes rather than applying the strict letter of the law. In the changing moral climate, two young movie entrepreneurs felt confident enough to take an option on the novel and look for a deal with one of the studios. These were James B. Harris, a producer, and the young director, Stanley Kubrick, who had received plaudits for two pictures, *The Killing*, a low-budget heist thriller and *Paths of Glory*, an antiwar tract based on a true story of mutiny in the French army during World War I. Kubrick had had dealings with the Production Code during the filming of *Spartacus*, having had to trim a tentative homosexual encounter between Laurence Oliver and Tony Curtis and several sequences of brutal violence.[4]

In 1959 they canvassed the film capital in vain for a distributor. None of the big names was willing to bite unless a PCA seal could be guaranteed in advance. Release through an independent or one of the majors' art film subsidiaries might have resulted in a version truer to the spirit and letter of the book. Neither Kubrick nor Harris was willing to go that route with the diminished audience that that would imply. Both were convinced that the Production Code was a dinosaur whose extinction was imminent.[5] In early 1960 things came together. The film rights were purchased for $250,000; Nabokov gave up his professorship at Cornell and came to Los Angeles to write the script; and Seven Arts, a television company bloated with cash, agreed to finance the project and look for a distribution link through MGM.[6] The casting of the title role required the author's assent, and he agreed to the fourteen year old Sue Lyon, who had some television and modeling experience. It was decided to shoot the picture in London, partly to enable Peter Sellers (who was to play Quilty) to meet other commitments there and partly to benefit from British government financing. In addition, the farther the production was from Shurlock's ken, the less interference could be expected. During the course of filming, Kubrick and Harris sought out Martin Quigley to play his accustomed role of facilitator. But Quigley was now persona non grata with the Legion, following *La Dolce Vita* and other contretemps, and his influence in Hollywood was similarly on the wane.[7] Surprisingly, Quigley found that much had already been done in the scripting stage to raise the tone from the "gutter level." Sue Lyon had been made up to look like a high school senior and the screenplay now had her as a fifteen-year-old. The motel seduction scene progressed with both participants clothed. Even the murder of Quilty, described in gruesome detail in the book, occurred mostly off-camera, with the character dying behind an oil painting. The major stumbling block was some dialogue in the seduction sequence, but a judicious fade-out removed what might be regarded as the most offensive words, leaving the rest to the imagination. With incredibly little fuss, *Lolita* won her seal of approval.[8]

At Legion headquarters, on the other hand, there was a sense of foreboding. For months it had received a stream of letters asking how the organization could prevent its filming. There were expressions of outrage that Kubrick could not be charged under the Mann Act for transporting a minor across a state line and then across the Atlantic.[9] Father Little could only respond weakly that the Legion had no *a priori* powers of censorship but must wait on the finished work. It was, indeed, regrettable in his eyes that the novel had been published, but now that it was a movie, concerned citizens could rest assured that the whole arsenal of Legion weapons would be used to ruin it if it did not pass muster.[10] Sullivan put the case succinctly. Violent antipathy of reviewers and consultors would be a reflection of the public attitude and would strengthen the Legion's case; acceptance would be an open sesame for "further revolting subject matter inasmuch as pictures [are] planned on lesbianism, incest, etc."; the age of Sue Lyon posed the question of whether the Church could, in conscience, sanction the corruption of a minor. Above all, he was acutely aware of the humiliating way in which the PCA was being manipulated and circumvented under the new guard. In a single year the percentage of objectionable films coming out of Hollywood had risen in the Legion's tally from 14.59 percent to 24.33 percent. The monstrosity that was *Lolita* was a sick symbol to be banished from the nation's screens, to be accomplished, if possible, with conviction and dignity.[11]

These commodities, however, were in shorter supply than the executive had hoped when the film was first screened on July 12, 1961. Of the fifty-five present, a large minority, twenty-six, were for a C, with the remainder evenly split three ways among B, S.C. and undecided between B and C.[12] This divisiveness was troubling in view of the expressed determination of Seven Arts to proceed with national release based on its possession of a PCA seal. Initial determination to impose the prevailing C verdict began to give way to questions of strategy predicated on a rating other than Condemned. Sullivan's personal reaction was still one of "profound distaste," yet he recognized that the central question was "the more effective control of the release" if the Legion could be even tangentially involved. A starting point might be to limit the age of admission. By its abdication of responsibility, Shurlock's organization had thrown open the doors of the country's theaters to every child who wanted to see it. What it had ignominiously ignored, the Legion might achieve by getting exhibitors to impose an eighteen-plus rule and have this carried in all advertising. Bolstering this assumption was the nature of the picture which, opined Sullivan, would not cause moral harm to adults. Many might be disgusted by the spectacle of James Mason lusting after a girl young enough to be his granddaughter, but such disgust could be salutary in arousing the public to demand that the PCA regain some of its former backbone. Together, the arguments for a Separate Classification over a Condemned rating had merit—and perhaps a *Lolita* bereft of controversy would be a box office failure.[13]

But before this daring principle could be evoked, Little thought it best to consult Bishop McNulty, chairman of the Episcopal Committee, especially in view of indecision at the Legion. His Excellency squelched hopes of anything other than the lowest rating after watching Nabokov's creation on October 12.

In his view, if offered the viewer "nothing but two and a half hours of exposure to an unrelieved concentration on sexual depravity which no amount of so-called restrained treatment could alter." If it purported to be a tragedy, he experienced no catharsis or even evidence of a contest between good and evil. The ruse of presenting Lolita as an older adolescent by increasing her age by three years was insupportable. The impossibility of this love and its ensuing tragedy were intelligible only in the context of the female as a perverse, minor adolescent. Her very behavior—gum chewing and popcorn eating—were the characteristics of a twelve year-old. McNulty also stated objections to specific scenes that other reviewers and consultors had raised. Quilty's conversation with the motel desk clerk provided "an object lesson on how to solicit for homosexual purposes." Particularly shocking, and without dramatic point other than cheap shock value, was the use of a portrait of the Madonna as a bedroom door prop while Humbert had sexual congress with Charlotte. In short, "this film, far from contributing anything positive to the commonweal . . . can only serve to lower the threshold of public resistance to moral depravity and deaden their sense of what is decent." The verdict had to be Condemned.[14]

Seven Arts's reaction to the announcement was one of barely concealed fury. David Stillman, their New York attorney, began by warning Father Little that legal action was underway to make *Lolita* a private property, meaning that the Legion could not comment publicly on it. Any long-term damage done as a result of the rating would cause his company to use all means at its disposal "to hold responsible any person or entity." Speculating on the "injustice" that had been inflicted, Stillman mused that it was probably done to balance the Legion's recent slipshod record of relatively favorable treatment "given to films which every informed person knows are far more condemnable on moral ground," or perhaps it was ignoring precedent by placing the novel on trial even though the picture was but a skeletal representation of the original. It would do well not to gloat over its action, otherwise the public might be unable to erase implications of incompetence from its collective mind.[15] Fathers Little and Sullivan were certain that Quigley's devious hand was behind this outburst because he had been unable to deliver on his promise of a smooth ride for the film at clerical hands.[16]

Neither art nor morality but money oils the wheels of the movie industry. The impasse over *Lolita* was broken from an unexpected quarter by the intervention of an eminent member of a temple of high finance. David G. Baird, the head of a prestigious Wall Street brokerage firm, had been approached by a group of Boston financiers to act as mediator in the affair. They had underwritten part of the film's cost and their apprehensions undoubtedly stemmed from a fear that the C rating would harm the film's chances at the box office to the extent that they would be unable to obtain a return on their investment. This, though, was not the impression that Baird tried to convey, at least during his initial meeting with the Legion. With charming ingenuousness he told Little that while he personally found the picture disgusting, he had been told that the

projected C rating would quadruple its business, which would surely nullify the
Legion's good works hitherto. Perhaps the existing version could be exhibited
without any classification whatever to avoid the notoriety of a rating that was
bound to divide libertarians and moralists. He revealed a little of the motive
for his visit before departing by insisting that if the Condemned label were to
go, his reward from an unnamed source would be applied to charity and not to
his considerable personal fortune. Sullivan and Little refused to be moved over
the consequences of their decision and flatly refused to create a precedent by
withdrawing it, and so nothing came of this peculiar encounter.[17] However, on
December 19 Baird was back to discuss specifics. The Legion was prepared to
listen to this "suave gentleman" as he itemized sticking points and the willingness
of Seven Arts/MGM to abide by an eighteen-plus age restriction.[18] On the
strength of this and subsequent discussion of McNulty's specific objections,
Harris spent the first three weeks of 1962 preparing an amended version.

At a gathering of surprisingly modest size on January 24, Sullivan rehearsed
the history of the dispute and asked the consultors and reviewers to judge between
two accounts of the seduction scene at the Enchanted Huntress—the original
in which Lolita would relate to Humbert the details of an affair she had had at
a summer camp (Camp Climax, no less!) with a thirteen-year-old boy, and an
abbreviated version with the confession omitted. The purpose of the longer
sequence was to alert the viewer to the girl's awareness of carnal desire in others
and to demonstrate that her knowledge of sex was not theoretical but experiential
and authentic. Establishing the fact of her tarnished virtue would mitigate the
seriousness of Humbert's guilt of statutory rape, since she was a willing ac-
complice. The shorter version would remove one lurid episode from a film not
lacking in those but leave open the issue of Humbert's sexual abuse of a minor.
On this and on the Legion's other concern about the age of Sue Lyon, several
consultors reassured their chief that the innate nymphomania of the character
was unmistakable throughout, while the characterization Kubrick had elicited
from Sue Lyon came from a performance whose nuances were probably unin-
telligible to one of her tender years, especially in the context of motion picture
production where scenes are seldom shot in sequence.[19] These rationalizations
were enough to cause Little to obtain McNulty's concurrence and so put an end
to five months of acrimony. *Lolita* had earned herself nothing worse than a
Separate Classification.

The atmosphere at Seven Arts was euphoric. Harris gladly accepted all the
conditions for exhibition including inclusion of the longer seduction scene and
an advertising campaign that would be closely scrutinized by the Legion for the
duration of the picture's run.[20] Normally the Legion did not go beyond a terse
three or four lines of observation on a specific title, but in view of the enormous
brouhaha, Sullivan felt obliged to defend what many considered insupportable
leniency. "Ten years ago people went to the movies to be passively entertained.
For audiences whose habit of entertainment is purely passive, the very subject
matter of *Lolita* would have seemed extraordinary and altogether shocking.

Audiences are more mature in the sense that they are more selective in film entertainment."[21] And so, perhaps, they were. But left unsaid was the realization that the Condemned rating was no longer the effective deterrent it once was. Priests were lamenting that more than ever the C list on the parish bulletin board was being scrutinized by adolescents as a guide to what was worth seeing.[22] Still, in retrospect, *Lolita* was not the trailblazer it first appeared to be. Nabokov had been forced to remove much of the perversely outrageous from his novel. In answer to the rhetorical question posed in the advertising slogan: "How did they ever make a movie of *Lolita?*" Bosley Crowther answered simply and truthfully, "They didn't." Casting an actress who looked seventeen not twelve removed the factor of perverted desire and rendered Humbert's passion more conventional.[23] There was nothing new in screen entertainment in having older men lust after younger women and finding their desires reciprocated. In the novel, Nabokov had purposely made his heroine old enough to experience menstruation and sexual arousal. Had she been any younger, she would have certainly been an innocent victim. By having her age pushed forward three years further, the screen Lolita was made into that convenient and reliable substitute for male guilt, the pubescent Eve tempting a weak, fallible, aging Adam. Theologically, that was acceptable or, at the very least, it was enough of an extenuating circumstance to allow the Legion to revise its verdict upwards. Nabokov's adaptation may also have mollified critics by its subtle shift in emphasis from father and stepdaughter to Quilty, a whimsical, arbitrary creature played with typical facetiousness by Peter Sellers. His posing set the tone of the film, which was not even a lame attempt at reversing the Henry Jamesian theme of New World corruption by the Old, but rather a tale of three immature people who are afraid to grow up.

The Legion's next full frontal attack—on Billy Wilder's comedy, *Kiss Me, Stupid!* (1964)—can be viewed either as a determined, if belated, flourish to regain its old fighting spirit in defense of decency or as a demonstration to those who had been dismayed by recent decisions of its inability to differentiate between the artistically meritorious and the meretricious.

Some felt that Wilder had only himself to blame. Ever since *Some Like It Hot*, with its cross-dressing, its diaphanously attired Marilyn Monroe and an outrageous, homosexual quip by Joe E. Brown at the fade-out, the director seemed to have been treading a fine line between adult humor and outright bad taste.[24] The Legion had narrowly decided against giving *Some Like It Hot* a C, and it viewed with only slightly less disfavor his next production, *The Apartment*, the story of an aspiring executive who lends his flat to superiors for trysts with their mistresses. The plot of *Irma La Douce*, following close on the heels of these, hinged on the relationship between a Parisian prostitute and her pimp.[25] Perhaps Wilder had exhausted the stock of whatever goodwill he may have had. In any case, the benefit of the doubt accorded to that trio was not to be extended to *Kiss Me, Stupid!* and the Legion applied its strictest label to a domestically made production for the first time since *Baby Doll*.

Loosely based on an Italian farce, *Kiss Me, Stupid!* is basically an extended gentleman's smoker joke, with outrageous dialogue but tame visuals. A popular singer, Dino, finds himself stranded in a small Nevada town, Climax, and at the temporary mercy of Orville J. Spooner, gas station attendant, part-time church organist and aspiring songwriter. To draw the crooner's attention to his musical compositions while his car is being repaired and, at the same time, cater to Dino's physical requirements, Spooner hires Polly the Pistol, a bar girl. It seems that unless Dino has sexual intercourse on a nightly basis, he develops a headache. A plot twist has the singer sleeping with Spooner's wife while Polly whoops it up with Spooner. In an epilogue, the dim Orville hears his song being performed but is unaware of what happened. His wife simply smiles a knowing smile and says, "Kiss me, stupid!."

In Legion eyes, the seventy-year-old Shurlock's decision to grant the film a seal appeared to be yet another instance of his capitulation to the rising tide of permissiveness. Not only was the foreign-language cinema making increasing inroads, but the hitherto relatively demure English equivalent had jettisoned its witty, civilized image, first for kitchen-sink drama and its attendant realism, and then for amoral, slightly sadistic spy thrillers. The phenomenally popular James Bond series posed a particularly acute problem with its succession of sexually charged women, including *Goldfinger's* indecently named Pussy Galore, who instantly succumbed to Sean Connery's charm. 1964 seemed to be a banner year for women of ill repute. *The Night of the Iguana*, *The Americanization of Emily*, *The Carpetbaggers* and *Where Love Has Gone* all revolved around practitioners of the oldest profession.

The only concession Wilder had made to PCA sensibilities—and it was at the behest of friends and cast members—was to amend the scene where Dino seduces Spooner's drunken wife. Dean Martin and Felicia Farr were recalled for the shooting of an alternative version giving the impression that the singer falls asleep without consummating the sex act although, teasingly, there was still some doubt left in the spectator's mind as to whether he had slept the entire night. This minimally bowdlerized version was submitted to the Legion on October 21, 1964. Relations between it and Shurlock had deteriorated so much over the previous twelve months that the former distrusted anything controversial bearing a seal. Sure enough, *Kiss Me, Stupid!* was, in the words of a reviewer, "so badly soiled that nothing less than a full-scale rinsing would permit even the possibility of a B."[26] The list of objections Sullivan presented to United Artists ran to five closely types pages and included twenty-three instances of offensive language and sound effects (the creaking of bed springs, for instance), suggestive costuming in the case of Polly (Kim Novak) and the name of the town where these gross acts occurred. The script seemed to be infested with double entendres. A dentist tells the insanely jealous Oliver, concerning his wife's treatment, "I am putting an inlay in her lower, left bicuspid." Dino, en route to Orville's garden, explains that his wife is going "to show me her parsley."[27]

These, and other objections, puzzled Wilder, who regarded them as nit-picking or the reading of meanings into perfectly innocent remarks. He was at a loss to understand what was improper in the line, "Whoever heard of a groom playing the organ at his own wedding?" when the character in question was an organist; and what tortured interpretation of, "You mean she's going to drink out of his shoe?" could render that statement offensive left him stumped. He also cautioned against the possibility of reshooting the questionable scenes. The sets had been dismantled and would be prohibitively expensive to rebuild. The players were scattered abroad or committed to other projects. (Kim Novak was in England filming another piece involving marital infidelity, *The Amorous Adventures of Moll Flanders*, which would displease the Legion in due course.) Still, the director felt he might be able to make sufficient revisions to appease the Church, specifically the elimination of the sound of creaking bed springs, the substitution of Thanksgiving for Palm Sunday in reference to the day on which the unsavory incidents occurred, and "stick" instead of "screw" in describing the means by which Polly kept a rhinestone attached to her navel. All of these alterations were contingent upon the Legion agreeing to lift its proposed C.[28]

Had there been extenuating circumstances, a compromise might have been arrived at. But there was too great a degree of unanimity among reviewers and consultors on the moral contamination of the script to permit a retreat. One after another had commented on the blatant disregard for Christian marriage, for the monotonous emphasis on sexual fulfillment as the most important aspect in life, and for the obscene, uncontrolled use of imagery such as the phallic cacti planted outside the house where most of the hanky-panky took place. Refusing to be moved, Little and Sullivan upheld the verdict and appended a lengthy rationale:

Satire on the foibles of its people has always been a sign of healthiness in a society. Through humor, the weakness of men can be exposed to a salutary recognition by all, and, many times much more effectively than by serious preachment. In the case of *Kiss Me, Stupid!*, however, not only has Mr. Wilder failed to create a genuine satire out of a situation about an amateur composer who attempts to sell his songs to a big name singer in exchange for the adulterous attentions of his alleged "wife" but he has regrettably produced a thoroughly sordid piece of realism which is aesthetically, as well as morally, repulsive. Crude and suggestive dialogue, a leering treatment of marital and extra-marital sex, a prurient preoccupation with lechery compound the film's bald condonation of immorality.[29]

Little reserved additional disapproval for United Artists' decision to release it through its art-house subsidiary, Lopert Pictures, a well-tried shoddy subterfuge that would fool no one.[30]

Neither side emerged with much honor saved. The movie swiftly faded at the box office, though it was arguable that the tired humor and feeble satire, not the Church's half-hearted campaign to enforce the C, led to its demise.

Wilder shrugged off the criticism, calling the Legion an anachronism in an era when *Lady Chatterly's Lover* and *Fanny Hill* were freely available in bookstores across the land. *Newsweek* also took it to task over what it viewed as its betrayal of the revised pledge, which had promised "to unite with all men of goodwill in promoting high and noble standards in motion picture entertainment." Incontrovertible evidence was at hand, said the magazine, in a perusal of the current list of Condemned films. Alongside Wilder's mediocre comedy were *Breathless, L'Avventura, Knife in the Water* and *Jules and Jim,* all highly regarded works of cinematic art by some of Europe's most prestigious directors. What had been graded A-I and presumably suitable for children of the faithful were *The Sins of Babylon, Snake Woman, The Earth Dies Screaming* and *Godzilla versus the Thing*—which Fathers Little and Sullivan could hardly defend as likely to elevate good taste.[31]

By 1965, and with all the enthusiasm of a child visiting the dentist for a tooth extraction, Hollywood was reluctantly having to contemplate the possibility of a classification system for its product. For as long as anyone could remember, its motto had been, "Let the parents beware," and its only concession to such a practice had been the Green Sheet, a parental guide to the movies containing recommendations of those suitable for children. With a circulation that seldom went above 30,000 from its first appearance in 1934, it had several deficiencies. The most glaring was exclusion of its verdicts from all film advertisements at the insistence of the Production Code Administration on the grounds that it would foster classification within the industry. That its costs were underwritten by the Motion Picture Producers and Directors Association laid it open to the charge that it was a house publication, afraid to bite the hand that fed it. Significantly, it limited its reviews to domestic pictures until 1963, when it somewhat reluctantly began to acknowledge the existence of foreign equivalents. Even with this addition, it reviewed, on average, only two hundred titles annually, or less than half the number exhibited in the United States. There were complaints from those in the hinterland that reviews appeared prior to a movie's general release whereas that same title might take up to six months to arrive at a rural destination. Even so, as the sixties progressed, the Green Sheet was excluding more and more from its listings of pictures suitable for children unaccompanied by adults. In 1963, it rated only six in this category.

Hollywood had a number of reasons for obstinately maintaining its opposition to a classification system. It pointed to the impossibility of establishing a chronological cut-off age for children. Many a sixteen-year-old, the argument went, had the sensibility and sophistication of an adult, while others in that age bracket were still children emotionally. Whose standards would prevail? Whose taste or judgment would determine the particular rating? Labeling certain titles "adult" would simply whet the curiosity of teens lacking parental supervision and looking for sensation. Thus, classification might have the unforeseen result of attracting the undisciplined rather than keeping the disciplined away. Most diligent parents were well informed via the Legion and other rating services. Classification would deny them the right to make up their minds by foisting the opinions of others on them. Nor, in the last resort, was it fair to ask a harassed ticket saleslady to judge age without recourse to birth certificates or similar documentation.[32]

These objections pointedly ignored salient facts. Most Western nations already had government-controlled classification systems in place and these functioned efficiently on the whole. Regardless of the interpretation of "maturity," state governments established age levels below which individuals could not do certain things, such as drive automobiles or consume alcohol. There was no reason why an arbitrary limit should not be set for viewing certain films. Precensorship already existed, being predicated on movies being available to all. The inevitable consequence, long in evidence, was a certain blandness in the domestic product when compared to its foreign counterpart. Classification would allow a change in approach by allowing adults to see adult films.

Stripping away the platitudes about free speech and freedom of choice, one would find beneath a crass commercial motive for the reluctance to change. Hollywood wanted to have its cake and eat it too. It was committed to the belief that its freedom to make adult pictures must not exclude the right of all ages to see them, and never would the industry admit that allowing universal access on all occasions might be wrong. It would not countenance the fact that the price to be paid for the degree of artistic freedom available to European filmmakers was government or voluntary classification.

Of course, the Legion's interest in the controversy was by no means academic. Boycotts, picketing and C ratings had not staunched the flow of ever more daring Hollywood films. If the industry were willing to have some kind of advisory classification carried out by a statutory agency, perhaps an offshoot of the PCA, it would find the Church willing to meet it half way. Sullivan had listened to Spyros Skouras's grim prophecy that classification as a green light for adult fare would also be a signal for pornographers to enter the legitimate market, but the Legion chief was willing to give the industry the benefit of the doubt in changing times.[33] Already, in 1963, the Special Classification had been changed to A-IV, to which was appended the somewhat vague and clumsy definition, "Morally unobjectionable for adults, with reservations." The intent was to widen the application of the rating, hitherto applied, as has been noted, to sex hygiene dramas and ostentatiously proleftist or theologically questionable documentaries, to films that treated "serious themes in an adult way" but, "while not morally offensive in themselves, require caution and some analysis and explanation as a protection to the uninformed against wrong interpretations and false conclusions."[34] Tennessee Williams's *Suddenly Last Summer*, with its intimations of cannibalism and homosexuality, would have almost certainly been placed in the B or C category a decade earlier, and the same held true for Joseph Strick's adaptation of James Joyce's *Ulysses*, which retained much of the lurid language, even though the novel was on the curriculum of many Catholic colleges' English Literature departments.

In a further concession to shifting mores, the Legion made a number of dramatic pronouncements in 1965. The first was a change of name to the less censorious National Catholic Office for Motion Pictures (NCOMP). This resulted from a bishops' meeting in Rome that summer. More than semantics was involved. Though it was suggested in official communiques that there was no question of compromise on moral principles because the office would continue to exercise its mandate of condemning unsuitable entertainment, there was an acknowledgement of "the legitimacy of responsible adult films." It could also be guaranteed that the old guard would protest vehemently at this further dismantling of the old fortress, as the official statement from the Episcopal Committee recognized:

No transitions are accomplished without pain, and there undoubtedly will be misunderstandings about the present work of the NCOMP, especially by those whose background predisposes them to dismiss movies as merely escapist entertainment. But it is necessary that the Catholic film apostolate cultivate this proper appreciation of films that reflect the concerns of real life as well as it has fostered and continues to promote the family entertainment film. If the film apostolate in the United States aspires to leadership in influencing both the film artist and his audience, it must accept responsibility in welcoming the appearance of every good film, whether it is meant for the few or the many.[35]

Another initiative, which would surely have caused Father Daly, the Legion's first director, to smile, was the institution, also in 1965, of annual awards for films "whose artistic vision and expression best embody authentic human values" in various categories. This effectively laid to rest the negativism of past Legion judgments by seeking out meritorious titles. While none objected to selection of the undersea documentary, *World Without Sun*, as Best Film of Educational Value and few took exception to the choice of *The Sound of Music* as Best Film for General Audiences (except, perhaps, for its syrupy sentimentality), a fair number of eyebrows were raised over John Schlesinger's *Darling* as Best Film for Mature Audiences. Rated X in its homeland by the British Board of Film Censors, the amoral tale of a beautiful woman who drifts from man to man seeking sexual and emotional fulfillment contained adultery and abortion. Quigley would no doubt have agonized over yet another betrayal of original principles, but cancer had claimed him in 1964. His friend and kindred spirit, William Mooring, made a despairing case for the traditionalists. In a *Tidings* editorial, headlined "Art In, Morals Out with the New Awards," he berated NCOMP for surrendering itself to "an artistic vision and expression" in films that mocked moral values. Sympathetic support for his view came in letters to the editor of various Catholic magazines, several of which asserted that viewing *Darling* only half a dozen years before would have been considered an occasion of sin even for adults. Was there any reason for taking the pledge when its application had become meaningless?[36]

That was no rhetorical question and raised yet another contentious issue. The Legion pledge had become the object of criticism, dissatisfaction, indifference and even hostility before the fifties were out. In the wake of Vatican II it was increasingly branded as a pathetic anachronism by some of the laity as well as the film industry. The latter took exception to the negative attitude, wearily rehearsing its oft-repeated claim that if a bad film warranted condemnation, a good one deserved some form of approbation. It added to the image of the Church as the patron of boycotts. Its negative wording effectively excluded American Catholics from having a positive impact on the moral content and style of the mass media. These were criticisms that the Legion took to heart as the Episcopal Committee worked on a revision, which was ready for December 1959. The new version read:

In the name of the Father and of the Son and of the Holy Spirit

I promise to promote by word and deed what is morally and artistically good in motion picture entertainment.

I promise to discourage indecent, immoral and unwholesome motion pictures, especially by my good example and always in a responsible and civil-minded manner.

I promise to guide those under my care and influence their choice of motion pictures that are morally and culturally inspiring.

I promise not to co-operate, by my patronage, with theaters which regularly show objectionable films.

I promise, as a member of the Legion of Decency, to acquaint myself with its aims and to consult its classifications and to unite with all men of goodwill in promoting high and noble standards in motion picture entertainment.

I freely make those solemn resolutions to the honor of God, for the good of my soul and for the welfare of my country. Amen.[37]

Noteworthy was the elimination of the word "condemn" and the substitution of "promote" and "guide." But old habits died hard and by a small majority, the bishops, meeting in Washington that year, voted to retain the old pledge, and allow individual dioceses to choose between the two versions. Even so, by 1963, and in the spirit of *Miranda Prorsus*, 95 percent of churches were administering the new pledge. When the winds of change picked up to gale force, the very concept of pledge-taking came under scrutiny. The old objections to conformity, peer pressure and the authoritarian command of the clergy were revived and found few defenders. It took a short time to go from a procedure where the congregation sat passively while the priest read the text of the pledge to a moment of silence in church which permitted each individual to reflect "freely and generously" on his commitment to God over attendance at immoral films, or not, as he saw fit. It hardly seemed worthwhile to ascertain whether the congregation was of a mind to rally even to this modification of the old battlecry; the assumption was that it had become irrelevant. By 1970 the ceremony was a thing of the past except in a few die-hard parishes.

With negative capsule reviews and the annual pledge well on their way to becoming obsolete, the last great controversy with which the Legion had to struggle was its attitude toward nudity. The furor over *The Pawnbroker* (1965)

raised yet again and in acute form the nature of the censorial structure that had been constructed for Catholics. Whatever else its purpose might have been, it had not been designed primarily (one could argue even tangentially) for an artistic perception of screen entertainment. As events since 1957 had shown, the rigidity of the criteria for evaluating motion pictures that had been developed over the Legion's lifetime interposed a barrier against acceptance of a deeply felt work and a creative impulse of its author. No matter how well a movie might be perceived in terms of its intrinsic worth, a single unacceptable element negated the positive and dictated a negative course of action. The rank and file were required to discard the entire apple because of one blemish on its skin. The Legion's respect for the artistry of a creative talent when balanced against the presence of unpalatable aspects in the creation must always be found wanting.

In *The Pawnbroker*, the title character, Sol Nazerman (played by Rod Steiger), is an aging Jewish survivor of the holocaust. His wife and children were murdered by Nazis in a concentration camp. Emotionally numbed by the tragedy, he lives behind an emotional barrier every bit as forbidding and unassailable as the serving cage in his Harlem, N.Y., pawnshop. Nothing is allowed to touch his soul, neither the adoration of his young, black apprentice nor the kindliness of a neighborhood social worker. He seems oblivious to the parade of piteous individuals that daily winds its way to his counter, part of the "stench" of humanity. He has decided, instead, to dedicate the rest of his life to making money. But love and sadness cannot be entirely sublimated. The past keeps returning, unbidden, to his memory in a series of flashbacks that grow ever so slightly longer as his will yields to them. In one of these, a subway train he has boarded becomes a cattle car full of fellow Jews bound for Auschwitz. In a closing sequence he kneels before the dying body of the youth who has saved his life and utters a silent scream that means to equate the casual violence of the ghetto with that of the extermination camp. Suffering is the theme of the picture. Its resolution in redemption is indeterminate, as the pawnbroker stumbles down the street, his face etched with agony.

The producers had approached a number of major studios with their adaptation of the Edward Wallant novel but only MGM evinced much interest, warning that major revisions would have to be made to make the story more upbeat. Had negotiations concluded successfully, Metro would almost surely have had qualms about the inclusion of a short scene where a young black prostitute bares her breasts in front of Nazerman in the hope of getting a better deal for some trinkets she wants to pawn. Her action calls to mind the stripping and brutalization his wife had received at the hands of the S.S. guards prior to her rape and death. Though dramatically justified, the sequence contravened the Production Code's ruling on nudity, and Shurlock invoked the clause in declining to give *The Pawnbroker* a seal even if, in private, he acknowledged the inarguable artistic merit of the remainder. Allied Artists, a minor company that belonged to the MPAA, agreed to handle distribution, and launched an appeal. The Appeals Board sat for four and a half hours viewing the picture and cited Section

6 of its procedure to overturn Shurlock's decision. The clause in question read: "If it should be of the opinion that the circumstances in connection with any appeal are such that, despite the provisions of the Code, as applied by the Production Code Administration, an exemption should be afforded, it may be granted but solely with respect to the picture under review." The decision was variously hailed as "a precedent-shattering step" and "a milestone" in recognizing that good taste and artistic merit had triumphed over an archaic rule. In a sense, though, the poison chalice of the nudity problem had been handed back to Shurlock. The leeway that had been granted in this instance would surely be used by others with claims to similar, morally uplifting pictures.[38]

This is precisely what alarmed Little when asked for his reaction to the Appeals Board verdict. The Legion had watched the movie on March 2, 1965 while the appeal was in process, and reluctantly decided on a Condemned rating solely because of its utilization of nudity in plot resolution. However, it had decided to postpone announcement of the decision to avoid giving the company the opportunity to capitalize on what might be construed as Legion obscurantism when contrasted with the prerelease reviews, most of which were laudatory in the extreme. It also clung to the forlorn hope that the appeal would fail. The Appeal Board's action, said Little, was a distressing development. Not only was it precedent-setting for a domestic film, it would impact on producers of titles currently in release whose nude scenes had not fared as well. Those included *The Sandpiper*, with a momentarily exposed Elizabeth Taylor and Al Zugsmith's *Fanny Hill*, with considerably more nudity to its discredit. Still, in both instances their makers could protest that they were moral in intent and meaning.

Yet, when it came to invoking moral principles, even the Legion was not entirely blameless. Since the start of the decade it had been turning a blind eye to partial frontal nudity in subtitled foreign films with limited drawing potential such as the French *Cleo from 5 to 7* (1962) or in sequences where the glimpse of unadorned flesh was so momentary as to be missed if the eye blinked at the crucial moment. Elizabeth Taylor's massage in *Cleopatra* was an example. It had also decided to make a distinction between full rear male nudity and the female equivalent, holding that the former was not sexually stimulating to women and "normal" men, whereas the latter was stimulating to heterosexual males—a masculine view of female attitudes toward eroticism that was not necessarily correct.[39] This had permitted Anthony Quinn to flaunt his posterior in *Zorba, the Greek* and Alan Bates his in *King of Hearts* without their films earning the lowest rating.[40] But in the case of *The Pawnbroker*, insisted Little, the nudity was frontal female. Furthermore, the same point could have been made by shooting the sequence from behind the woman so that only her back was seen or by having a close-up of her face. Support for this view came from a surprising but welcome source. The fall issue of the academic *Film Quarterly* pointed out that the producers had taken liberties with the text of the novel. In the novel the woman does indeed try to entice the pawnbroker, but without removing her blouse, and Nazerman's memory of his wife's degradation occurs elsewhere in the plot. It also criticized the impromptu striptease as artificial in execution, suggesting burlesque, rather than a cunning appeal to a man's sexual urge and thus failing to make a convincing trigger for the brutally realistic memory the pawnbroker has of his wife's degradation. Instead, the journal continued, the episode came across as a gratuitous shock effect rather than a unified experience.

Meanwhile, and in response to those uncharitable enough to inquire of the Legion as to whether the exhibition of nudity in art galleries, including the Vatican's own, was equally reprehensible, Little drew the well-worn distinction between patrons of museums and movie theatergoers. The one group was well able to restrain its collective emotion; the other, immature and impressionable, would be stimulated in its baser instincts. Too, there was an aeons-old tradition that recognized the undraped state of the human body in painting and sculpture as a legitimate art form. For the Johnny-come-lately cinema it was never an artistic necessity. This might have been a sound argument in the days of McClafferty, but it had a distinctly hollow ring when laid side by side with recent pronouncements on the artistic mission of the motion picture. Martin Landau, the film's producer, appealed over Little's head to Archbishop Krol and the Episcopal Committee, making an impassioned defense of the film's noble intentions and reminding them of the prestige that had attached to the production as a result of its being selected as the official American entry at the 1964 Berlin Film Festival. There the sequence in question had occasioned no comment.[41]

Krol and the bishops refused to be moved. Nakedness was nakedness, said the archbishop, and the Legion was to be praised in its effort to close the floodgates when a torrent of unadorned female flesh was threatening to inundate the screen. Hollywood had used its ingenuity in the past to conform to the Production Code and it could continue to find means to suggest the unclothed state without having to resort to blatant exposure.[42] But this caused counter-reaction in the liberal Catholic press. In her *America* film column, Moira Walsh acknowledged "the elder statesman reputation the Legion had acquired as the most listened-to voice in film regulation outside the industry," but argued that surely the only appropriate regulator of a work of art was the artistic conscience of a skilled and responsible practitioner. Outside regulation was unnecessary for the honest artist and, by the same token, ineffective for the irresponsible one who, while abiding by the letter of the law often violated its spirit. *Ramparts* and *West Side News*, two examples of leftist political opinion, were far more condemnatory. Where, they wanted to know, had the Legion of Decency been for the past thirty years when infinitely more was at stake than the exposure of a pair of black breasts? Was it only myopia that had caused it to ignore the greater obscenity visited on black people by Hollywood, to wit its portrayal of that race as, variously, shuffling, servile Sambos and Aunt Jemimas or mentally deficient comedians? To compound this sin of omission and to humiliate further, blacks had been forced to watch these insulting images in segregated theaters.

Nowhere had the Legion's voice been raised in protest. Its stand on *The Pawn-broker* was surely hypocrisy of the worst sort.

But, having nailed its colors to the mast over this particular movie, the Legion grimly stuck to its decision, hoping for a commercial failure.[43] The prayer was answered. For all the critical kudos that had accompanied it, *The Pawnbroker*'s overall bleak view of life, its lack of stars and even its black-and-white pho-tography conspired to cause its lack of success with the general public. When the ailing Allied Artists sold the rights to American-International in 1966, the new owners hastened to comply with NCOMP suggestion.[44] The offensiveness of the scene was nullified by substituting a close-up of the woman's face, and the rating immediately became A-III.[45] Even that was not the end of the story. Copies of the unexpurgated version that had been circulating in Europe emerged in art theaters from time to time, and a Jesuit-sponsored conference on the cinema, held at Fordham University in 1967, also screened the original in a discussion on the cinema and censorship. Sullivan could only offer up the lame excuse that since NCOMP had no legal contact with a distributor, it depended on his word of honor that the sanitized copy was being exhibited; but this hardly explained the presence of the original in a Catholic institution except, perhaps, in terms of elitism.[46] Academics, it seemed, were less likely to be corrupted than the common throng.

The Pawnbroker was to be one of NCOMP's last flourishes against nudity as the sole rationale for a C rating. Monsignor Little had announced his resignation from the Legion in September 1966 to take up pastoral duties at St. Bartho-lomew's, one of the largest and most prominent churches in the Brooklyn diocese. Though he jocularly explained his decision as a desire "to die in the Stations of the Cross not looking at Gina Lollobrigida,"[47] he had been in office for seventeen years, the last half dozen or so in the firing line. It is sometimes forgotten that while Vatican II had paved the way for a more positive relationship with the media, this new relationship was not welcomed everywhere. Some saw it as sowing the seeds of disruption. Attitudes toward film morality were a case in point. Cardinal McIntyre and conservative elements had viewed, with in-creasing dismay, the implementation of a forward policy, and whether or not they saw the hand of the Young Turk Sullivan behind each move, they were inclined to believe that Little, as his superior, far from pulling rank and re-straining his subordinate, had allowed himself to be swept along on the per-missive tide. Sullivan himself is convinced that there was a definite element of ecclesiastical coercion in Little's disappearance. That Sullivan did not follow his superior into oblivion was due, in part, to the support of Krol and to the practical difficulty in replacing two experienced staff people with newcomers on short notice.[48]

NCOMP policy over the most controversial picture of 1966, *Who's Afraid of Virginia Woolf?* and the considerably less controversial *Hawaii* almost certainly brought matters to a head. When the NCOMP chose to classify *Who's Afraid* of *Virginia Woolf?* A-IV, it knew it was making one of the most contentious decisions in its brief existence as Legion successor. A landmark judgment was rendered, marking a definite break with yet another principle of Legion philosophy. The decision was to occasion more correspondence, most of it hostile, than any film before or since.[49] For those who agreed with *Time* that NCOMP had once and for all jettisoned the bleak negativism it had inherited for a critical recognition of moral goodness embedded in a sinful topic, there were more numerous—and shrill—voices who saw it as irrefutable proof that the institution had ceased to be a reliable moral guide. For the one camp, the rating arrived at was the only possible decision for a Church agency trying to encourage American Catholics to adopt an intelligent, literate approach to contemporary themes; for the other, it was an act of betrayal of millions of ordinary 'Catholics' and, no less deplorably, of the Production Code by the Code's one-time closest friend.

Edward Albee's critically acclaimed Broadway hit of 1962 was deemed to have forfeited its chance for a Pulitzer Prize because of its raw language. The setting is a New England college campus where an academically mediocre history professor, George, and his shrewish wife, Martha, exist in a marital hell that they have created for themselves over the years. They invite a young biology instructor and his wife back for drinks after a faculty party. For the remainder of the night the quartet participate in a game of vicious character assassination. When the verbal abuse palls, Martha seduces the visitor but finds him to be a flop in bed. Her entire married life has been dominated by the fantasy that she has a son. Near play's end, George informs her that "the little bugger" has been killed in a car accident and proceeds to read the *Dies Irae* from a fake missal. Martha tearfully protests that he must not destroy the illusion, the only thing that has bound them together in their self-made inferno. Finally, the guests gone, they decide to remain together, stripped of their pretence and possibly less pessimistic about the future.

The most obvious problem in trying to translate the play to the screen was the uninhibited language, with eleven "goddamns," five "sons of bitches" and assorted graphic phrases such as "up yours" and "hump the hostess." There were also unflattering anatomical references to "melons bobbling" and "ass." Though the Production Code had long-since permitted "damn" and "hell," no single movie script submitted to it had ever contained such a concentration of salty language. To permit an unadulterated transcription from the play would have destroyed what vestiges remained of the Code's prohibitions against bad language. On the other hand, to limit the profanity would be to dilute the flavor of the Broadway success—or such was Albee's view when he politely refused to substitute new lines for the "potent dialogue" at the request of Warner Brothers, who had paid $500,000 for the rights.[50] The company turned to Ernest Lehman, a veteran Hollywood scriptwriter, to come up with something more to Shurlock's liking. Ironically, Lehman's most recent effort had been for the saccharine *Sound of Music*, an exercise in unadulterated blandness.

For several weeks he wrestled with the intractable lines in a despairing attempt to launder them and still remain true to the spirit of the original. "You son of a bitch . . . " became "You dirty, lousy . . . ;" and "Hump the hostess" was trans-mogrified into the strange and unlikely "Hop the hostess." But soon he was forced to agree with director Mike Nichols that such substitutions were dishonest and reprehensible. Nichols reminded him of an absurdity of the past that had fooled no one. It had occurred in a Gary Cooper movie where the lead had remarked, "He's so poor he hasn't got a pot to put flowers in." Frankness had to be the order of the day. "People do and say certain things in bed that we all know they do, and people say certain things to each other that we have all heard. The whole point of the sexual revolution . . . is to let these things take their place and then go back in proportion. We feel the language of Woolf is essential to the fabric."[51] The alternative strategy of releasing through an art-house subsidiary was not possible in this instance. Warners had hired two of the industry's most expensive stars, Elizabeth Taylor and Richard Burton, to play George and Martha. Their salaries, added to that of Nichols, sent the budget soaring to $7.5 million, which it could only recoup in first-run theaters. In any case, Warners did not even own such a subsidiary. For better or worse, *Virginia Woolf* would have to be a major production with equivalent box office expectations.

By the summer of 1966 only two bodies counted in the censorship stakes, the PCA and NCOMP. State and local groups had fallen one by one, the victims of court challenges to their constitutionality under the First Amend-ment's protection of free speech or of frustration in making their edicts stick in the case of specific titles. With Shurlock, at seventy-one, on the verge of retirement and Jack Valenti of the MPAA still an unknown quantity, Warners sensed that the battle over *Virginia Woolf* would be won or lost with the Catholic Office. Anything less than a C would put pressure on the Code-minders to modify their stand, and even that rating would not be disastrous if it were equated in the public's mind with high-class, adult entertainment. Additionally, the Appeals Board might take a liberal view, given the credentials of the piece. By design, the company shipped a heavily guarded print to New York on April 30, a few days before Shurlock saw the picture. Accompanying it was a dec-laration that Warners acknowledged the adult nature of the drama and was prepared to impose a restriction against admission of children under eighteen unless accompanied by a parent. This it would enforce on all exhibitors, and its advertising would be tailored accordingly.[52] This *de facto* recognition of industry-imposed classification was heartening to NCOMP and played a role in the final decision.

An analysis of the verdicts of the ninety-one reviewers and consultants in attendance at the Warners preview theater on May 2, shown in Table 2, provides further confirmation of the gap that had widened between the two groups, the one still containing remnants of the old guard, the other increasingly populated by individuals with knowledge of "cinema" rather than "movies."

Table 2
Final Voting Statistics for Who's Afraid of Virginia Woolf?

	Reviewers	Consultants	Total
A-II	0	1	1
A-III	2	7	9
A-IV	3	41	44
B	3	11	14
C	11	7	18

Unable to give precise rating:

A-III or A-IV	1	1	2
A-IV or B	1	1	2
B or C	0	1	1

On the objecting side were verdicts of "vulgar, disrespectful, obscene, just plain dirty, no positive values, no sufficient moral frame of reference, no clear-cut condemnation of evil," and that old bugaboo, "sacrilege." As one reviewer acerbically noted, if the office had condemned the nudity of The Pawnbroker on principle, it could hardly maintain that oft-repeated blasphemy was less serious; therefore it ought to act accordingly. Several clergymen lamented the taking of the Lord's name in vain, one suggesting that "Jack Warner" was a more fitting oath. But the majority begged to differ and, for the most part, submitted rationales that were far more detailed and no less deeply held. One priest, a specialist in communications media, submitted four typewritten single-spaced pages holding that Virginia Woolf was fundamentally a highly moral film, a brilliant, tragic revelation of the sadness and powers of deception within the human heart. Others felt that, in recommending the picture, NCOMP could go some way toward expunging the stereotype held in show business circles of what church groups looked for in religious movies:

It is not things like The Trouble with Angels. Too long moral garbage like Doris Day films have escaped censure because they break none of the rules. They merely contradict flatly every value of realistic ethics that Dan Lord had in mind when he made up the Code. There is no advocacy of immorality here, but a moan of resignation that immorality can touch people of wit and literacy as well as such toy people as the young couple. The bawdy allusions are placed where they belong: in a despicable context.

The imposition of the A-IV classification together with restrictions on age and advertising to which Warners had given prior consent did nothing to assuage the indignation of those of the laity with memories of Fathers Masterson and McClafferty. For them the last straw of permissiveness had been placed on the back of decency's camel. Martin Quigley, Jr., taking up the torch from his recently deceased father, rightly observed that the NCOMP decision would place Shurlock in an untenable position and make a positive Appeals Board verdict a formality. Nor did he see it as a single-case scenario. The entire Production Code had been "destroyed as a force for screen decency." Blasphemy, profanity and obscenity were absolutes and nothing had changed since 1929 to make them less so. Yet, by this one stroke, the office had succeeded in lowering moral standards of screen acceptability en route to demolishing the machinery of screen regulation that his father had laboriously constructed.[53] As if anything were needed to add fuel to the flames, *Life* magazine ran an intemperate feature with a three-page photo spread on the NCOMP decision. By chance it appeared on June 10, the day on which the appeal was upheld. The photographs, featuring an uninhibited, impromptu dance by Elizabeth Taylor in a roadside diner, conveyed an impression of sexual abandon that the film lacked in reality. The accompanying article contained an admission by Little that, although he had never encountered some of the words uttered in *Virginia Woolf* on the screen up to that point, he had heard them at Coney Island. Sullivan acknowledged that their predecessors in the Legion would indubitably have savaged the picture, but times were different. One might as well have said that a girl who appeared bikini-clad on a beach in 1800 rather than in 1966 would have suffered the same obloquy.[54]

Both were to rue these flippant comments. Within days of the *Life* feature, the NCOMP was deluged with outraged protests. A pastor in North Dakota was among the most vituperative but not untypical in writing, "Send us none of your bulletins. You are a disgrace to the Holy Roman Catholic Church, or are you intending to differ with that organization, too—the last bastion of morals but fast being invaded by liberals and freethinkers like the NCOMP? There is nothing I can do for you but remember you at Mass and ask Almighty God to bring you to your senses or knock you out of existence!"[55] A group of female parishioners in La Jolla, California, began a grass-roots campaign to urge abolition of NCOMP by means of a petition to be circulated nationwide. The intention was to send it to Cardinals Spellman and McIntyre. Rumor also had it that some of the more vexed among early signees wanted a rider that Little and Sullivan be defrocked for their sins.

From the besieged battlements of NCOMP headquarters, Sullivan tried to calm the storm by suggesting that the time had come to clarify the intent of the A-IV rating. What he proposed was a supplement to the *Catholic Film Newsletter* in the form of a round-table discussion on NCOMP's attitude to mature themes and their legitimate screen treatment, with space given over to the specifics of the *Virginia Woolf* case as an example of the philosophical application of the criteria. He was adamant that the project should not be construed as an apologia for the rating, but as a reasoned explanation as to why controversial pictures with serious themes deserved to be evaluated on the basis of "Christian criticism".[56] This gambit did nothing to placate critics, who continued to bombard the office throughout the summer with complaints and subscription cancellations.[57] The acid test of compliance with the self-imposed age limit came with the film's release in July. Theater owners, pusilanimous as ever, grumbled about the eighteen-plus clause with its requirement to check customers to determine age, fearing, too, that they would be prosecuted for airing an immoral picture. Marshall Fine, president of the fifteen thousand–strong National Association of Theater Owners (NATO), made a public display of contrition, agreeing with Martin Quigley, Jr. that there was no such thing as good taste in blasphemy, profanity and obscenity.[58] Privately, the membership basked in the publicity that preceded and accompanied *Virginia Woolf* and breathed a collective sigh of relief when their places of entertainment were not busted. Yet old habits soon reasserted themselves. By the time it went into second release, in the fall, the stringent requirements were no longer in place. "Parent" had become "adult" and drive-ins turned a blind eye when couples turned up, as was their custom, with kids in the back seat.

Even so, the office remained unrepentant. It insisted that to have issued a Condemnation would have had even less effect than in the case of *The Moon Is Blue*. Whether veterans of the pledge believed it or not, *Virginia Woolf* was a piece of cinematic literature, not to be lumped with the exploitationist drivel that was pouring into theaters from all parts of the world.[59]

During the furor over *The Pawnbroker*, Arthur Krim, president of United Artists, had asked Little for a ruling on nudity in connection with a multimillion dollar film version of James Michener's *Hawaii*, already in production.[60] There were other potentially difficult elements in this three-hour account of Christianity's conquest of the islands, not the least of which were incest in the Hawaiian royal family and the personality of the main character, a dour, Calvinist minister, played with the requisite amount of fanaticism by Max von Sydow. But the central censorship issue was a scene in which native women, naked above the waist, paddle and swim out to greet the arrival of the missionary's ship. For the naysayers in the IFCA there were no mitigating circumstances. Subjectively speaking, the women in *Hawaii* were younger, more attractive and indubitably lighter-skinned than the female in *The Pawnbroker*, and the scene in question was more likely to arouse prurient interest than the morose, unconsummated seduction attempt on Nazerman.[61] Nevertheless, Little gave a startling assurance to the United Artists president that the Legion had always exempted documentary sequences containing shots of unclad natives, and the nudity presented in *Hawaii* was, presumably, "a verisimilitude of native conditions prior to the white man." Given a company promise that no major female character would appear in a similar state of déshabille, the Legion secretary threw his weight in favor of an A-III rating.[62]

More than women's breasts were at issue. *Variety* found the decision worthy of comment in view of the fact that the subject of incest had a prominent place in the plot and was treated sympathetically. True, it occurred within a framework of non-Christian culture, but the film carefully avoided condemnation of the practice and left it to the audience to decide whether it was "right" for the Hawaiian royal family for whom it was a sacred institution. The portrait of the missionary, though he was a non-Catholic, was so negative as to leave the impression that conversion of the heathens was a tragedy. The anticipated flow of mail to the Legion and individual bishops spoke of "the Church double-crossing women," lamented that "decency appears to be dead," and deplored NCOMP's apparent "resignation from the fight for decent entertainment." NCOMP seemed to believe that some nudes were less dangerous to morals than others.[63] After 1966 a response to this line of reasoning would have to come from Father Sullivan alone.

The new executive secretary of NCOMP was well aware that he personified the organization's new spirit. NCOMP had become a very different beast from its predecessor and there could be no turning back of the clock. But developments in 1967 on the film censorship front forced Sullivan to cry halt. If NCOMP seemed to be charting a new course, Hollywood was plunging into unknown waters with reckless abandon. By year's end Sullivan had established a record of sorts by placing seventeen features in the Condemned category, more than the Legion had done in any single twelve-month period in its history.[64]

His actions were in response to the moviemakers' determination to cash in on the popular culture scene as their receipts continued to plummet. School principals had not long-since ordered male students sporting Beatles haircuts to have them trimmed above collar level before allowing them to return to class. But by 1967 miniskirts, see-through blouses and topless swimsuits were the stuff of fashion magazines. Sexual freedom via The Pill, trial marriages or cohabitation with no thought of marriage at all, simulated sex on the stage and raunchy rivals to what was becoming, by comparison, an ever more pristine *Playboy* seemed to give proof that puritanism in the United States was dying. The Hollywood scene was changing more rapidly than in any comparable period in its existence. Conglomerates looked enviously at the studios, not necessarily for their prime function of making movies but for their undervalued real estate and their vast film libraries that could be used to feed the voracious monster that was commercial television. Runaway production, as it had been termed in the fifties—the shooting of pictures overseas with international casts and budgets— seemed to be the rule rather than the exception. The MGM lion and Columbia's lady with the torch did not necessarily signify a production from the studio but could simply be the convenient logo under which a film was released. Also, far from the prying eyes of American censors, scenes and dialogue could be inserted with impunity. Profit or loss, not prestige and purity, were the prime concerns of the corporate owners. Since the television set had acquired color, the one ace left for the movie industry to play in its struggle to hold on to the fragmented audience was frankness.

NCOMP lurched about in response, scattering C ratings with abandon.[65] But they no longer amounted to very much. Its imposition on Michelangelo Antonioni's *Blow Up* (1966), which was distributed by MGM and contained glimpses of female public hair in a display of nudity, was tempered by Sullivan's reply to a lay inquiry. "Where a family man is equipped to interpret a film like *Blow Up* and guide discussion of it for and with his family, we would, of course, have no objection nor more than we would do to the study of this film and others carrying C ratings in a film education class. . . . We made no attempt whatever to limit distribution of the film. In all cases the ratings are intended as a guide, a reference and a very minimal one at that, rather than a rigid set of 'do's' and 'don'ts.' "[66]

Without renouncing the old ratings system, such utterances and those of the consultors progressively undermined its spirit and goals, so much so that the IFCA formally dissociated itself from NCOMP in 1969. The handling of *Rosemary's Baby* must have wistfully reminded remaining veterans from Mrs. Looram's glory days of a time when a hint of blasphemy was enough to banish a work. Its director, Roman Polanski, was already the recipient of three Cs, for *Cul De Sac*, *Repulsion* and *Fearless Vampire Killers*, when he turned his hand to an adaptation of Ira Levin's tale of devil possession. The heroine is impregnated by Satan and bears his child in an erotically charged parody of the birth of Christ. The witches and sorcerers assembled greet her with cries of "Hail, Rosemary!" and inform her that she was chosen among all women for the honor. Comparisons were made with *The Miracle*. More to the point, it was seen as the ultimate test as to whether NCOMP had retained any of its power over the movie industry. It condemned *Rosemary's Baby* for "the perverted use which the film makes of fundamental Christian beliefs, especially in the events surrounding the birth of Christ, and its mockery of religious persons and practices,"[67] adding that the various prolonged scenes of nudity would, in themselves, have brought an identical rating.

Variety was correct in its speculation that the decision would strike thoughtful observers as ironic. Rather than defining *moral* in the strictly sexual aspect, they felt the Catholic Church should deal with the moral import of films in a wider sense. As always, it was liberal churchmen taking that viewpoint who tended to disagree with NCOMP on those occasions when it had to address religious elements.[68] Moira Walsh, with her accustomed perspicacity, claimed it was logical for characters with a commitment to pure evil to act out baleful mirror images of Christian beliefs and practices. This was far from saying that the film made perverted use of Christian beliefs, as the NCOMP condemnation implied. As far as the general public was concerned, the debate was irrelevant.[69] The impact of the Legion/NCOMP's most recent condemnations of *Hurry Sundown*, *Kiss Me, Stupid!* and *Reflections in a Golden Eye* was difficult to gauge, because none of them had much box office potential and ended up no better than breaking even. Of *Blow Up*, *The Pawnbroker* and *The Fox* (the last an adaptation of a D. H. Lawrence story of the sexual impact of an itinerant sailor on two lesbians living on an isolated farm) it might be said that each could be marginally defined as an art-house offering. But who could deny that *Rosemary's Baby* was the quintessence of commercialism? In challenging a James Bond spy-thriller for box office champion of the year 1968, it narrowly missed the prize.

The pundits had their proof. A Condemned rating was an irrelevance. The legendary power that the Catholic Church had exerted over the motion picture industry was at an end.

NOTES

1. NLOD file, "Lolita." The unsigned, undated pamphlet also castigated Louella Parsons for publicizing the casting of Sue Lyons, and James Mason for lowering himself to play Humbert Humbert.

2. Leff and Simmons, pp. 218–19, summarize the tortured history of the manuscript's fight to be published.

3. *Commonweal*, November 28, 1958.

4. According to the *Hollywood Reporter*, October 13, 1958, Harris and Kubrick had pledged to Shurlock that "it will not be dirty but will be presented to you in script form first." Such a procedure was uncommon; normally only completed scripts were considered. An unexpurgated *Spartacus* was released commercially in 1991.

5. Kubrick had told a *Look* magazine reporter: "The Code has become loose suspenders that hold up the baggy pants of the circus clown. . . . It allows the pants to slip dangerously but never to fall." Jack Hamilton, "Hollywood Bypasses the Production Code," September 29, 1959, p. 80.

6. Alvin Tofler, "Interview with Vladimir Nabokov," *Playboy*, January 1964, pp. 35–45.

7. Quigley had further irritated Legion sensibilities with his insistence that he be treated as a middleman in all dealings between it and MGM. Sullivan informed the company that the Legion would continue direct negotiations with both it and Embassy Pictures. NLOD file, "The Law," Sullivan to Mary Ryan, July 15, 1959. Quigley charged that the proposed C rating for *Lolita* was a manifestation of vindictiveness against him, personally, to settle old scores. He maintained that the Legion was initially for an A-III or B until it learned that he was personally involved in the production in London. QP Box 3, Quigley to Spellman, October 20, 1961. There is no evidence that this was so.

8. NLOD file, "Lolita," Shurlock to Little, September 14, 1961.

9. Ibid. Among the dozens of letters were several suggesting that charges of pedophilia should be filed.

10. Ibid., Memorandum, undated.

11. NLOD *Annual Report*, 1960, p. 6.

12. NLOD file, "Lolita," Memorandum, July 13, 1961.

13. Ibid., Sullivan to Little, September 26, 1961.

14. Ibid., Little to David Stillman, October 10, 1961. The Legion had had preliminary discussions with Harris and Seven Arts representatives on September 21 when there was agreement on an eighteen-plus age limitation and a carefully monitored advertising campaign (Little memorandum, September 25, 1961).

15. Ibid., Stillman to McNulty, October 13, 1961. He demanded to know why precedent had been ignored. *Lolita* was the only instance in Legion history where the chairman of the Episcopal Committee had unilaterally imposed his will.

16. Ibid., Memorandum, undated.

17. Ibid., Memorandum, October 26, 1961.

18. Ibid., Memorandum, December 20, 1961.

19. Ibid., Consultor to Sullivan, January 26, 1962.

20. Ibid. Eliot Hyman to Little, February 6, 1962. Among the conditions was no tie-up with the novel. McNulty had absented himself from further screenings and left the chairman's task to Archbishop Kroll. See, also, Little to McNulty, February 15, 1962.

21. Quoted in the *New York Herald Tribune*, July 15, 1962.

22. This had always been true to a degree. But now, lax parental supervision aggravated the situation. The problem was discussed at the National Catholic Welfare Conference meeting on November 29, 1961.

23. *New York Times*, June 14, 1962.

24. The capsule comment read, in part: "This film, though it purports to be a comedy, contains screen material elements that are judged to be scandalously offensive to Christian and traditional standards of morality and decency." NLOD *Ratings Guide*, December 1959.

25. Ibid., "a coarse mockery of virtue."

26. NLOD file, "Kiss Me, Stupid," Miscellaneous ballot sheets, October 21, 1964.

27. Ibid., unsigned and undated memorandum.

28. Ibid., Wilder to Robert Benjamin, United Artists, November 6, 1964.

29. NLOD, *Ratings Guide*, December 1964.

30. NLOD file, "Kiss Me, Stupid," Little to David Picker, United Artists, November 28, 1964. The film would be resubmitted for rating in 1970, at which time it was classified G.P.

31. *Newsweek*, December 28, 1964.

32. These reservations were detailed in the *Journal of the Producers Guild of America*, September 1961.

33. Father Sullivan in conversation with the author, May 1990.

34. Corliss, p. 49

35. National Catholic Office for Motion Pictures, *Annual Report*, 1966.

36. Leff and Simmons, pp. 252–53.

37. Revised pledge reproduced in NLOD Report, 1960, pp. 8–9.

38. NLOD file, "The Pawnbroker," Little to Kroll, April 28, 1965.

39. Corliss, p. 54. A statement to this effect appeared in the *New York Times*, April 20, 1967.

40. NLOD file, "The Pawnbroker," April 21, 1965.

41. Ibid., Krol to Landau, May 10, 1965.

42. Ibid., Press release, October 14, 1965.

43. According to *Variety*, February 23, 1966, Loews broke with precedent by booking a C-rated picture, albeit not for its showcase theaters.

44. *New York Times*, August 3, 1966.

45. Corliss, p 54.

46. Leff and Simmons, p. 274.

47. Sullivan believes that Little was under constant pressure by Quigley and his supporters for having allowed himself to be led by those who, they insisted, had come, on Sullivan's coattails, to wield calamitous power over the Legion since the late fifties. Interview with author, May 1990. Little's comment on Lollobrigida is in Alexander Walker, *Sex in the Movies: The Celluloid Sacrifice* (Baltimore: Penguin Books, 1968), p. 258.

48. The NLOD file contains over three hundred letters and transcripts of phone calls.

49. *Variety*, December 18, 1963.

50. NLOD file, "Who's Afraid of Virginia Woolf?" undated.

51. Mike Nichols quoted in "A Surprising Liz in a Film Shocker," *Life*, June 10, 1966, p. 92.

52. Ibid., Martin Quigley, Jr. to Spellman, July 27, 1966. "It is sad that an agency of the U.S. Hierarchy should be a source of scandal."

53. Ibid., Little to George P. Hunt, June 15, 1966.

54. NLOD file, "Who's Afraid of Virginia Woolf?" Little complained to *Newsweek's* editor over its June 10 feature which, he alleged, gave the impression that the film was an obscene exercise by quoting out of context. Little to George F. Hunt, June 15, 1966.

55. Ibid., Father Frederic J. Nelson to NCOMP, August 28, 1966.

56. Ibid., Sullivan to John L'Heureux, S.J., July 6, 1966.

57. Ibid. Of the entire episode Sullivan would comment: "I have been at this office nine years. There has been one storm after another with *La Dolce Vita*, *Suddenly Last Summer*, *The Knack*, *Tom Jones* and *Darling* to name a few. But *Virginia Woolf* is a hurricane in comparison." Sullivan, Memorandum, undated, but almost certainly 1966.

58. *Catholic News*, July 14, 1966.

59. NLOD file, "Who's Afraid of Virginia Woolf?" Sullivan to M. H. Jahn, July 12, 1966.

60. NLOD file, "Hawaii," Krim to NCOMP, June 9, 1965.

61. Ibid. Of the sixty-five votes, only one (a consultor) was for a C and six (consultors only) voted for a B. None of the IFCA voted lower than an A-IV.

62. Ibid., Little to Kroll, October 14, 1966.

63. *Variety*, September 28, 1966.

64. See Appendix 1.

65. "Record Catholic Pix Nixes," *Daily Variety*, December 27, 1968.

66. Quoted in *Hollywood Reporter*, December 29, 1966.

67. NLOD file, "Blow Up," Sullivan to Timothy Evans, August 4, 1967.

68. *Variety*, July 19, 1968.

69. *America*, July 13, 1968.

_____ *Chapter 8* _____

Decline

The high hopes that NCOMP entertained for the establishment of a revised Code and voluntary classification system were to be dashed shortly after their inception. By 1970 a joint report by NCOMP and the Broadcast and Film Commission of the National Council of Churches concluded that the program was "in proximate danger of failure" unless remedial action was taken immediately.[1] At its inception there had been an expectation in Church circles that the Ratings Administration and NCOMP might work in tandem in some semblance of a reincarnation of the good old days of Breen, McClafferty and Masterson. Instead, the ratings system progressively lost all credibility in NCOMP eyes.

There can be little argument that classification was forced on an unwilling industry determined to cling to the outmoded concept of "the parental facilitative exercise" until no longer practicable. As late as May 1968, barely six months before the system was introduced, the new czar of the MPAA, Jack Valenti, insisted Hollywood's obligation went no further than providing parents with information that would enable them to decide whether or not their children should see a particular movie. In fulfillment of the idea, the MPAA had, for some time, been designating certain productions SMA (Suggested for Mature Audiences). To a limited extent, this complemented NCOMP thinking by giving an approximation of self-policing.[2] But two Supreme Court rulings that year forced Valenti's hand. The first, known as the *Dallas* decision, struck down a municipal ordinance that had excluded "young persons" from *Viva Maria*, a light-hearted, amoral action picture with Brigitte Bardot and Jeanne Moreau.[3] The other, decided the same day as *Dallas*, upheld a New York statute that prohibited the sale to minors of material that they, though not necessarily their parents, would find obscene.[4] The apparent contradiction between these two judicial opinions could be explained by the vagueness in the wording of the

Dallas ordinance. It did not preclude a carefully enunciated film classification system—which is precisely what the Texas city proceeded to implement.

Valenti continued to cling to the increasingly threadbare concept of parental decision making. He was willing to concede that the industry might wish to classify some films as unsuitable for persons under sixteen as long as they were exempt from that restriction if accompanied by a parent or guardian. His advice to the industry was "to exercise responsibility and restraint."[5] Obscenity cases would be won or lost in the courts through criminal prosecution of specific titles. Unintentionally or not, the consequence of this approach would be to remove the onus from producers and distributors and place it on theater owners and their staffs. That was buck-passing at its worst, and exhibitors were not slow to recognize the implications. Cashiers, projectionists and managers would be on the firing line for having sold tickets, run the equipment and supplied the house of ill repute for an allegedly obscene show. It was enough to alarm Julian Rifkin, president of the National Association of Theater Owners (NATO), who saw another dire consequence. If, through industry lethargy or abdication of authority, state or local governmental censorship came to be imposed, about half of all films currently being exhibited would probably be off-limits to juveniles. He reasoned that a government system would almost certainly have more stringent standards than one put in place by the industry.[6]

Valenti was forced to meet secretly with the leaders of NATO on May 22, 1968. He continued to press stubbornly for the parental facilitative approach, though he was resigned to a system that would include a clause excluding unaccompanied children under sixteen. Rifkin, in contrast, was adamant that any plan must, of necessity, contain a category to proscribe attendance by young teens under any circumstances. This, he reckoned, would have the double purpose of protecting theatrical managements from lawsuits filed by or on behalf of irate parents of minors who might discover or decide obscenity existed only when seated in the theater, or by civic and religious groups citing precedent elsewhere and similarly bent on protecting minors. At the same time, it would forestall government action by demonstrating that both arms of the movie business were conscious of their responsibilities.[7] The device chosen was the unfortunate letter X, which soon became associated in the public mind with se-X and has ever since been synonymous with pornography. Independent film distributors were not displeased to see this rating, regarding it as an exploitable commodity to be linked to the three-letter work, thereby helping attract the adults-only audience for which their product was always intended. That only a nominal fee was to be charged to an independent who submitted such a picture for classification was undoubtedly another point in its favor. The ratings categories, G (General, for all audiences), M (Mature, soon changed to GP and later still to PG for Parental Guidance), R (Restricted to persons under 16) and X (off-limits to all under 16, upped to 17 in 1970), came into official existence on November 1, 1968.

NCOMP tried to keep an open mind in judging the efficacy of the innovation, but within a year it was expressing serious misgivings in the areas of public education, enforcement, advertising and even the ratings themselves. No attempt had been made by the MPAA to enlighten the public on the gradations beyond a summary, one- or two-line explanation of the alphabet soup. NCOMP asserted that parents were being led to believe that the system rated films for overall quality, whereas they were actually evaluated only as to suitability for children. It found the GP designation, wittingly or unwittingly, too closely associated in the public mind with General Patronage and lamented the disappearance of the letter M, which more clearly identified a picture as containing mature material. As far as exhibitor implementation of the rating plan was concerned, public opinion, judging from complaints received by the Church, indicated that hordes of unaccompanied children were being admitted to R movies. However, it was impossible to ascertain the magnitude of the abuse with accuracy because of the casual, indifferent attitude of NATO members, all 13,000 of whom had been canvassed by their organization. Of the 25 percent replying, half admitted that they took a lackadaisical approach to admission because, in their experience, unlike that of NCOMP, complaints from parents had been few. The paucity of the response was differently interpreted by NCOMP. It was suspicious that theater owners were reluctant to confess and therefore overall compliance was at a low level. Still, it was willing to admit, by way of mitigation, that business logic was not entirely unsupported by compelling facts of the popular cultural scene. Bland films would find it hard to compete for leisure dollars in a society where violence and liberated sex ran rampant. Miniskirts, see-through blouses, topless waitresses, sexual promiscuity made possible by the pill, cohabitation by young adults without benefit of clergy and simulated sex on-stage of the *Oh, Calcutta!* variety were going largely unchallenged by law—cumulative proof, as if any were needed, that the American puritanical tradition was terminally ill. If some recalled the glory days of the Legion when a sensational advertising campaign had alone been sufficient reasons to move a film from a higher to a lower rating, the willful abuse of the new system as it applied to print material was further evidence of its inefficacy. To attract as many youngsters as possible, advertisers often made the R symbol all but illegible on posters and the entertainment page. The X, by contrast, was often enlarged out of all proportion, justifying the Church's concern that the symbol was tailor-made for sexual exploitation.[8]

The faulty mechanism of the ratings system was one problem; its enforcement at the production level was another that had equally serious shortcomings. NCOMP had reservations about the in-house structure of the board charged with appending the appropriate label. Employees of the MPAA were responsible. Independents rehearsed the long-standing grievance that their products were subject to harsher criteria than those applied to the major studios, a charge difficult to sustain in the first year of operation, when United Artists' *Laughter in the Dark*, Paramount's *Medium Cool* and MGM's *Best House in London* were all rated X. Still, the suspicion that the profitability of MPAA member companies rose or fell according to the ratings imposed on specific titles by certain of their employees was difficult to refute in practice. Moreover, the Appeals Board was open to a similar charge of collusion, since it was composed largely of MPAA and NATO members. Jack Valenti launched a broadside against the Danish sex comedy, *Without a Stitch* (with a self-imposed X), which played at one of New York's plushest cinemas. He described it as "trash," "pornographic" and "unfit for major showcase exposure," urging a boycott by other first-run theaters.[9] This was regarded by its distributor, Tonylyn, as partisan politics of the most blatant kind. That it considerably outgrossed Paramount's lackluster, M-rated musical *Paint Your Wagon* in those theaters where it became a replacement was, perhaps, a portent of where audience tastes were heading in the early seventies.[10]

The NCOMP could only contemplate both current and retroactive rating results with equal dissatisfaction. In 1969, the cause of its ire only five years before, *Kiss Me, Stupid!*, was classified GP, a category it shared with two previously Condemned pictures, *Wedding Night* and *That Splendid November*. The fault, according to NCOMP, lay in their being judged in terms of language and visuals and superficial aspects rather than in overall treatment and theme. Even if no overt adult visual material or salty language were present in a film, said NCOMP, its approach and general ambience might be such as to merit placement in the R category at least. It seemed apparent from even a cursory glance at 1969 results that many pictures had received a GP rating by avoiding or editing out brief moments of profanity or nudity. While that might bring young people into the theater, it could only destroy the long-term credibility of the system in the eyes of responsible parents. In sum:

The seeds for audience alienation were planted a long time ago. . . . No longer can Hollywood rely upon Catholics to take an annual "Decency Pledge" that will then be used to keep producers and exhibitors in line. The Vatican Council has stressed personal responsibility freely discharged; pledges are not part of the renewed Christian's life, but social involvement, including writing to his Congressman and Senators, and ecumenical collaboration to heal the ills of society are. Somehow the entire film industry must find a way to work with the 100 million alienated potential patrons in order to ward off censorship and to redirect the tremendous potential of the medium towards the enlightenment and progress of people everywhere. A first step will be placing a priority on social conscience over profits."[11]

Just how far the NCOMP had diverged from the Ratings Administration was illustrated by the case of *Midnight Cowboy*. The latter had imposed an X, chiefly for an abortive homosexual encounter in a Times Square washroom involving Jon Voight. NCOMP's official organ, the *Catholic Film Newsletter*, justified its relatively lenient A-IV for what it defended as "a strong and at all times masterful story of the imperceptible growth of friendship between two outcasts who, in being reduced to one another, find a rich and poignant relationship that, however unlikely, has the ring of humanity at its purest."[12] For those who saw the cinema as an art form with the power to educate and inspire, it was hard not to dismiss Hollywood's ratings system as a vast neglected opportunity whose aesthetic possibilities were never realized or were allowed to drain away. Years of competition against television for the viewer's dollar had driven producers to embrace lurid sensationalism as their main weapon. Faced with anonymous hard-nosed accountants who had replaced the legendary studio heads as dictators of policy, would-be supporters of cerebral, thought-provoking entertainment for adult viewers got nowhere in the ratings game. Still, their disappointment ought to have been tempered by the realization that Hollywood had never laid great store by culture. The jibe, "If you have a message, send it by Western Union," contained an essential truth. Once the initial shock of turning away juveniles was over, old habits reasserted themselves among showmen.

Equally discouraging for NCOMP was Hollywood's failure to support or even sufficiently acknowledge its program of encouraging film education in schools. This, the outgrowth of a decision taken at Mundelein College in April 1959 to "prepare young people to profit from the best creative efforts new film makers had to offer" had, by the late sixties, blossomed into a scheme under which NCOMP was servicing over six thousand film education programs nationwide. The distributors of 16mm prints reaped a bonanza, but the industry as a whole remained distant, regarding the project in the same light as college movie clubs providing welcome additional revenue from titles that had usually exhausted their commercial potential by the time the Church came to book them.[13]

As Skouras had prophesied, and Sullivan came to appreciate, the game was to find out how far you could go in the inclusion of racy ingredients and negotiate with the Appeals Board over the contentious issues it caught, perhaps losing some but retaining enough to give your film the appeal intended. Before he left to devote himself to other endeavors, including public broadcasting—the shining exception to the cultural wasteland that commercial radio and television had become—Sullivan withdrew NCOMP support from the Ratings Administration on the justifiable grounds that it had long since failed to enforce the Production Code. For many Catholics it was a welcome, if belated, decision.

The changing moral climate brought adult movie theaters to hundreds of towns and cities throughout the land. With Linda Lovelace's demonstration of her remarkable thoracic talents in *Deep Throat* catapulting the film to a place among the twenty-five highest-grossing productions of 1972–73, and Marilyn Chambers, the Ivory Snow girl, turning the $100,000, XXX-rated *Behind the Green Door* into another multimillion dollar hit, it was difficult to wax overly indignant about Monty Python's *Life of Brian*, with its spoof of a look-alike Jesus crucified in place of the real one. The media paid less and less attention to NCOMP, whose remonstrances seemed to become increasingly muted as the decade progressed. Financial considerations led to its closure in 1980 and subsequent merger with the National Catholic Office for Radio and Television. The two became the Department of Communication under the aegis of its parent body, the United States Catholic Conference. The *Catholic Film Newsletter* with its reviews of "better films currently in release" also ran until 1980 when it, too, fell victim to economic exigency. At the time of its demise its circulation had fallen to four thousand.[14]

The U.S. Catholic Conference Office for Film and Broadcasting (USCC) continues to rate movies on a regular basis. In 1982 the Episcopal Committee decided that the continuation of the B and C ratings made little sense. If a film was morally offensive, it was up to the individual to decide the degree of offensiveness. Consequently, B and C were merged into an O (morally offensive) rating. USCC reviews of current and upcoming motion pictures, videos and television programs are contained in the weekly *TV and Movie Guide*.[15] In singling out recommended pictures of unusual merit it duly acknowledges Pope John Paul's recent message for the annual observance of World Communication Days:

Whether the media serve to enrich or impoverish man's nature depends on the moral vision and ethical responsibility of those involved in the communications process and of the recipients of the media's message. Every member of the human family, whether the humblest consumer or the most powerful producer of media programs, has an individual responsibility in this respect.[16]

NOTES

1. *Joint Report: National Catholic Office for Motion Pictures & Broadcasting and Film Commission of the National Council of Churches* (privately printed), May 20, 1970.

2. *NCOMP Films*, 1969/70, "The Year in Review," pp. 5–10.

3. Douglas Ayer, Roy E. Bates and Peter J. Herman, "Self-Censorship in the Movie Industry: An Historical Perspective on the Law and Social Change," *Wisconsin Law Review* 3 (1970), pp. 818–19. The ordinance did not require the board to provide a rationale for its decision. However, two members stated publicly that the farcical portrayal of a clergyman and the sexual promiscuity of the two female leads had influenced the decision. *Interstate Circuit, Inc. v. Dallas*, 390 U.S. 376 (1968), revising 402 S.W. 2d 770 (Texas, Ct. Civ. App., 1966).

4. *Ginsberg v. New York*, 390 U.S. 629 (1968).

5. *Variety*, April 24, 1968.

6. Ibid., May 15, 1968.

7. *Daily Variety*, March 18, 1970. Commenting on the need for an industry initiative, it headlined its article, "Tidal Wave of Censor Bills, Almost Every State Has One on the Fire; Film Industry Facing Monumental Fight."

8. *NCOMP Films* 1969/70, pp. 8 and 82–83.

9. *Variety*, January 28, 1970.

10. Tonylyn sued Loews for cancellation and withdrawal of its prints from two of its first-run New York City theaters. Paramount had also threatened to withhold product if Loews did not comply.

11. *NCOMP Films*, 1969/70, p. 10.

12. NCOMP file, "Midnight Cowboy," July 16, 1969; also Richard Hirsch to J. R. Heisey, September 12, 1969. Several complainants wanted to know why the office had given a relatively lenient classification when the Ratings Board had imposed its lowest.

13. Sullivan to author. Sullivan bemoans the fact that film distributors, by and large, refused to acknowledge the pedagogical value of the scheme and refused to give reduced rental rates for what they lumped together with commercial screenings.

14. Herx acknowledges that circulation could not sustain production and distribution costs. Herx in conversation with author, June 1990.

15. Catholic newspapers carry USCC reviews supplied via the Catholic News Service. The weekly *T.V. and Movie Guide*, the *Monthly Film Guide* and the *Family Guide to Movies on Video* are available from the Office.

16. Message for the twenty-fifth annual observance of World Communications Day, May 12, 1991.

_____ Chapter 9 _____

Conclusion

For a generation whose exposure to movies has occurred entirely within the past twenty-five years, the history of the Legion of Decency must appear as a slightly surrealistic saga abstracted from a bygone age. Nearly all of the pictures that raised clerical ire to apoplectic levels half a century ago could be shown on prime time television today without incident.[1]

The so-called "adult" theater, the purveyor of hard-core pornography, has declined in numbers of late but only because its fare is increasingly sampled within the confines of the home. In an era in which the VCR has supplanted the cinema as a regular source of visual entertainment, few contemporary video stores worth their salt are without an X-rated section. There, the customer can browse casually and without interference among the hundreds of examples produced annually depicting a myriad of permutations on the sex act, and not even the most dedicated could hope to watch more than a fraction of the cumulative total. In the more respectable part of the same shop, unexpurgated versions of movies that were trimmed to obtain the commercially acceptable R are sold and rented with equanimity, to be watched by an audience whose individual ages no morality force can hope to police. In domestic privacy, naked bodies can be seen entwined and cavorting in the most remarkably gymnastic of positions, the air rent with four-letter words describing the apparatus and execution of the act of coition. Moral authority is obviously not what it used to be.

How different it was for their parents and grandparents. For three decades a handful of influential Catholics was able to dictate the content of motion pictures in the United States with a greater degree of effectiveness than they could the written word. The *Index Prohibitorum* might keep certain printed pieces out of the hands of the faithful but it could not deny them to the remainder of the population. The Condemned film rating, on the other hand, was a magisterial judgment that usually consigned the guilty object to ostracism and swift oblivion. Given the paucity in numbers of movie prints as distinct from books, that was easily achieved. In this aspect of its endeavors, the Legion acted as a sort of revising chamber or upper house for the Production Code Administration. For while Breen, his associates and acolytes in Hollywood kept a vigilant eye on infractions of the Code, there was always some degree of horsetrading going on in the film capital. Here a lustful kiss might be allowed if there an expletive were deleted. Rhett Butler could throw the word "damn" at Scarlet O'Hara in exchange for only the hint of a brothel in *Gone With the Wind*.[2] But when the piece in question arrived in New York, it was forced to undergo a more rigorous adjudication whose outcome was not a simple "pass" or "fail" verdict but assignment into one of up to six categories, the lowest of which usually spelt financial ruin for its owners. This is not to suggest that there was antagonism between the PCA and the Legion. On the contrary, the two worked in tandem until Breen's retirement, the one bolstering the power and stiffening the resolve of the other. The superficially affable Breen often imposed his will by reminding his clients that if he were to relax standards, his coreligionists three thousand miles to the east would indubitably compensate.

Amazingly, the Church's arm, which decreed the ultimate fate of each picture, was run on a shoestring and by a handful of clerics. The annual budget for the Legion in the 1930s never exceeded $15,000.[3] In considering the power it exerted over many millions of people, one is struck first by the pusillanimity of the motion picture industry and second by the acquiescence of the population as a whole. The assumed right of a religious minority to threaten a legally established business with financial ruin by way of a boycott because of a single infraction was but feebly protested by exhibitors' associations. Though the names Louis B. Mayer, Harry Cohn, Adolph Zukor and David O. Selznick have become synonymous with business guile and ruthlessness toward underlings and competitors, these and other giants of the halcyon days of the American cinema bowed low before monsignors threatening sanctions. A discreet murmur or a telling phrase couched in ecclesiastical rhetoric was usually sufficient to convince them that visual and aural discretion was the better part of valor. But nowhere is there evidence in the Legion's voluminous files to suggest that the wholesale acts of butchery committed on pre-Code, post-Code and foreign pictures in particular, were expressions of the general will. Most moviegoers of the thirties, forties and fifties were neither shocked nor disgusted by the nudity of Hedy Lamarr, the double entendres of Mae West, the promiscuity of Brigitte Bardot or the semi-transparent frocks worn by Jean Harlow and Marilyn Monroe. They were certainly not unaccustomed to bad language and off-color jokes. Rather, the outcry came from kindred spirits, a minority of rigid moralists who agreed with the agenda drawn up in 1934. Zealots among them were elevated to awesome positions of local power as Legion representatives. The habit of obedience to authority was well established in American Catholic society; the Legion representatives ensured that it was maintained. The omnipotence of the priest in the confessional booth was extended to the movie screen, and few dared to suggest there was no need for his ministrations.

The Legion's ethical position was unequivocal. It was based on the contention that morality is timeless and unchangeable. Like the Production Code, its standards were rooted in the Ten Commandments. To have called for their dilution, it insisted, would be tantamount to demanding a revision of the Decalogue. Of course, the Legion maintained that it was not against the portrayal of violations of these commandments provided there were proper compensatory moral values, including punishment of transgressors. Objections that this was a simplistic or even disingenuous approach were met by reference to the commercial motion picture as primarily and essentially an entertainment for the proletariat. In Quigley's words, the picture show might be trivial and commonplace, but it fulfilled a useful social function in harmlessly occupying the leisure time of a public "lacking in interior resources, to whom idleness is often an opportunity for mischief."[4] Recreation, while necessary for the working class, had to be morally healthy, otherwise it was potentially dangerous.

Besides sounding insufferably patronizing, this attitude consigned film to the function of an innocent opiate, a useful social tool in the hands of the few to divert the mindless majority for several frivolous hours in the darkness of a theater. As a consequence, most of what Hollywood produced in the quarter century following formation of the Legion was pitched at the level of the young adolescent. Ideally, Catholic taste should have been frozen at the A-I or A-II level, in which case the Legion's continuing existence would have been unnecessary. Walter Kerr, the distinguished drama critic, and himself a Catholic, deplored what he termed the "purity-with-popcorn" norm imposed by the Church's creation.[5] Although for most of its existence it distanced itself from any conclusions as to artistic excellence and insisted that only moral evaluations were being made, the Legion's dominant position as a pressure group inevitably involved some degree of artistic culpability. In a single-minded obsession with morality divorced from art, it was all too often guilty of abstracting the theme from the totality of the work, praising or deprecating irrespective of authorship, as if the subject of incest, for example, were inherently unsuitable whether treated by Sophocles or Mickey Spillane. The cuts that producers and distributors made by the thousands after 1934 can only be seen as acts of appeasement to placate a religious pressure group in the light of its interests and dogmas. By way of rebuttal it could be said that, in a democratic society, any and all constituencies are free to exert pressure and, axiomatically, such pressure can be resisted by counterpressure. While, in theory, this has a superficial attraction, the practical consequences for the movies are mind-boggling. Had Hollywood made the same obeisance to Jewish, Quaker, Presbyterian or other denominational sensibilities as it did to Catholic, the content of resulting pictures would have been impossibly bland.

Freedom, as the Catholic press never wearied of asserting, does not mean that a man has the right to poison the mind of his fellowman, and some pictures did little but exude pure evil, or so it was claimed. The responsibility for determining the degree of toxicity and the point at which pressure to keep such poison off the screen overrides the right of the individual to choose for himself, was assumed by the Church. It claimed to speak for a membership that was not exclusively denominational. But while the lethal dose of a poison of chemical nature can be calculated through laboratory and physiological analysis, the toxicity of a literary theme does not lend itself to such an objective determination. As the case of *The Miracle* proved, in a secular society with separation of church and state constitutionally enshrined, it was difficult to define sacrilege. Divorce was anathema to the Catholic Church but was legal in every state in the union; there was no injunction in the Bible against double beds, the exposure of female navels or even children's genitalia, and yet all three were frowned upon and invariable deleted as a result of Code and Legion pressure.

In prohibiting films not in conformity with the precepts of Christian morality, the Legion of Decency's philosophy and conduct could be found wanting. Movies that successfully ran the gauntlet of IFCA and consultor scrutiny were held to be in conformity with those precepts. Yet they seldom, if ever, portrayed life as it was, but rather showed life as it should have been. In so doing, these films represented a world that did not exist—of good invariably triumphing over evil, of justice fairly meted out or of impossibly happy endings achieved through some highly unlikely plot mechanism that made all well between a feuding boy and girl or errant husband and wife. To insist that motion pictures always be consistent with lofty moral principles was to rob them of their ability to be faithful reflections of reality. Sin and imperfection are unfortunate constants in any society. The oft-repeated demands of Quigley and his cohorts for the elimination of words and ideas from films not in conformity with Catholic belief because of the influence of the motion picture on the impressionable had an unfortunate consequence. It gave films a tone of hypocrisy that robbed them of much of their moral force. Even the least analytical of viewers could not help but note that everyday existence was seldom portrayed with accuracy on American screens. Because of Legion intervention in *A Streetcar Named Desire*, to take a notorious example, Stella Kowalski punishes her violent, brutish husband by refusing to continue living with him. In the world of the forties and fifties, economic reality and societal pressure denied most abused, working-class women this alternative. Certain institutions were sacrosanct. The American political system, banking and organized religion were all above reproach. If sins were committed in their name, the problem was not systemic but with the individual sinner. The movies were full of crooked lawyers but the American legal system was always held to be the fairest on earth. All that was required of the Senate to disown the scheming politician of *Mr. Smith Goes to Washington* was a conscience-rousing, we-the-little-people speech by James Stewart. Equally serious problems of rape, abortion, child abuse and racial discrimination, to name but a few, no American film could address honesty until recently. The affluent physician of *Detective Story* had his profession changed from abortionist in the stage play, to "baby farmer" in the film version, since the former topic was taboo in the eyes of both the Code and the Legion.[6] But it made nonsense of the plot, which hinged on the discovery by a self-righteous detective that his wife had undergone the procedure by the same doctor prior to their marriage. Was it any wonder, therefore, that the spectator came to associate the screen with unreality and subscribed to a "this can only happen in the movies" mind set?

In this state of affairs lay the explanation for the comparatively harsh treatment meted out to foreign language pictures, especially those from continental Europe. It would be unfair to blame the Legion exclusively, since its conduct was but one aspect of the paradox of American morality in general—to abhor eroticism and shrug off violence. The nation has always been surprisingly narrow and remarkably liberal at the same time. Brutality has long enjoyed a vogue in popular culture, from the mindless mayhem of the hockey arena and the sim-ulated barbarism of the wrestling ring to the calculated sadism in Bret Easton Ellis's novels. The contentious issues for the Legion and the Production Code Administration were almost entirely in the realm of sex and sensuality, as the roster of banned and mutilated films bears witness. Only very occasionally was an institutional voice raised against graphic violence or organized killing on the screen. It is no exaggeration to state that for Hays, Breen, McClafferty, Mas-terson and other arbiters of public taste, the possibility of humankind's anni-hilation by nuclear warfare was less alarming than the total exposure of a single female breast.

The European cinema stood accused for its emphasis, real or imagined, on scenes of intimacy or group lust calculated, in the Legion's favorite phrase, to arouse "prurient interests." The sexual behavior of Gina Lollobrigida, Silvana Mangano, Martine Carole and other temptresses was not romantically idealized but crudely presented as the expression of carnal desire. Blame for their existence could be laid at the door of moral indifference. The superior record of the United States was taken as an eloquent exemplification of the dictum, "By their fruits shall you know them." By the same token, the proliferation of films of low moral character originating mostly in France, Italy and Sweden in the immediate postwar era was seen as proof that no equivalent organization of Christian origin, character and purpose like the Legion of Decency existed in these countries to counterbalance rampant, godless hedonism and exert a wholesome influence. The sad consequence, said the Church, was an attitude of tolerance of things forbidden under the eternal verities of moral law for the sake of transient values of physical satisfaction. For a time, too, the equation of Communism with moral subversion ran a close second as an obsessive fear, and it was priggishly tempting and politically profitable at the height of the Cold War for moralists to combine the two and see leftist propaganda as a second string in the bow of pornographers conniving at the downfall of the United States. To allow examples of such depravity access to American audiences was to connive at the fatal corruption of home, youth and family values.[7]

And yet, for all the Mother Grundyism of the times, it cannot be denied that they were contemporaneous with the golden era of the American cinema. The heyday of the Legion was also that of the great studios, the legendary stars and the most enduring pictures. Perhaps the very existence of censorship and classification acted as a stimulus to the imagination as creative talents wrestled with ways to circumvent the mines strewn in their path by the Code and the C rating. Not infrequently the purpose was achieved in a subtle, mature manner that is preferable to the stark overstatement—one might say the sledgehammer approach—of today's more literally minded filmmakers. When Clark Cable blew his toy trumpet and caused the blanket between his bed and Claudette Colbert's (which he called the Walls of Jericho) to fall in *It Happened One Night*, there was no need to tell the audience that the marriage was about to be consummated. Familiarity, and the passage of time, would render other conventions—the pounding of the sea against rocks or fireworks to indicate orgasm—risible.

In the fifties a number of factors conspired to loosen the Legion's grip. A liberal U.S. Supreme Court and sympathetic local judiciaries extended to the movies the constitutional protection for artistic endeavor that had been denied them since the infancy of the cinema. The shoddily made picture might still have few defenders, but the seriously intentioned one could no longer be dismissed with a stroke of the judicial or ecclesiastical pen for some narrow, doctrinal reason. The decline of the studio system and the rise of the independents meant that many actors, producers and directors were no longer governable contractees but free agents more able to thumb their collective noses at the Code's authority. At the same time, *Miranda Prorsus* forced the Church to look beyond the confines of its outmoded handbook of morality and accept the motion picture for having at least the same potential to express as wide a range of human emotion and behavior as any of the other expressive arts. The result was a noisy shifting of gears and a chorus of dismay from reactionaries as the Legion jettisoned much of the intellectual debris of the past to acclimatize itself to the new spirit. Harsh economic facts, especially the challenge of television, drove Hollywood to make pictures for a selective audience that was younger, more sophisticated and morally more permissive than its predecessor. As a consequence, the industry was forced to institute a ratings system not unlike the Legion's which, gloomy prognostications to the contrary, did not damage its profitability or destroy its business.

The degree of breast exposure in *The Outlaw*; the use of the word *virgin* in *The Moon Is Blue*; the innocent, fleeting reference to family planning in *Panic in the Streets*—how remote and irrelevant these issues seem today and how laughable it is to contemplate the vision of adult men spending many tedious hours over their resolution! There is a tendency to dismiss all of it as a tempest in a tea cup, the concerns of a vanished era whose only valuable lesson is to illuminate an obscurantism and petty-mindedness from which we have happily escaped. But the difficulty with this interpretation is that it supposes the battle has been won, that freedom of expression reigns supreme and that the kinds of emasculations performed on *Duel in the Sun* or *Tea and Sympathy* are impossible in a contemporary context. No one would deny that the degree of license afforded to filmmakers since the establishment of the ratings system and the mellowing of NCOMP allowed a more honest, forthright approach to themes that could not have even been alluded to a generation ago. A picture like *Henry and June*, based on Henry Miller's Parisian experiences, with a husband supportive of his wife as she embarks on an odyssey of lesbian self-discovery, can be completed without interference from a latter-day Breen or Quigley. Even so, the battle for control of the screen is far from over. On one level it is still fought over ratings. Clauses in directors' contracts frequently insist that the finished product must merit nothing lower than a Restricted label, since that is the minimum classification permitted for juvenile attendance. Many shopping malls in which theaters are increasingly located also forbid the screening of X-rated movies, and many "respectable" newspapers will not accept their advertising. The proposed compromise, NC-17, the proponents of which claim will give legitimacy to an adult work without the stigma attached to the "skin-flick X" has drawn the fire of the Catholic Church, which sees it as a surreptitious means of covering the essentially unregenerate pornographic movie in a cloak of respectability.

Beyond this specific issue is the continuing assault on movies and inevitably—given its major role as the purveyor of film—television, by the fundamentalist right, based on the belief that certain films pose a danger to youth and family values. It should be remembered that the Legion of Decency was founded during a period of profound economic decline, the worst Western society has experienced in this century. It has been argued that periods of clerical domination coincide with depressed times. Confirmation of a sort has been supplied of late by the campaign of Dr. Theodore Baehr, chairman of the Christian Film and Television Committee. His release, in 1992, of a twenty-page document outlining a new code to govern motion picture content was accompanied by an expression of regret that the Catholic Church had abdicated responsibility with the closure of the Legion of Decency. In words that echo those of seventy years ago, he deplored the vacuum that was "soon filled by the Gay and Lesbian Alliance Against Defamation, the Church of Satan, and other special interest groups who presently influence Hollywood." Moral support, together with a call for voluntary compliance with a new morality code eerily reminiscent of Hays's version, was voiced by Cardinal Roger Mahoney.[8]

The shadow of clericalism has not dissipated. Loquacious electronic evangelists in three-piece suits may have replaced the self-effacing, black-coated monsignors of yesteryear. Father Lord and Bishop Cantwell may be gone, but their spirit, weaker and more attenuated, lives on.

NOTES

1. The full, 124-minute, unexpurgated version of *The Outlaw* is frequently aired on cable television.

2. After days of discussion, the Motion Picture Association board members meeting to consider the last line of dialogue in *Gone with the Wind* devised a rule that "hell" and "damn" would continue to be banned except where their use was "essential and required

for portrayal, in proper historical context, of any scene or dialogue based upon historical fact or folklore, or for the presentation in proper literary context of a Biblical, or other religious quotation or quotation from a literary work provided that no such use shall be permitted which is intrinsically objectionable or offends good taste." Selznick's wearisome fight for inclusion of "the 'D' word" is recounted in Leff and Simmons, pp. 97–105.

3. Father Sullivan recounted to the author that, when first appointed in 1957, he was offered a salary of $1,200 per annum. Since that was less than he was paying for room and board, it was reluctantly raised to $1,800. Even so, both he and Little had to supplement their earnings from the Legion with pastoral work. Little's stipend was then $120 monthly with free accommodation. Mrs. Looram was paid only travel expenses although later she was given a small, undisclosed honorarium.

4. *The Production Code: Its Character and Purposes.* Privately printed (1950) and un-paginated.

5. Quoted in the *New York Post*, "The Legion of Decency and the Movie Code," May 27, 1955.

6. NLOD, *Annual Report*, 1953, P. 11. Masterson was of the opinion that any reference to abortion would "incite a morbid and dangerous curiosity which might well lead to a desire for imitation." He was instrumental in having a line of dialogue removed that hinted that the cop killer, Joseph Wiseman, might also have indulged in "perversion," i.e., homosexual behavior.

7. Director Paul Graetz, whose *Diable au Corps* had been critically acclaimed in its native France and elsewhere on the continent but condemned by the Legion and refused a seal, asserted that it was "impossible to produce pictures in Europe within the regulations put in place 20 years ago for the makers of Hollywood films." He proposed that the Hays Office exempt all foreign movies from the Code and leave their exhibition to the discretion of local theater owners. *Variety*, March 15, 1950.

8. For critical comments on both Baehr and Mahoney see *Los Angeles Weekly*, February 7–12, 1992 and *Los Angeles Reader*, February 7, 1992.

Appendixes

Appendix 1
Comparative Statistics on Feature Films Reviewed and Classified, 1938–1970

Year	Class A-I No.	%	Class A-II No.	%	Class A-III No.	%	Class A-IV *** No.	%	Class B No.	%	Class C No.	%
*	780	61	380	30					89	8	13	1
1938	332	62	164	31			2	0.1	32	5.9	5	1
1939	312	54	200	35			2	0.5	50	8.5	9	2
1940	271	50	210	39					47	9	10	2
1941	267	51.25	197	37.81					50	9.6	7	1.34
1942	271	51.13	202	38.11					51	9.62	5	0.95
1943	229	52.16	151	34.40					55	12.53	4	0.91
1944	191	44.52	184	42.89					51	11.89	3	0.70
1945	143	38.1	189	50.4					43	11.5	0	0
1946	155	39.64	176	45.01					60	15.35	0	0
1947	195	44.32	172	39.09					70	15.91	3	0.68
1948	174	38.58	188	41.69					82	18.18	7	1.55
1949	193	41.33	165	35.33					96	20.56	13	2.78
1950	179	39.0	169	36.82					103	22.44	8	1.74
1951	148	33.49	195	44.12					85	19.23	14	3.16
1952	182	40.81	172	38.56					78	17.49	14	3.14
1953	148	38.6	142	37.1			1	0.25	89	22.95	4	1.1
1954	138	39.20	127	36.08					78	22.16	9	2.56
1955	94	28.74	115	35.17					110	33.64	8	2.45
1956	98	29.88	141	42.99			1	0.3	80	24.09	8	2.44
1957	139	33.25	131	31.34					137	32.78	11	2.63
1958	132	33.42	109	27.59	73	18.48	2	0.51	74	18.73	5	1.27
1959	70	25	91	32.5	68	24.2	1	0.4	43	15.4	7	2.5
1960	80	20.09	55	20	67	24.37	1	0.36	64	23.27	8	2.91
1961	88	30.45	65	22.49	49	16.95	6	2.08	71	24.57	10	3.46
1962	73	26.55	80	29.09	51	18.54	10	3.64	46	16.73	15	5.45
1963	70	26.62	71	27	63	23.95	11	4.18	37	14.07	11	4.18
1964	52	20.15	71	27.52	60	23.26	14	5.43	45	17.44	16	6.20
1965	74	25.96	74	25.96	67	23.52	12	4.21	43	15.09	15	5.26
1966	68	25.96	64	24.43	76	29	8	3.05	34	12.98	12	4.58
1967	50	20.41	58	23.67	76	31.02	12	4.90	32	13.06	17	6.94
1968	43	12.99	55	16.64	114	34.44	17	5.12	71	21.45	31	9.36
1969	26	8.25	47	14.92	126	40	28	8.89	48	15.24	40	12.70
**1970	17	10.12	12	7.14	70	41.67	16	9.52	30	17.86	23	13.69

*   First period covers films reviewed February 1936 to November 1937
**   Six month period only
***   Separate classification becomes A-IV on June 11, 1963

Appendix 2
Organization of the Legion of Decency

Chairman

Episcopal Committee for Motion Pictures

Chairman

International Federation of Catholic Alumnae

Executive Secretary

National Legion of Decency

Board of Consultors

Diocesan Directors

Local Branch Reviewers

Publicity and Liaison

Priests (sermon pledge)

Appendix 3
Controversial Films Examined in 1952 (NLOD *Annual Report*, 1952)

Detective Story (Paramount)

This picture was based on a successful Broadway play of the same name to which we objected on two scores. (a) Perversion—which was established in a line of dialogue, and (b) Abortion—which we thought was present both in dialogue and by impression. Our protest effected the deletion of perversion and considerably lessened the impression of abortion. The picture was eventually classified 'A-II', or—morally unobjectionable for adults.

Las Vegas Story (R.K.O.)

This film, starring Jane Russell, reflected the acceptability of divorce, contained light treatment of marriage and was suggestive in both costuming and dialogue. As the picture stood with these objectionable elements we were strongly inclined to condemn it. We presented our objections to RKO who acceded to our objections and substantially reduced the offensiveness to get the picture into a 'B' category. It was still a bad picture after a considerable number of deletions, but the original elements of objectionability were considerably lessened.

Monkey Business (20th Century Fox)

We informed 20th Century Fox, after seeing their film, that we intended to condemn it. While this picture was a comedy and the theme might be said to be moral, we felt that the multiplicity of suggestiveness in situations, costuming and dialogue, as well as the acceptability of divorce, constituted a serious threat to proper Christian standards. We met serious opposition from the Fox people who finally capitulated in view of a condemnation. About five or six changes were made which, while not curing the original objections, nevertheless substantially changed the situations and took it out of the 'C' class. 20th Century Fox, as you may recall, was the producer and distributor of *Forever Amber* which is always a constant reminder to them of what a condemned picture implies.

Singing In The Rain (M.G.M.)

As we have already insinuated, MGM offers the Legion every possible cooperation. In this instance, an otherwise innocuous film which could easily have been rated 'A-I' was marred by the unnecessary use of a suggestive dance sequence. We communicated with MGM officials with the hope that the sequence could be eliminated. We were informed that technical difficulties made any deletion untenable. Therefore no change was made.

Wild North (M.G.M.)

We did not think this picture was condemnable. As a matter of fact it was a film made for family consumption but which unfortunately was marred by several adult situations which could not be corrected, as well as by an unnecessary line of dialogue which would portray suicide sympathetically and which could be conveniently deleted from the film. As such, the film would have fallen automatically into the 'B' category. Knowing the cooperation which has been given us by MGM in the past, we brought this fact to their attention. They investigated the technical possibilities of deleting the line which established the suicide. We withheld our rating until this investigation was completed. MGM reported a willingness to delete the objectionable element and, therefore, the picture was rated as 'A-II.' It might be noted that this picture played for only a short time as a 'B.' The note of change in all prints was brought to the attention of Legion subscribers.

Wild Heart (formerly titled *Gypsy Blood*) (Selznick International)

This picture, widely distributed in England and on the Continent, was brought to this country by David O. Selznick. A note of superstition and fatalism pervaded the story which contained a condonation of immoral actions as well as suggestiveness and offense to religion. As such it was condemnable. Mr. Selznick thought that our objections were unreasonable and presented a strong front against any corrections in his film. In response to economic pressure Mr. Selznick added a foreword to his film, deleted a line we thought offensive to religion and attempted to mitigate the offensiveness. The principal character of this film was a Welsh minister who, we thought, did not represent religion too well. We were able to classify the film as 'B' after corrections had been made. To the best of our knowledge, the film has not had great commercial success.

Models Inc. (Mutual Productions)

This was a low budget film of Mutual Productions, an independent company, purporting to show the evils of present-day "model agencies," but which were actually an outlet for immorality. We particularly objected to the elements of white slavery which we considered to be present. In addition there were several sequences which violated common decency. Substantial changes were obtained resulting in mitigation of the offensiveness.

Room for One More (Warner Bros.)

This was the first time, to the best of our knowledge, that a major company has introduced sex instruction into a film. This instruction was given quite realistically in one sequence and, in view of the traditional stand of the Legion on sex hygiene, we thought that a protest was in order to Warner Bros. The picture in itself was not condemnable, although objectionable from the viewpoint of suggestiveness besides the sex instruction. We sincerely felt the presence of this material was contrary to the Motion Picture Code. We informed Warner Bros. that it was not our intention to condemn the film but explained to them our concern about the subject matter. They promised to investigate the possibility of a deletion but later informed us regretfully that nothing could be done.

Rashomon (Japanese) (R.K.O.)

We suggested to Mr. Robert Mochrie, formerly Vice-President of RKO, that this picture could readily be lifted from 'B' by reason of suggestive sequences to 'A-II' with convenient cutting of the realistic presentation of the rape scene. No action was taken by RKO in this regard and they settled for a 'B' classification.

Tomorrow Is Too Late (Italian) (Joseph Burstyn)

This film was made in Italy and received a prize from the Office Catholique International du Cinéma at a film festival in Uruguay. The theme stresses the necessity of proper sex instruction and reflects Catholic thinking in its treatment. It was classified 'A-II.'

CONDEMNED FILMS

Latuko

This was the only American picture condemned and not corrected during the past year. The Legion objection read as follows: "Although this picture might be judged to have certain scientific value, nevertheless it contains unsuitable material for entertainment motion picture theaters and for this reason constitutes a serious danger to Christian and traditional standards of morality and decency." *Latuko* has received considerable publicity throughout the country. It is a documentary film made in Africa in 1950 by Edgar Monsanto Queeny of St. Louis. The film describes the life of the Latuko tribe in Equatorial Africa and includes various scenes in which nude males appear. The Legion could see the scientific value in the picture but as an entertainment piece in public theaters thought it was fraught with danger. Mr. Lesser, the distributor of the film, offered as evidence the testimony of two priests who had seen the picture and who were reputed to have commended it both orally and in correspondence. Their opinion was predicated, it seemed to us, on the scientific value of the film. The picture is said to have had a successful run in several St. Louis theaters as well as in Los Angeles. It was not passed by the New York State censors and on appeal the State Board of Regents confirmed the original opinion of the censors. The picture had also created national publicity in Newark, N.J. where it was originally condemned by the police department, but a court order that followed revoked the initial stand of the police authorities. The American Museum of Natural History has an interest in this picture. At writing the *Latuko* issue seems to be dead.

La Ronde (French) (Commercial Pictures)

This film in the story it tells condones and glorifies immoral actions and contains immoral sequences. This motion picture has enjoyed considerable success particularly in London. It has been refused a license by the New York State Censor Board on the grounds that it would corrupt public morality. Presently an appeal is being made in court against the original ban. It has been shown in art houses in Washington and in Los Angeles where it has been hailed for its artistic values. The theme of the picture is the portrayal of various forms of profane love. It is a sophisticated treatment of illicit amours and we consider it a dangerous picture.

Marie Du Port (France) (Bellon-Foulke International Productions)

This picture in the story it tells condones immoral actions. Here again we revert to the glorification of a prostitute.

Miss Julie (Sweden) (Trans-Global Pictures Inc.)

This picture in the story it tells condones illicit actions. Moreover, in treatment it seriously offends Christian and traditional standards of morality and decency. The film received some sort of prize in Europe for its artistic achievement but both in theme and treatment was a glorification of illicit love.

It's Forever Springtime (Italian) (A.F.E. Corporation)

This picture in the story it tells seriously offends the Christian and traditional concept of the sacrament of matrimony. Moreover, it is offensive to religion and the name of the Deity. Suggestive sequence.

Young and the Damned (Mexican) (Mayer-Kingsley)

This picture in the story it tells seriously offends Christian and traditional standards of morality and decency. Moreover, it contains material morally unsuitable for entertainment in motion picture theaters. This is the story of juvenile delinquency in Mexico which might have some value to a specialized audience of social workers but which in treatment contains various obnoxious sequences which would constitute a serious threat to morality if shown in public.

Paris Nights (French) (Discina-International Films Corp.)

This picture in the story it tells seriously offends Christian and traditional standards of morality and decency. Suggestive costuming and situation. This film was nothing more or less than a burlesque show transferred to the screen and as such was intended as a lustful presentation.

The Raven (French) (Lopert Films)

The manner in which this story is told condones immoral actions of various kinds. Moreover, the film tends to promote disrespect for religion. Suggestive dialogue and situations.

The Thrill That Kills (Alternative title: Cocaine) (Italian) (Distinguished Films)

This film in the story it tells condones and glorifies illicit actions. Moreover, it contains material morally unsuitable for entertainment motion picture theaters. This film purports to be sociological in its message. It portrays the ill effects of the illicit use of cocaine, but, unfortunately, would arouse undue curiosity about drugs. Besides, it has sequences that would appeal to the prurient-minded.

Women Without Names (Italian) (Lopert Films)

This film contains material unfit for general motion picture audiences. Furthermore, it condones immoral actions and has suggestive sequences. Under the guise of portraying the plight of post-war women in Italy this film was replete with perversion and suggestiveness.

Scarred (Italian) (Casolaro Films Distribution Co.)

This picture in the story it tells condones immoral actions; contains material offensive to religion; suggestive sequence.

The Stroller (French) (Discina-International Films Corp.)

This picture in the story it tells seriously offends Christian and traditional standards of morality and decency. This is a vivid presentation of prostitution.

Lover's Return (French) (Lopert Films)

This film in the story it tells condones immoral motives and actions. It is disrespectful towards religion and contains suggestive sequences.

Appendix 4
Sample Ballot Form of IFCA

Name of Picture:	Club de Femmes	Location:	55th St. Playhouse
Date:	October 24, 1937	Producer:	Not Known
Stars:	Danielle Darrieux	Distrib.:	Jacques Deval
Domestic Production:		Feature:	X
Foreign Production:	X	Short:	
Language:	French		

I.   Content Classification:

Biographical	Fantasy	Social Drama	
Detective	Historical	Society	X
Comedy	Musical	Western	
Drama	Mystery	Documentary	
Educational	Scientific	Propaganda	

II.   Audience Suitability:
- A-I   Unobjectionable for General Patronage
- A-II   Unobjectionable for Adults
- B   Objectionable in part
- C   Condemned   X

Reasons for above classification of audience suitability

This picture is suffused with sex; it is decidedly a sulphurous brooding over sex as the mainspring of life which leads the picture either to romanticize the heroine's illegitimate motherhood or to portray the Sapphism between two of the girls in unmistakable terms.

Reviewer: _____
(It is the policy of the Committee not to publicly list the name of the reviewer of a Condemned film)

III.   Entertainment rating:

Excellent	Fair	X
Very Good	Poor	
Good		

Appendix 4 (cont.)

IV.   Objectionable aspects, scenes or remarks:

       1.   Daring costume—style of strip-tease.
       2.   Condones motherhood of unmarried girl.
       3.   Condones loose morals of the associate members of the club.
       4.   Suggestive looks, words and actions.

V.   Special comment on non-moral matters:

The author of this play, Deval, is trying to show the effects of repression upon a group of young girls. In spite of a lot of forced gaiety, he has not succeeded in ridding his film from the usual clinical odors such themes carry with them. The picture flaunts sex as the omnipotent god before whom all must bend a craven knee.

VI.   Outstanding scene or episode in detail: None.

VII.   Synopsis:

The Club de Femmes is supposed to be something of a grandiose residence or hotel where working girls live in order to avoid "the perils of Pauline" in the big city. It is called "Cite Femina" to indicate that it is a fortress against predatory men. Claire, a dancer, who lives here is in love with a music student. Unable to see him as much as she wants, she gets him in the club in feminine disguise where, of course, the author's thesis bends over backwards to prove itself.

Greta, a Danish girl from Copenhagen, comes to live in the club. Not succeeding as an art student she accepts an invitation from Helene, the switchboard operator, to meet a certain "gentleman" who may help her. That she is little more than a procuress is made quite evident when Greta returns the next day, bearing all the marks of a party girl.

Helene, however, continues to ply her trade. Her next victim is an over-simple Juliette. She, too, returns in a morally mangled condition. But the procuress has not reckoned well this time. It seems that this Juliette is watched over by another girl, Alice, with a devotion which is unfortunately a clear case of Sapphism. This Alice is a serious, brooding figure who never takes part in any of the games of the other girls, but manifests an unnatural affection for Juliette. Embittered by what has befallen the object of her care and surveillance, Alice poisons the telephone operator. The doctor of the house (a woman of course), Gabrielle Anboy, who is about the only likeable character in the film, has her sent away to serve as a nurse on a leper colony in the South Seas.

At this point the romanticization of Claire's episode begins. It soon becomes known that she is enceinte, and all the girls spend their time knitting tiny garments for the expected child. When this event takes place, the entire Club is a bedlam of laughter, tears and whatnot and even Mme. Garfeton, the stern and severe directress of the establishment, is on her knees by Claire's bedside, weeping to her heart's content.

The last scene shows her making a speech in which she admits the rules and regulations are of no avail against the omnipotence of love. She sums up the author's thesis with the words—"Je sais maintenant que vous autres jeunes filles ne peuvent jamais changer" (I know now that you young women can never change).

Appendix 5
Presidents and CEOs of the MPPDA and PCA, 1922–1971

Presidents of the Motion Picture Producers and Distributors of America.*

Will Hays	1922-1945
Eric Johnston	1945-1963
Ralph Hetzel	1963-1966
Jack Valenti	1966-

*Name changed to Motion Picture Association of America in 1945.

Chief administrators of The Production Code Administration.*

Joseph I. Breen	1934-1941
Geoffrey Shurlock	1941-1942
Joseph I. Breen	1942-1954
Geoffrey Shurlock	1954-1968
Eugene Docherty	1968-1971

*Name changed to Ratings Administration in 1968.

Select Bibliography

Adler, Mortimer J. *Art and Prudence*. New York: McGraw-Hill, 1953.

Ames, Roy S. "The Screen Enters Politics." *Harpers* 171 (May 1935), pp. 116–26.

Ardrey, Robert. "Hollywood's Fall into Virtue." *Reporter* 16 (February 21, 1957), pp. 8–14.

Ayer, Douglas; Bates, Roy E.; and Herman, Peter J. "Self-Censorship in the Movie Industry: An Historical Perspective on the Law and Social Change." *Wisconsin Law Review* 3 (1970), pp. 791–838.

Baxter, John. *Hollywood in the Thirties*. New York: A. S. Barnes, 1970.

Behlmer, Rudy, ed. *Memo from David O. Selznick*. New York: Viking Press, 1972.

Benedict, John. "Movies Are Redder Than Ever." *American Mercury* 91 (August 1960), pp. 3–23.

Bergman, Andrew. *We're in the Money: Depression America and Its Films*. New York: New York University Press, 1971.

Bergman, Mark. "Hollywood in the Forties Revisited." *Velvet Light Trap*, no. 5 (Summer 1972), pp. 2–5.

Blanchard, Paul. "Roman Catholic Censorship II: The Church and the Movies." *Nation* 166, no. 19, part 1 (May 1948), pp. 499–502.

Carey, Gary. *All the Stars in Heaven: Louis B. Mayer and M.G.M.* London: Robson Books, 1981.

Carmen, Ira H. *Movies, Censorship and the Law*. Ann Arbor: University of Michigan Press, 1966.

Le cinéma dans l'enseignement de l'eglise. Vatican City: Commission Pontificale pour le Cinéma, la Radio et la Télévision, 1955.

Cooney, John. *The American Pope: The Life and Times of Cardinal Francis Spellman*. New York: Times Books, 1972.

Corliss, Richard. "The Legion of Decency." *Film Comment* 4, no. 4 (Summer 1968), pp. 24–61.

Davis, Mike. *City of Quartz*. New York: Verso, 1990.

De Grazia, Edward, and Newman, Roger K. *Banned Films: Movies, Censors and the First Amendment*. New York: R. R. Bowker, 1982.

Delpar, Helen. "Goodbye to the Greaser: Mexico, the MPPDA and Derogatory Films, 1922–26." *Journal of Popular Film and Television* 12, no. 1 (1984), pp. 38–41.

Ernst, Morris, and Lorentz, Pare. *Censored: The Private Life of the Movies.* New York: Jonathan Cape and Harrison Smith, 1930.

Facey, Paul W. *The Legion of Decency: A Sociological Analysis of the Emergence and Development of a Social Pressure Group.* Ph.D. diss., Fordham University, 1945. New York: Arno Press, 1974.

Farber, Stephen. *The Movie Rating Game.* Washington, D.C.: Public Affairs Press, 1972.

Forman, Henry. *Our Movie Made Children.* New York: Macmillan, 1933.

French, Philip. *The Movie Moguls: An Informal History of the Hollywood Tycoons.* London: Weidenfeld and Nicholson, 1969.

Friedman, David F. *A Youth in Babylon: Confessions of a Trash-Film King.* Buffalo: Prometheus, 1990.

Furhammar, Lief, and Isaksson, Folke. *Politics and Film.* New York: Praeger, 1971.

Gardiner, Gerald. *The Censorship Papers: Movie Censorship Letters from the Hays Office, 1934–68.* New York: Dodd, Mead, 1987.

Giglio, Ernest David. The Decade of the Miracle, 1952–62: A Study in the Censorship of the American Motion Picture. D.S.S. diss., Syracuse University, 1964.

Gomery, Douglas. *The Hollywood Studio System.* New York: St. Martin's Press, 1986.

Gow, Gordon. *Hollywood in the Fifties.* New York: A. S. Barnes, 1971.

Handlin, Oscar. *Al Smith and His America.* Boston: Atlantic-Little Brown, 1958.

Haskell, Molly. *From Reverence to Rape: The Treatment of Women in the Movies.* New York: Holt, Reinhart and Winston, 1973.

Hays, Will H. *The Memoirs of Will H. Hays.* Garden City, N.Y.: Doubleday, 1955.

Higham, Charles. *Hollywood at Sunset.* New York: Saturday Review Press, 1972.

Inglis, Ruth. *Freedom of the Movies: A Report on Self-Regulation from the Commission on Freedom of the Press.* Chicago: University of Chicago Press, 1947.

International Motion Picture Almanac. New York: Quigley, 1935–1986.

Jarvie, I. C. *Movies and Society.* New York: Basic Books, 1970.

Javits, Arthur R., Jr. "The Payne Fund Reports." *Journal of Popular Culture* 25, no. 2 (Fall, 1991), pp. 127–40.

Josephson, Matthew, and Josephson, Hannah. *Al Smith: Hero of the Cities.* Boston: Houghton-Mifflin, 1969.

Jowett, Garth. *Film: The Democratic Art.* Boston: Little, Brown, 1976.

Koppes, Clayton R., and Black, Gregory D. *Hollywood Goes to War.* London: Collier Macmillan, 1987.

Knight, Arthur. *The Liveliest Art.* New York: Macmillan, 1957.

Kracauer, Siegfried. "National Types as Hollywood Presents Them." *Public Opinion Quarterly* 13, no. 1 (1949), pp. 153–72.

Leff, Leonard J., and Simmons, Jerold L. *The Dame in the Kimono: Hollywood Censorship and the Production Code from the 1920s to the 1960s.* New York: Grove Weidenfeld, 1990.

Lord, Daniel A., S.J. *Played by Ear.* Chicago: Loyola University Press, 1956.

MacGowan, Kenneth. *Behind the Screen.* New York: Delta, 1965.

Martin, Olga G. *Hollywood's Movie Commandments.* New York: H. H. Wilson, 1937.

Mast, Gerald. *A Short History of the Movies,* 4th ed. Chicago: University of Chicago Press, 1988.

Moley, Raymond. *Are We Movie Made?* New York: Macy-Masius, 1938.

———. *The Hays Office.* Indianapolis: Bobbs-Merrill, 1945.

National Catholic Office for Motion Pictures Film Catalog, 1936–65. New York: NCOMP, 1966.

Nizer, Louis. *New Courts of Industry: Self-Regulation under the Motion Picture Code.* New York: Jerome S. Ozer, 1961.

Oberholtzer, Ellis P. *The Morals of the Movies.* Philadelphia: Jerome S. Ozer, 1971.

Occhiogrosso, Peter, ed. *Once A Catholic.* New York: Ballantine, 1987.

O'Neill, William L. *Coming Apart: An Informal History of America in the 1960s.* Chicago: Quadrangle Books, 1971.

Peet, Creighton. "Our Lady Censors." *Outlook,* December 25, 1929, pp. 645–47.

Phelan, John S. *The National Catholic Office for Motion Pictures.* Ph.D. diss., New York University, 1968.

Phelps, Gary. *Film Censorship.* London: Victor Gollancz, 1975.

Powdermaker, Hortense. *Hollywood: The Dream Factory.* Boston: Little, Brown, 1950.

Quigley, Martin S. *Decency in Motion Pictures.* New York: Macmillan, 1937.

Randall, Richard S. *Censorship of the Movies.* Madison: University of Wisconsin Press, 1968.

Rosen, Marjorie. *Popcorn Venus.* New York: Coward, McCann and Geohegan, 1973.

Russo, Vito. *The Celluloid Closet: Homosexuality in the Movies.* New York: Harper and Row, 1987.

Schumach, Murray. *The Face on the Cutting Room Floor.* New York: Morrow, 1964.

Seligman, Ben B. *The Potentates: Business and Businessmen in American History.* New York: Dial Press, 1971.

Shafer, Ingrid. "The Catholic Imagination." *Journal of Popular Film and Television* 19, no. 2 (Summer 1991), pp. 50–57.

Skinner, James M. "Cliche and Convention in Hollywood's Cold War, Anti-Communist Films." *North Dakota Quarterly* 46, no. 3 (Summer 1978), pp. 35–40.

———. "The Tussel with Russell: The Outlaw as a Landmark in American Film Censorship." *North Dakota Quarterly* 49, no. 1 (Winter 1981), pp. 5–12.

Sklar, Robert. *Movie Made America: A Social History of American Movies.* New York: Random House, 1975.

Stone, Judy. "The Legion of Decency, What's Nude?" *Ramparts* (September 1965), pp. 48–56.

Stuart, Frederic. *The Effects of Television on the Motion Picture and Radio Industries.* New York: Arno Press, 1975.

Thorp, Margaret. *America at the Movies.* New Haven, Conn.: Yale University Press, 1939.

Turan, Kenneth, and Zito, Stephen S. *Cinema: American Pornographic Films and the People Who Make Them.* New York: Praeger, 1974.

Vardac, Nicolas. *From Stage to Screen.* Cambridge, Mass.: Harvard University Press, 1949.

Vizzard, Jack. *See No Evil: Life Inside a Hollywood Censor.* New York: Simon and Schuster, 1970.

Walker, Alexander. *Sex in the Movies: The Celluloid Sacrifice.* Baltimore: Penguin Books, 1968.

Westin, Alan. F. *The Miracle Case: The Supreme Court and the Movies.* Alabama: University of Alabama Press, 1961.

Wills, Gary. *Reagan's America.* New York: Doubleday, 1987.

Young, Kimball. "Review of the Payne Fund Studies." *American Journal of Sociology.* September 1935, pp. 250–55.

General Index

Film Title Index

About the Author

JAMES M. SKINNER, Professor of History and Film at Brandon University in Manitoba for twenty-six years, has contributed several articles on film censorship to journals in Canada and the U.S.A. He was exposed to the control of film content in his position as vice-chairman of the Manitoba Film Classification Board. Dr. Skinner was also director of the Brandon Film Festival for twenty-two years. He is the author of *France and Panama: The Unknown Years, 1894–1908.* He is presently sessional lecturer in History and Film at the University of Victoria, British Columbia.

ISBN 0-275-94193-0

DATE DUE